South Shropshire's First World War

To my latest grandchild Zahra who has entered this world.
Also to two friends who have recently left it: Colin Lamb and Dave Richardson.
I miss them both.

South Shropshire's First World War

Bishop's Castle, Bridgnorth, Church Stretton, Craven Arms, Ludlow, Much Wenlock
and surrounding villages

by

Derek Beattie

Logaston Press

LOGASTON PRESS
Little Logaston Woonton Almeley
Herefordshire HR3 6QH
logastonpress.co.uk

First published by Logaston Press 2014
Copyright © text Derek Beattie 2014
Copyright © illustrations as individually acknowledged 2014

ISBN 978 1 906663 82 7

Typeset by Logaston Press
and printed and bound in Malta
by Gutenberg Press

Contents

Acknowledgements

My thanks to the staff at all the local libraries throughout south Shropshire and beyond and to those at the Shropshire Archives. Thanks are also due to the local history societies at Craven Arms, Leintwardine, Bishop's Castle and Ditton Priors for their invaluable and kind help. Special mention must be made of Ina Taylor of Much Wenlock, Janet Preshous of Lydham, Jane Smith of Worfield and Daniel Locket of the Ludlow Museum and Resource Centre for their labours on my behalf, all of which were greatly appreciated. Finally, I must thank Andy and Karen Johnson at Logaston Press for their constant support and advice.

Derek Beattie
Ludlow
January 2014

1 THE OUTBREAK OF WAR

On Tuesday 4 August 1914 Britain went to war against Germany. After German forces had entered Belgian territory as part of Germany's long laid military plans to attack France, the British government issued an ultimatum on 3 August that if the German forces were not withdrawn, a state of war would exist between Britain and Germany as from 11pm (midnight Central European time). The pretext for this was an 1839 treaty signed by the main European states that guaranteed Belgian neutrality. As news of the declaration of war spread, cheering crowds, many waving Union Jacks, began gathering in Trafalgar Square and Downing Street and outside Buckingham Palace. But it was not only in London where crowds awaited and then greeted the news, but also in towns and cities throughout the nation. South Shropshire was no exception.

The assassination of the Archduke Ferdinand in Sarajevo on 28 June had aroused little interest in Shropshire, and the consequent declaration of war by Austria Hungary on Serbia only claimed a short paragraph on page 8 of the *Bridgnorth Journal.* However, when, on 31 July, Russia ordered general mobilisation in support of Serbia against Austro-Hungarian aggression, tension began to mount locally. This increased as Germany, to fulfil her commitments under an alliance with Austria-Hungary, sent an ultimatum to the Tsar. This was followed by Germany formally declaring war on Russia, as a result of which France ordered mobilisation of her armed forces under the Dual Alliance of 1894 in order to support Russia. Quickly and inexorably, all the major nations of Europe were being drawn into conflict. The question now was what Britain would do. In Bishop's Castle it was observed that:

> Not within the recollection of the eldest resident has the borough and district been in such a fever of eager expectancy as in the present European crisis. It is the sole theme of gossip everywhere. The daily and evening papers are very speedily cleared out and the police station noticeboards eagerly inspected.[1]

In Ludlow the first hint of imminent war came when the local railway company cancelled two excursion trains at noon on Monday 3 August; they had been destined to carry groups from the Wesleyan Sunday School to Llandudno and Blackpool. On

Tuesday the Town Crier, Richard Morgan, dressed in his full regalia, paraded the streets of the town calling upon the people to gather outside the Town Hall for an address by the Mayor, Samuel Valentine. Since it was the last week of the annual local holiday many heeded the call. Just after 10am a crowd began to gather. The local company of territorials, led by Captain William G. Lane and Lt Donald M. Marston, who had just been recalled from their annual camp, took up position facing the council chamber. A platform decorated with the standards of England, Wales and Scotland had been erected and it was from here that the Mayor, formally attired in robes and chain, addressed a crowd of between two and three thousand

The mayor of Ludlow, Councillor Valentine, reads out the official declaration of war from the balcony of the old Town Hall in Castle Square on 4 August 1914 to a crowd of between two and three thousand people. By his side Captain Lane of the local territorials holds aloft the Union Jack, encouraging the gathered crowd to cheer and sing the national anthem. As it was the time of the local holiday, many of the crowd are wearing their summer best including a preponderance of fashionable straw boaters. At the front can be seen members of the local territorial unit who had just been recalled from their annual camp at Glan Rheidol near Aberystwyth. The following day would see them leave the town for war duties. (Courtesy of Shropshire Museum Services)

people. Before he spoke Captain Lane waved the Union Jack to raucous cheering. News of the failure of the German Government to heed the ultimatum was given followed by three cheers for the King, and three cheers for Captain Lane and his flag. Voices were then raised in an impromptu rendering of the National Anthem.[2]

To understand the welcoming of war by the British population it is necessary to understand the nation's pride in its position at the head of the greatest Empire in the world, and its possession of the largest navy, and the growing fear and distrust of Germany, which, in the popular imagination, was a growing threat to both.

Since 1902 the nation had celebrated Empire Day. At every school on 24 May schoolchildren would stand to attention in lines and salute the Union Jack that was hoisted on the school flagpole. They would be told stories about the exploits of Empire heroes such as General Wolfe at Quebec, General Gordon at Khartoum and Robert Clive in India. Then they would be given a half day off in order to take part in marches, maypole dancing, concerts or parties. The fact that this small nation was in control of nearly a quarter of the globe, and saw itself as a civilising influence on the world's peoples, made the British population, even the ordinary working man or woman, feel superior to the people of all other nations. Any threat to its expansion or continued existence was viewed with anger, and Germany appeared to pose just such a threat. Kaiser Wilhelm openly expressed his desire for the Germans to have an empire and their 'place in the sun', and as part of her effort to achieve this, Germany had begun to expand her naval strength from 1898.

This was viewed as a threat to the Royal Navy. Britons believed that as long as our fleet ruled the waves these islands were safe from their enemies. Any upset to the naval balance of power was therefore perceived as a danger to all British citizens. The Germans' decision to expand their navy began a naval race which led Britain rapidly to develop the new Dreadnought class of battleship, the first of which was launched in 1906. When Germany responded to this by building equivalent ships, public concern in Britain grew and demands rose for yet further expansion of the Royal Navy. As far as the British public were concerned, the only reason for any nation to expand its navy was in order to threaten Britain or its empire.

In the face of this perceived threat, there was a rise in militarism in Britain during the Edwardian years, and in the same period the British Army was reformed, the South African War of 1899-1901 having highlighted weaknesses in the army's ability to fight a foreign war. A fully equipped expeditionary force ready to proceed abroad at a moment's notice was established, and in 1908 the Territorial Army was formed, based on the mounted Yeomanry regiments that had been raised during the Napoleonic Wars and the local Volunteer Corps that had been formed after the Crimean War, but given modern uniforms, equipment and training. The founding of the Boy Scout movement in 1908 by Sir Robert Baden Powell, the hero of Mafeking during the South African War, was part of the same trend, with its khaki uniform

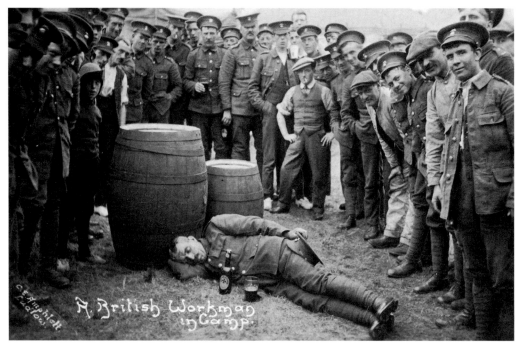

Reservists, Territorials and the Yeomanry all had to attend annual camps as part of their contract. This was to ensure that if war came they would be ready to be called or recalled to the colours at a moment's notice. C.E. Amphlett, a Ludlow photographer, took this shot at one of the camps held locally. Whether the man lying on the ground knows he is being photographed or not is not known, but the picture shows the camaraderie of the men and helps explain why they willingly went off to war together. (Courtesy of A.T.D. Evans)

and its emphasis on patriotism, physical fitness, outdoor camping, tracking and observation. As will be seen, these skills being honed by the young were soon put to use for home defence when war was declared. In addition, because of concerns about the numbers of volunteers for the South African war who were found to be physically unfit for foreign service, physical training in schools now became based on manuals prepared by the military.

In the hours prior to the outbreak of war a number of preparatory actions had already been carried out. The first was the call up of the reservists: civilians who had service experience. Telegrams for men on the naval reserve list began to arrive on Saturday 1 August, and they boarded trains at local stations to report for duty on the following Monday and Tuesday. From Monday, telegrams began to arrive at the homes of those in the army reserve as well. These army reservists were made up of four groups. The first was of men had completed their army service and had undertaken that for two years after they had left the army, they would be prepared to re-join in any emergency. Such men received 7/- a week and had to undertake twelve training days a year. The second, larger group included those men who were

After many volunteers wishing to serve in the South African War at the turn of the century were found unfit for foreign service, the government decided that physical education in schools should be overhauled. A new syllabus, based on the military training manual, was introduced and some schools were even issued with rifles to help in the teaching of drill. In this photograph the pupils of the National Boys' School in Bishop's Castle proudly show off the 24 Martini-Henry carbines which they received in 1902 for use in their physical training lessons. (Courtesy of Janet Preshous)

serving their normal period on reserve (usually five years) after leaving the forces. They received 3/6 per week and also had to attend twelve training days a year. This group could only be called up when a general mobilisation was called. The third group consisted of those who, after their five years in reserve, agreed to another four years on the same terms. The final group served in the Special Reserve, which was mainly made up of part-time soldiers. These men had not served in the regular army but had undergone six months full-time training and had to attend three to four weeks training a year. A former regular could join if he wished after he had completed his Army Reserve term.

After quickly putting their affairs in order, informing their employers that they would not be returning to work and hurriedly saying farewell to their families, these men boarded trains at stations all over south Shropshire on Wednesday 5 August. At Ludlow, the 10.13 train to Shrewsbury was especially busy as men headed off to the King's Shropshire Light Infantry (KSLI) depot; the platform was crowded with mothers, wives and children waving farewell.[3]

Within a day of war being declared the local territorials were ordered to report for war duty. Here, at Knighton Station, the local unit await their special troop train whilst being seen off by their families and friends to the music of the local Boy Scout band. Similar scenes were seen at Bridgnorth and at Ludlow where it was estimated that a crowd 4,000 strong waved them goodbye. (Courtesy of A. T.D. Evans)

The next group to go were the county territorials who made up the 4th Battalion KSLI. In south Shropshire were based the F (Bridgnorth) Company, which recruited in the south-east of the county and G (Ludlow) Company, which covered the south-west. These part-time soldiers had been on their annual camp at Glan Rheidol near Aberystwyth and were recalled to their hometowns on the Monday. Some men who lived in outlying villages stayed the night at their local drill hall in order to be on hand when the expected mobilization orders arrived. This duly happened the following day at 4pm.[4] Those who could get home to say their farewells did so, but all had to return to report for duty early on Wednesday morning for medical inspection. Here they then stayed until marching off together later that day.

Their send off was emotional. At Bridgnorth, F Company, under the command of Captain William Horace Westcott and headed by the town band, 'marched down the High Street amid the cheers of the spectators to the railway station', where they caught the 5.45pm train to Shrewsbury. G Company, in Ludlow, caught a special troop train at 8.55pm, no doubt with other units of the 4th Battalion already aboard, to take them to billets in south Wales. To bid them farewell, crowds had been gathering from 7pm when the shops closed. Hundreds crowded on to the platform despite attempts by officials to hold them back. Others gathered on the footpath leading from the station to Gravel Hill over the tunnel which 'became choked with a living mass'. As yet more arrived, the crowd moved into the field on the other side of the railway line where they stood four or five deep. Many men and boys even clambered over the hedge onto the railway embankment. It was estimated that when the soldiers marched onto the platform the crowd numbered 4,000. As the troop train left:

> As if with one voice the multitude gave one terrific roar ... Women waved their handkerchiefs and regularly squealed at the top of their voices so excited were they, while men waved their hats and even their sticks ... and cheered till their throats refused to give sound to further utterances. An answering cheer was heard from the train.[5]

They were departing as heroes on the crest of near hysterical patriotism.

The mounted Shropshire Yeomanry were ordered to prepare to move out as well. C (Ludlow) Squadron, who also drew their recruits from Craven Arms, Clun and Bishop's Castle as well as towns just over the county border in Herefordshire and Worcestershire, were told to assemble at the Town Hall on Thursday 6 August. About one hundred men, with their horses, were billeted around Ludlow. Just before 11am on the Saturday they assembled on the Castle Green where they were given a civic farewell and then, cheered on their way through crowded streets, they rode two abreast to Bridgnorth via Burwarton.[6] Members of the Yeomanry who lived in and around Bridgnorth and Much Wenlock belonged to D (Wellington) Squadron and they were ordered to join up with their comrades. The Much Wenlock troop was given a hero's farewell. Led by the town band they rode in procession through

As part of their training, members of the Shropshire Yeomanry attended a two-week camp each year to practise manoeuvres. In 1912 this took place at Walcot Park and here a group of them can be seen refreshing their horses in the estate grounds.
(Courtesy of A.T.D. Evans)

As soon as hostilities were declared the part-time Shropshire Yeomanry was mobilised. On the Castle Green in Ludlow, C Squadron, recruited mainly from the Ludlow, Craven Arms, Clun and Bishop's Castle area, gather on Saturday 8 August 1914 to prepare for a civic send off before riding out of town to take up their war duties. (Courtesy of Ray Farlow)

The Shropshire Yeomanry was made up of four squadrons. This is the Ludlow troop, which belonged to C Squadron. This squadron covered the area south of Craven Arms and over the county border to Kington, Tenbury, Leominster, Hereford and Ross-on-Wye. (Courtesy of A.T.D. Evans)

the streets cheered on by the local populace waving flags. Following a blessing by the vicar they were sent on their way against the backdrop of Auld Lang Syne.[7] All four squadrons of the Shropshire Yeomanry then made their way to Oswestry to await further orders.

The general public's appetite for khaki ensured that all troops travelling through any of the south Shropshire towns in these heady first days and weeks of war found a warm and often raucous welcome waiting. The people of Bridgnorth turned out in large numbers, complete with town band, to welcome members of the Shropshire Yeomanry who had ridden in from Ludlow to stay overnight. Ludlow itself, being on the main road between Hereford and Shrewsbury, saw many troops passing through to their collecting depots and here too crowds always appeared to cheer them on their way. A number of units stopped overnight in hastily arranged billets. The Herefordshire Yeomanry rode through on Saturday 8 August on its way to Shrewsbury. A small detachment of the 2nd Battalion Monmouthshire Regiment came into town the same evening also travelling to Shrewsbury, whilst on the Sunday large crowds gathered in Old Street, High Street and the Bull Ring to see the arrival of around forty men of the 3rd Battalion Monmouthshire Regiment together with 60 horses and 14 transport wagons.

As mobilisation occurred in August 1914 a number of units passed through the south of the county on their way to various collecting depots. Many travelled with transport wagons. For example, on Saturday 8 August a detachment of the 2nd Battalion Monmouthshire Regiment billeted in Ludlow for the night. With them they brought 60 horses and 14 transport wagons. Such a unit is photographed resting, whilst the horses were refreshed and fed, as it passed through Churchstoke. (Courtesy of A.T.D. Evans)

The inhabitants of Bishop's Castle, forewarned by the local police sergeant and constable who had been serving billeting notices on the ten local hotels and inns, came out in force to meet the 198 men and horses of the Montgomeryshire Imperial Yeomanry. A full civic welcome awaited their arrival at 3.30pm, with the Mayor and Town Band greeting them in streets festooned with bunting. The following morning they left to ride via Lydbury North and Craven Arms to their billets in Ludlow, where 43 men and 50 horses of the Monmouth Territorials joined them. The next morning the Yeomanry rode off to Hereford whilst the Territorials travelled on to Shrewsbury. In addition, troop trains continued to pass daily through Ludlow, Craven Arms and Church Stretton, and local children would sit by the tracks waiting to wave.[8]

The economic benefits of troop visits to these small south Shropshire towns were not lost on local councillors who, for the most part, were tradesmen. Hoteliers and innkeepers received War Office payments of 6d per bed per night for soldiers, 2/- for officers and 1/9d for the stabling of each horse, plus set payments if they supplied any breakfasts, lunches or suppers.[9] Seeing no reason why the wider business community should not also benefit, councillors in Bridgnorth, Church Stretton and Ludlow all asked their Town Clerk to contact the War Office and offer their towns as places where the permanent stationing of troops would be welcome.

Army officers came to inspect each place. Bridgnorth Council were excited at the prospect of a contingent of Royal Engineers but were later disappointed to learn that they would not be coming. After Ludlow was visited, the town was awash with rumours of the imminent arrival of troops. To local delight, it was confirmed that in May 1915 a hundred officers and 2,000 men of the South Wales Mounted Brigade would be encamped just outside the town on the racecourse at Bromfield. A gratified mayor, who also happened to have a thriving grocery business, explained to his fellow councillors that 'the soldiers in our midst are bound to make a considerable difference to the trade of the place'. But to the chagrin of local businessmen, the War Office, offering no explanation, suddenly cancelled their plans. Likewise, Church Stretton appeared to have hit the jackpot when the army came to inspect two possible campsites. They estimated that 5,000 infantrymen could be accommodated on land at Ashbrook, along with a medical corps and members of the Royal Army Service Corps and 300 horses. In addition, it was felt that 500 cavalry could camp on land adjoining Sandford Road. The council were soon debating what they could charge for supplying water to the troops, but they too were disappointed when they were informed that the units would no longer be coming. The council tried again in September 1915, explaining to the War Office that they could accommodate 1,000 men in various billets around the town. Again the potential economic benefits were the main reason behind the request, and the council was reminded 'it would be a good help to the town during the coming autumn and winter'.[10] This effort to bring war prosperity to the immediate area was also doomed to failure.

Craven Arms was the only place to have servicemen billeted for a period of time when a small unit of the Army Veterinary Corps took over the Horse Repository next to the Auction Yard. There they stayed from August until November 1914 as

The army needed horses not only as cavalry mounts but also to pull all forms of military transport. From August to November 1914 a unit of the Army Veterinary Corps took over the Horse Repository in the centre of Craven Arms. Their job was to inspect the horses brought in by the Army Remount Department, having been compulsorily purchased from farmers, traders and private individuals. Here, members of the corps are parading on land beside the repository. (Courtesy of A.T.D. Evans)

Five Shire horses are paraded for the photographer after being passed fit by the Army Veterinary Corps in Craven Arms. The horses collected at the repository were then taken to the railway and loaded onto special trains to start their journey to one of the war fronts. (Courtesy of A.T.D. Evans)

the army combed the area requisitioning horses.[11] This caused the farmers some upset. Members of the Army Remount Department arrived at Ludlow's Monday Animal Market and eleven horses were compulsorily purchased from both carriers and farmers who were in town for the day. Next it was the turn of the town's traders. Eighteen of their horses were examined in the yard of the Feathers Hotel and five chosen and taken. The Remount Unit then descended on the Norbury District on a Saturday in November requisitioning 16 animals. They moved on to the Lydbury area, and a further nine horses were taken. At the Friday market in Bishop's Castle farmers and carters went home twelve horses short. Such visits were to become frequent over the coming months and years and were always unannounced. At a May Fair in Bridgnorth the Army made a surprise entry and took twenty horses away, so that a number of farmers had to walk home leaving their carts behind.[12] Not only did the farmers dislike the inconvenience of losing their work horses; they were especially incensed that they were paid £10 under the market price for them, while at the same time having hay requisitioned, also at below market price.[13] Patriotism took second place in such instances.

But as the Reservists reported to their regiments for duty and the Territorials and Yeomanry went to their collecting depots there was a need for more troops. Britain only maintained a small regular army of just below 250,000 men, most

Groups of soldiers would descend unannounced on town market days and requisition any horse that they deemed suitable for army use, often leaving farmers and traders to walk home. Here horses are being inspected outside the Ship Inn at Tenbury. The owners of horses chosen would be given a requisition note with a set price detailed on it that could be claimed through the War Office. (Courtesy of Roy Winton)

of whom were stationed across the globe protecting the outposts of empire. The Army reserve that had been recalled to the colours totalled 150,000, the special reserve 63,000, and the Territorial Army added only a further 63,000. This gave Britain, in August 1914, an army of just over half a million, compared to France's 4 million men, Germany's 4.5 million, Austria-Hungary's 3 million and Russia's 5.9 million. Unlike other major European countries Britain had no system of conscription so would have to rely on volunteers to increase the number in the ranks. Lord Kitchener, the Minister for War, at first called for 100,000 volunteers aged between 18 and 30 to serve for three years or until the war ended; it was felt that the war would be a short one but that a period of three years would also allow for an army of occupation afterwards. 'Or until the war ended' was an insurance policy which was, of course, needed. On 28 August he called for a further 100,000 and raised the age limit to 35, and in the following month he called for yet more recruits to bring the total number in the army to one million. By 21 December the required figure had risen to four million, and south Shropshire was expected to play its part in helping to fill this seemingly bottomless pool of recruits. These volunteers would form the 'New Army'.[14]

At the beginning of the 20th century many young men emigrated to parts of the Empire to begin a new and hopefully more prosperous life. When war broke out in 1914 some felt it their duty to return to fight for their mother country. One of these was Private Alfred William Morris, whose parents lived at Brooklyn Farm, Culmington. He joined the Canadian Infantry and is photographed here on board a train in Canada (on the right leaning out of the window holding a cap) beginning his journey to Europe. Aged just 21, he was killed at Ypres in August 1916. (Courtesy of Shropshire Museum Services)

Since Britain only had a small standing army, the call went out in August 1914 for the formation of a 'New Army' of volunteers. In the small hamlet of Munslow eleven men immediately came forward. Here they are pictured in their best suits with many still wearing the ribbons presented to them by the local gentry in recognition of their willingness to serve. Notice how one young man has knelt on paper in order to protect his trousers from the damp earth. How many of these men returned unscathed is not known. (Courtesy of A. T.D. Evans)

Local recruiting offices were set up in Ludlow and Bridgnorth, and men could either sign up at one of these or travel to Shrewsbury to enlist there. The Ludlow office was at 8 Corve Street, a property owned by the Marsden family, and the Recruiting Officer was Edmund Richard Marsden, a local solicitor. At Bridgnorth an office was opened at 60 High Street, where a Captain Welch was in charge. Pressure to enlist was at first put on the men on the National Reserve Class 1 and 2 lists. These were men who had military experience but had served their compulsory time in reserve. In Ludlow such men were called to a meeting in the Drill Hall by the recruiting officer and asked to volunteer. As a result it was made public that of the 62 men in Class 1 (those under 42 years of age), thirteen had already gone off to serve, whilst another twelve had now volunteered and were waiting to go. Of the others, seven said they were too ill to enlist, and seven were postmen or railway men who could not be spared from work. The remainder claimed good reasons for not having volunteered. As for the 42 men in Class 2 who were aged 43 or over, four were already serving, five had also now volunteered, twelve had joined the Local

On 8 September 1914, five young bellringers from Claverley church, all aged between 18 and 22, enlisted in the army at Bridgnorth. Four travelled together from Claverley: Ernest Drew, standing on the far left, Dennis Boucher, standing second from the right, William Owen, kneeling on the far left and Cyril Boucher, kneeling second from the right. Probably arriving from his parents' home at Bobbington is the fifth friend, George Thomas, standing second from the left. After training they were sent to France in July 1915. They all survived the war, though two, George Thomas and Cyril Boucher, were discharged in 1917 due to wounds suffered. (Courtesy of A.T.D. Evans)

Guard, seven were said to be medically unfit, seven were clergy, postmen or rail-waymen who were needed at home, which just left seven who claimed, for various reasons, that they could not serve at the moment.[15]

The main drive for volunteers, however, was amongst the young men of south Shropshire who had no previous military experience. Such young men came forward for a number of reasons. For some it was patriotism. Others were driven by a thirst for adventure. The furthest that many had ever travelled was to the next market town or for a day out to Hereford or Shrewsbury, or (in the case of a lucky few) a short holiday to a Welsh seaside resort. Enlisting gave these young men a chance to go abroad and see sights they had only read about in school books or seen pictured on cigarette cards. For agricultural labourers in particular, whose social horizon in the first years of the 20th century was usually limited to a handful of public houses and the occasional sporting fixture against the next village, this was a once in a life-time chance to break the claustrophobic bonds of everyday life. It is not surprising that the Chief Recruiting Officer of the county admitted that farm workers were the easiest of all to persuade to enlist.[16] Some, however, were encouraged rather more forcibly. It is claimed that Squire Rocke of Clungunford House, an ex-military man, marched his young estate workers and tenants to Ludlow to enlist, and Sir William Rouse-Boughton of Downton Hall also actively encouraged the younger members of his staff to join up.[17]

South Shropshire did not universally conform to the traditional view of a constant stream of the nation's youth pouring into recruitment offices. It certainly happened in the heady, patriotic, early weeks especially in the rural communities, helped partly by appeals from the pulpit. In the parish of Claverley, 58 men had enlisted by mid October 1914, most being volunteers for Kitchener's New Army. At Ditton Priors 25 had left to fight by mid November whilst at Lydbury North, in a parish of just 806 inhabitants, 54 men had enlisted in the New Army by the end of the year. However, only five men out of a population of 539 in the Bromfield parish answered the call. In the larger villages and small towns enlistment was also quite strong at first, but lessened as the months progressed. In the parish of Clun, 30 men had enlisted by the end of September, whilst at Bishop's Castle the figure was 97 by the end of November, many of these being volunteers for the New Army. However, in Ludlow and Bridgnorth the percentage of recruits was far smaller, perhaps partly due to the wider variety of occupations and social opportunities available in these places. Reasons for falling enlistment

The recruiting office in Ludlow was at 8 Corve Street and here new volunteers line the pavement before walking off to the railway station to catch the train to take them to the army depot at Shrewsbury. (Courtesy of Shropshire Museum Services)

figures in the Ludlow area given by Sir W.M. Curtis, the chairman of the Ludlow Recruitment Committee set up in November 1914, included the low rates of allowances given to the wives and dependants of those who went off to serve and the small pensions to be given if they were killed or disabled. In addition there was the fear of unemployment once the war was over, since employers did not have to keep jobs open for those who went off to fight. Perhaps this worry was not felt to the same extent in the agricultural community. One other reason, though this was rarely mentioned at the time, was the state of health of the young men of the area. In October, six men travelled from Bishop's Castle to Shrewsbury to enlist but only two passed the medical. At one recruiting rally in Ludlow, of the six men persuaded to step on the stage to join the forces, three later failed their medicals. The ravages wrought by poverty and poor housing meant that even though some men wanted to join the forces, a number of them were judged not fit enough to die for their country.[18]

To encourage voluntary enlistment, Lord Kitchener, Minister of War, began the formation of 'Pals' battalions. This allowed friends to serve together, not only in a battalion but also in a company or even a platoon. The sad corollary of this was that when the men went into battle the list of casualties could include many men from just a few streets or a single village, causing untold communal grief. This photograph shows some of the recruits to the 6th 'Pals' Battalion of the King's Shropshire Light Infantry assembling at the regiment's depot in Shrewsbury. (Courtesy of Shropshire Regimental Museum)

For some the numbers enlisting were just not enough. In Ludlow, a letter published in the local newspaper at the end of August from 'One Who Has Enlisted' claimed that only twenty men in the borough had so far volunteered. 'It seems,' he lamented, 'almost incredible for a place the size of Ludlow that so few have responded to the call at such a time as this.' By the end of October, in a town with a population of over 5,000, only 52 men had joined Kitchener's New Army. In Bridgnorth, the mayor appealed for local recruits, hoping to raise enough men from the town and the surrounding district to form a company in the KSLI so that friends could all serve together. Two hundred recruits would be needed, but when the battalion was formed, it could only be done by joining the 120 raised there to the 80 so far raised in both Ludlow and its surrounding district. Disappointed, the mayor could at least claim that the Bridgnorth area had found 'rather more than our share'.[19] The recruits served together in D Company 6th Battalion, known as the 'Pals' Battalion. By July 1915 they were fighting side by side in France.

It was decided in both towns that more would have to be done to persuade young men to enlist. As a result, recruitment drives were instituted. In Ludlow a rally was held in the Town Hall in early September with Field Marshall Lord Methuen as guest speaker. Following his exhortations, when men were asked to come up onto the stage to volunteer and be given a ribbon and a handshake, 28 rose to their feet. The following month a patriotic concert was held at the Town Hall and a fresh plea for volunteers was made to the audience. Yet a further attempt to persuade young men to enlist was organised in December when the Town Hall was once again 'profusely adorned with flags and bunting, Union Jacks being conspicuous'. Men home on leave were invited to attend dressed in their khaki uniform to add further psychological pressure. Speeches were made and songs were sung, but at the end only six men stood up and one of these was found to be under age. Such recruitment rallies took place throughout the south of Shropshire. At Church Stretton in October, Rowland Hunt M.P. addressed a public meeting, and another was held in Bishop's Castle at the Crown Hotel.[20]

These efforts were certainly required in parts of the county as the monthly enlistment figures for the Ludlow Recruiting Office show. This office was the focal point of recruitment not only for the borough of Ludlow but for the surrounding rural district including Craven Arms. It has to be borne in mind that their figures incorporated the re-enlistment of men with military experience in the National Reserve who had served their compulsory time on the reserve list and had been persuaded to volunteer. August saw 61 recruits, September 119 but October saw only five men come through the door. There was an increase to 15 recruits in November and 24 in December but the figures were far from satisfactory given the numbers being called for.[21]

The same pattern seems to have been replicated in the Bridgnorth area. By early September, only 41 men from the borough had volunteered for Kitchener's New

Army whilst 80 had come forward in the rural district. Even in the villages, after the first burst of patriotism, the tide of volunteers was receding. At Claverley, after 58 had joined the forces in the first two months of hostilities, the remainder of the year saw only an average of four new recruits per month. As a result, as well as holding similar recruitment rallies, the authorities in Bridgnorth attempted to bring community pressure to bear. A detailed street list was published in the local newspaper giving the full names and addresses of all those serving in the armed forces: regulars, territorials, reservists and New Army volunteers. It was hoped that this would encourage inter-street rivalry driven by community and peer pressure. To this end those streets that were deemed the most patriotic 'and appear to have done the best so far' were singled out for praise: Cartway with 46 men serving from a total of 74 houses, Bernard's Hill with 42 men from 76 properties and Severn Street with 32 in the armed forces from just 50 homes. Such tactics appear to have brought results since by the end of 1914, the borough of Bridgnorth was congratulating itself on its achievement in having 438 men in the armed forces out of a population of 5,463. This they claimed, if repeated across the nation, would mean a total of 3.6 million men under arms.[22]

Other methods of community and peer pressure were exerted on young men to encourage enlistment. The landlord of the Queen's Head at Church Stretton was proud of the fact that he had encouraged twelve of the thirteen local lads whose football team had their headquarters at his public house to enlist. Lady Catherine Gaskell of Wenlock Abbey would entertain volunteers for luncheon before arranging for the local band to play as they marched to Much Wenlock railway station. Proud relatives, neighbours and friends would turn out to cheer them on their way. At Diddlebury, Captain and Mrs Wingfield-Stratford of Delbury Hall gave the first three recruits for the New Army a meal in the local schoolroom along with their family and friends. Each of the three young men was then presented with a pipe and tobacco. This was followed by a dance to which the village was invited. All this was done to encourage other villagers to answer the call for men.[23]

Yet another method of boosting enlistment was by encouraging mothers, wives and girlfriends to exhort young men to serve by questioning their manhood. A letter to the *Ludlow Advertiser,* signed 'One of the Girls,' stated that:

> Our town has done well, but there are still many more all round who could try. It is to those who ignore their country's call through laziness or selfishness that we say 'Cowards die many deaths; but the valiant only one.'

A second letter claimed that 'as women we have no use for the man who will not fight for his King and Country because he is not fit to be the father of our children', whilst yet a further one made the veiled threat that 'women will, no doubt, deal faithfully with any shirkers here'. Such views were encouraged at recruitment rallies where speakers asked the ladies to use 'your good influence to spur on the young men to join the KSLI or Lord Kitchener's Army to defend our nation'.[24] Churchmen also got involved. At Lydbury North, via the parish magazine, the women were asked to urge their young menfolk to enlist.

> And who can induce them to? You, their mother, and those of you who look forward to being the wives of them one day. And let this be the way in which you tackle them. 'I don't want you to go, but if I were you I should go.'[25]

Though the expansion of Britain's armed forces was at the top of most people's agenda at this time, it was not the only worry that troubled both the leaders of the nation and the ordinary man or woman. One fear that was prevalent in 1914, just as it would be again in 1940, was the fear of invasion. Following Prussia's successful invasion of France in 1870, General Sir G.T. Chesney published a short story in *Blackwood's Magazine* entitled 'The Battle of Dorking' that saw Britain invaded by German-speaking soldiers. It apparently touched a fear in the public's imagination and began a literary genre that would see over four hundred 'invasion' works published by 1914. Military men wrote a number of these, or had them ghost-written, which gave the idea some form of respectability. *The Invaders* by Louis Tracy, published in 1901, saw both French and German soldiers infiltrate Britain disguised as young men on walking and cycling holidays, whilst Erskine Childers' *Riddle of the Sands*, published in 1903, described a plot by Germany to invade Britain using hundreds of barges filled with soldiers. The most successful of all was William Le Queux's *The Invasion of 1910,* published in 1906, which sold over one million copies. It is not surprising, therefore, that one of the first reactions both of the public and of the military was to fear an invasion coupled with an outbreak of sabotage by enemy agents. Whilst an editorial in the Ludlow parish magazine gave a rather exaggerated description of seaside towns on the east coast that 'have been turned into camps, houses pulled down, trenches cut, earthworks thrown up and wire entanglements laid', many of the territorial units, including those from south Shropshire, indeed found themselves immediately dispatched to guard Britain's coastline and sensitive port installations.[26]

The fear of Germans infiltrating the country either as a precursor to invasion or in an attempt to spy on our defences or even commit sabotage, was one that even troubled those left at home in south Shropshire. Anti-sabotage precautions and the whole question of Home defence was at the top of the local agenda as well. The first group to be asked to help was the Boy Scout movement. As soon as war was declared Sir Robert Baden-Powell sent a telegram to Lord Harlech, commandant of the movement in Shropshire:

Hope you can supply 1,000 scouts under district Commissioners to aid local, civil or defence authorities in such duties as collecting or distributing information re supplies, billeting, guarding culverts and telegraph, assisting the Post Office, Police, Fire Brigade, Ambulance and Poor Relief distribution.

This request was in turn relayed to local Scout troops who responded immediately.[27]

That members of the Scout movement were expected to carry out such duties came as no surprise at the time, even to the boys' parents. It was well known that the movement was based on the Mafeking Cadet Corps, dressed in khaki uniform, that Baden-Powell organised when defending that town when it was besieged during the South African War. This corps was manned by boys too young to fight but able to carry messages to outlying posts, often up to a mile away, and to act as lookouts to warn the military of enemy movements. Even Baden-Powell's book *Scouting For Boys* was based on two earlier military manuals that he had written listing the skills and uses of scouting. Being asked to carry out duties to free soldiers for front line duty would come as no surprise to Scouts.

To begin with, Scout patrols acted on their own initiative. The troop from Bishop's Castle was sent out to search for anyone looking or acting suspiciously. Eight of their senior members carried out cycle patrols which covered an area a ten-mile radius from their town. But within days the Scout movement's contribution to home defence was set on a more organised footing. They were given the responsibility of guarding telegraph connections throughout south Shropshire as well as patrolling railway lines. Seventy Scouts covered the railway line between Wooferton and Church Stretton whilst checking on the telegraphic and telephonic wires at the same time. Different troops had a different area to cover. The Scouts from Richard's Castle guarded the Ludlow to Wooferton section of railway, soon to be joined by members of the Bridgnorth troop. They were camped in the grounds of Overton Grange and were on duty two hours on and four hours off, 24 hours a day. The Ludlow troop had the responsibility of guarding the section between Ludlow and Church Stretton and camped at the racecourse at Bromfield. The Scouts at Bishop's Castle were given the telegraph connections to safeguard from sabotage. This included the sections from Bishop's Castle to Hopesay in one direction and to Marshbrook in the other. These boys stayed under canvas on the summit of Oakleymynd. Before moving to the Ludlow area, the Scouts of Bridgnorth were at first stationed between Morville and Bewdley guarding the telegraph lines. The various troops of Scouts remained on duty, away from their homes for days at a time, until relieved in early 1915 by the 3rd Supernumerary Company of the 4th Loyal North Lancashire Regiment, who took over communication guard duties.[28]

The Church Lads Brigade was also asked to help and in early August they were under the control of the Army Council. Each boy was asked to volunteer to carry out whatever duties their country required them to do. After their parents had given them permission, all stepped forward and signed the relevant forms. A Captain Dodgson was given the duty of guarding the Birmingham water supply line and had responsibility for 70 miles of its length that mainly went through south Shropshire. To carry this out he was given 150 boys with their officers. As soon as the morning of Wednesday 12 August he sent off by train twelve lads from the Ludlow Brigade with a sergeant to begin guard duty. These young men were even armed. Later that day a further 16 boys and two sergeants were sent off by train. A number of units of the Brigade from near and far soon joined them, including a few from Birmingham who camped by the side of the Steventon aqueduct near Ludlow which they had orders to guard. The ranks of the young men under the command of Captain Dodgson soon rose to 400. In December a Ludlow contingent, who had been camped near Kidderminster, were sent to the Elan Valley in Wales to take over the protection of the reservoirs there.[29]

The fear that there could be a German invasion also led to the formation, all over the country, of local volunteer corps to help defend Britain's cities, towns and villages. These were the forerunners of what was to be the Home Guard in the

*The Boys Brigade or Church Lads Brigade was founded in Scotland in 1883 and by 1914 had branches all over the United Kingdom. The movement was designed to instil Christian manliness into young men through semi-military discipline, physical fitness and religious studies. As can be seen in this photograph of the Ludlow Brigade, the senior members were trained in the use of weapons. As a result, throughout south Shropshire these young men were used during the first months of the war to protect the water supply line from Wales to Birmingham against possible saboteurs.
(Courtesy of Shropshire Museum Services)*

The younger members of the Ludlow branch of the Boys Brigade gather in College Street prior to going out on cycle patrol in the local countryside. Their allotted task was to search for, and report on, possible German spies and saboteurs in the vicinity. Fears of a German invasion, aided by fifth columnists, were widespread even in Shropshire in 1914/15. (Courtesy of Shropshire Museum Services)

Second World War. The idea was that a Volunteer Training Corp (VTC), according to the Mayor of Ludlow, could be 'a useful auxiliary to our Home Defence in case of invasion', though the men would have to provide their own arms and equipment or have them donated. It was envisaged that those who would join would be men who were over age or had some other impediment to enlistment in the regular forces such as being in an occupation that was deemed to be in the national interest. By November 1914, Ludlow had set up a unit with 98 members. They divided into two platoons that were drilled and trained – one on Tuesday evenings and one on Friday evenings. A Sergeant Instructor by the name of John Flattery, who was the Town Hall Keeper, was responsible for the training at the Drill Hall. Rifle shooting was also practised at the miniature range there. The Mayor of Bishop's Castle, Alderman Dr Selwyn Hale Puckle, called for a VTC unit to be set up in his town within the first few days of war breaking out. About 30 men answered his call and they had weekly drills at the Girls' School. Another unit was set up at Church Stretton, commanded by Dr Horatio Barnett, and in December it was decided that a contingent should be formed in Much Wenlock; this became a reality in April 1915. In November 1914 even the small parish of Ditton Priors formed their own VTC, numbering 40

Because of the constant fear of invasion of these shores by German forces or sabotage by fifth columnists, a Home Defence Force was positioned to guard both our coasts and what were deemed strategic installations throughout the country. Such units were usually made up of men who were deemed too old or too unfit for foreign service. Fourth from the right on the back row is Alfred Taylor of Richard's Castle, who had been an estate worker at Moor Park. (Courtesy of Jean Giles)

members, and so, a little later, did the hamlet of Quatt. Surprisingly, Bridgnorth lagged behind in this aspect; the mayor only called a public meeting to form a unit in June 1915 and initially only 20 men came forward, though a Mr W.H. Foster of Apley Park donated £500 towards the purchase of equipment. Another laggard was Cleobury Mortimer, where a VTC unit was set up in September 1915.

As well as the usual drill and rifle practice these men took part in training exercises. To get fit the platoons in Ludlow took part in route marches, the first being from the Drill Hall to the policeman's house on the Bromfield Road and back, a distance of four miles. Men from the Church Stretton, Much Wenlock and Broseley VTCs went on a field day at Lutwyche Hall carrying out various manoeuvres, whilst the Bridgnorth VTC held manoeuvres in fields around Lodge Farm, Dudmaston.[30]

The constant fear of German spies, sabotage or even invasion of this country led to a growing hatred of Germans that at times bordered on hysteria. People's imaginations began to run riot and some began to see spies everywhere. The proprietor of the Corve Street garage in Ludlow became suspicious of a man who wanted to hire a motorcar. He immediately telephoned the police claiming that there was a German at his premises and that he would attempt to detain him until they arrived. He failed, but the police soon found the suspect in a nearby public house only to discover that

A number of men who had not joined the regular forces volunteered to join their local Volunteer Training Corps (the forerunner of the Home Guard in the Second World War). In the village of Hopesay the social hierarchy was kept in that the sergeant in charge on the left was the local school's headmaster Arnold Pugh. From left to right the others were Charles Evans a general labourer, James Parton a gardener, H. Jones a farmer, William Owens a railway signalman, George Lloyd a blacksmith and George Davies a chauffeur. (Courtesy of Keith Rudd)

he was a gentleman who had come to Ludlow for the races and just wanted to get home. At Craven Arms a man was seen 'going about in an aimless manner' and soon the police were being told of a German spy who said he was searching for fossils. When he was arrested he turned out to be a visitor from Redditch who was staying at the local hotel. At Clee Hill a man speaking with a strange accent, immediately branded a German, turned out to be a Londoner visiting a relative in the district. There were so many such mistaken sightings that the police had to ask the public to think more carefully before they raised any alarm.

> It would be very wise if people noticing anything which appeared to be unusual would follow the individual and satisfy themselves that there really was cause for alarm before informing members of the different bodies who have the work in hand. [This would save] busy men a deal of trouble and worry.[31]

One very nasty situation occurred at Church Stretton just after war was declared. The trouble started when a German waiter at the Long Mynd Hotel allegedly boasted to a drinker at the bar that his countrymen 'would trample us under their feet and make us slaves'. The newspaper reporter's own prejudices came to the fore when he then said that the German waiter was 'knocked to the floor with a good English right'. Shortly after this the waiter, and others who worked with him, attempted to go to the local railway station to catch a train south and, hopefully, return to Germany before they could be interned as enemy aliens. They were, however, forced to run the gauntlet of angry locals bent on venting their feelings not only verbally but physically. 'It was only with difficulty that the contingent managed to get to the station in a perfect condition.' Rumours then swept Church Stretton that the waiters had been turned back once they reached their destination, and a large, threatening crowd met each incoming train. Word then spread that the waiters had successfully returned to the hotel by another route. It was proudly claimed, 'they were now practically confined indoors when any of the Stretton "boys" were about'. It appears that the rumour of the waiters' return was not true, but the episode highlights the anger that was directed at any who were judged to be enemy aliens.[32]

In fact, rumours were rife throughout south Shropshire against certain individuals who were deemed to be of foreign origin. A few felt forced to threaten legal action and instructed solicitors to put warning notices in the newspapers. Osmund Pitman of Mayfield, Ludlow, asked his solicitors to state publicly that he was of pure English descent, even listing his forebears, in order to contradict statements that he was of German stock. He said that he would sue if they were repeated. For others, animosity was shown against them simply because they had foreign-sounding names. The solicitors of Henry Mahler of Bell House, Ludford, had to be instructed to take action regarding rumours circulating the town about him. They placed notices in the local newspapers stating that Mahler was born and bred in England and that his father was a British subject though of Swiss extraction. Again there was a threat to sue if the malicious gossip did not stop.

Even Rowland Hunt, the local Member of Parliament, was guilty of spreading wild rumours. He asked the Home Secretary, Mr McKenna, whether

> In view of the fact that telegraph wires had been cut, and bombs and firearms and carrier pigeons found in the possession of alien enemies, could he ensure that such people were tried by the military authorities and dealt with under military law.

The Home Secretary refused, telling him that no wires had been deliberately cut and no bombs discovered since the war began and that he was guilty of repeating unfounded rumours.[33]

Such fears, though, persisted. In a letter to the Mayoress of Bridgnorth, Lady Glanusk stated:

I consider that the wife of the man who is blind for life or has had both legs shot off etc. has the absolute right to demand that the enemy at present at large should be interned, or, if it could be arranged, sent out of the country. The fact that a man being naturalised when the war began hardly makes a patriotic Englishman.

As a result, local Bridgnorth women signed a petition, which finally amassed 2,050 signatures, asking that aliens within 30 miles of the coast should be interned.[34]

In Ludlow, in May 1915, 'German spies' were still being arrested.

Some excitement was manifested in the town on Monday night when a supposed 'spy' was brought to the police station under an armed escort. The incident happened at 7.30 at a time when a good number of people were about. The captured 'spy' turned out to be a well-known townsman, Mr William Melsome of Ashford, formerly living at Fishmoor, who is somewhat deaf.

It seems that members of the National Reserve, who were guarding the railway line at Ashford, had failed to receive satisfactory answers to the questions they were asking, and arrested him. The spying charges were dropped, but he was fined 10/- for being on land forbidden to the public.[35]

The actions of many of the wealthy upon the outbreak of war were also unedifying. As soon as war was declared, food prices soared, in anticipation of a possible reduction in food imports and the need to provision the army. The cost of sugar doubled whilst the price of bacon rose by a third. Meat, cheese and bread also saw large price increases. This situation was then compounded by the actions of those who could afford to stockpile food in their larders and outhouses. This led to panic buying; some grocers practically sold out of stock on the day war was declared. The finger of blame was pointed at both the moneyed classes and the shop owners who willingly took the windfall in profits by selling them the goods. In a barely concealed criticism of Ludlow's mayor, Councillor Valentine, who had a high-class grocery shop on Broad Street, the local newspaper stated that:

We regret the larger firms had not the courage of smaller shopkeepers in refusing to supply extra orders, particularly as in many cases the unusual orders came from people who ordinarily get their supplies from the London stores.[36]

The *Church Stretton Advertiser*, by praising those shop proprietors in Bishop's Castle 'who had loyally declined to supply any family orders above the ordinary order', also criticised by omission those who had not and the gentry families in their locality who had placed the orders. The anger that similar action was causing in Bridgnorth was articulated in a letter signed 'Fair Play':

> What a disgrace it is that the price of food has been forced to the present state to the wives and families left behind; and who is to blame? Not the Germans or the Government, but the well-to-do who have been so selfish as to purchase huge quantities of groceries and provisions etc. to save a few paltry pounds and to compel the working classes, who cannot afford to lay out money to either go without the necessities of life or to pay exorbitant prices.[37]

It was actions such as this that gave a warning that social conflict could be on the horizon. One local editor felt obliged to say that there could be 'another kind of war in this country when the present hostilities come to an end'.[38]

The outbreak of war had brought about tensions: fear of German invasion, fear of spies and fear of sabotage, all fuelled by a surge of xenophobia. In addition there was a fear of food shortage, which in turn resulted in rising class antagonism. Such tensions were to remain throughout the coming years, though their consequences for the local populace were to change as time went on. The war also brought heightened feelings of patriotism that, for some, presented a chance to break the shackles of a claustrophobic country life and sample what they believed at the time would be a short episode of adventure. The initial enlistment bubble, whilst not bursting, at least soon began to deflate and with a constant increase in demand for new recruits problems were bound to arise as to who would or should enlist. As a result, fresh tensions would grow between families whose men had gone off to war and those with no men in the army. In addition, as it became obvious that the war would not be a short one, the pressure for those at home who were unable to fight due to their age, sex or health to play their part in the war effort would grow.

2　The Continuing Saga of Recruitment

By Christmas 1914 the initial burst of young men rushing off to the recruiting offices was over. The numbers enlisting in 1915 were few and getting fewer as the year passed, though there was still a steady stream of young men who went off to enlist as soon as they reached the minimum age to volunteer. Recruitment was not helped by the news that filtered back to Britain of the terrible conditions being endured in the new trench warfare, and many men were soon considering how to avoid serving at the front. The result was not only a growing friction between those families that had men in the forces and those that had not, but also a growing realisation by those in power that moves towards compulsory military service would have to be instituted. Against this background was the need to keep a workforce that could supply the essential demands both of the Home Front and of the military.

In March 1915 only twenty men came through the doors of the Ludlow recruiting office to enlist, the number only increasing by one the following month.[1] As a result the local regiment, the KSLI, tried a direct approach to attract recruits. In April, their drum and bugle band arrived unannounced in Bishop's Castle on the noon train with two recruiting officers. It was the day of the crowded Friday market and they were soon to be seen 'buttonholing' any young men they could find. It appears they managed to shame or persuade six to accept the King's shilling, and these travelled by the first train on the Monday morning to Shrewsbury. A few days later the band descended on Ludlow, parading around the town 'playing lively airs' whilst the recruiting officers passed among the spectators, though it is not known with what success on this occasion. In October the KSLI band visited Ludlow yet again on another recruitment drive, this time accompanied by a full company of men, before moving on to Cleobury Mortimer and then Bridgnorth as part of a tour of the main population centres of the southern part of the county.[2]

A number of local initiatives, mainly based on bringing psychological pressures to bear, were also undertaken to encourage more to volunteer. In Bridgnorth, the street-by-street publication in the local newspaper of the names of those who had enlisted was kept updated, whilst in Ludlow full lists of those who had volunteered were also published. These provided details of all men who had joined the armed forces both in the borough and in the local district.[3] In addition, Rolls of Honour listing the names of those who had joined up were displayed in many places. The Mayor and Mayoress of Ludlow paid for specially commissioned boards to be affixed to the walls of the three elementary schools – the National School on Lower Galdeford, the British School on Old Street and East Hamlet School – to display the names of past students who had volunteered to fight. On its unveiling, the board at the National School listed 190 names, whilst that at the British School had 85 names. All were continually kept up to date.[4]

Churches too began to have Rolls of Honour hung in their porches, again being updated every time one of their parishioners enlisted. At the parish church in Bishop's Castle such boards were erected in the porch in September 1914 and by mid October they displayed 73 names. By the end of 1915 this total had risen to 170. The same happened at the parish church at Clun. At Hope Bowdler, by early 1917, villagers could read the names of 30 parishioners.[5] In small rural communities such as this where the church was a focal point of community life, the psychological impact and peer pressure on families that had yet to send anyone to war must have been great. Another tactic was the issue of large yellow cardboard shields to each family who had a man in the armed forces, which were meant to be displayed in their front window, thus making public that this household had sent a man to fight, and adding yet further pressure on neighbours that had not.

Giving public prominence to patriotic examples set by certain families was yet another way of inducing feelings of shame in households that contained men of enlistment age. The keenness of Richard Marsh of Bishop's Castle to join the Army was one such example highlighted. As soon as he reached the age to enlist he promptly set off to walk to Shrewsbury to be sworn in. He then returned the next day, once again by foot: a distance of 44 miles.[6] Stories of families who had sent a number of their menfolk into the armed forces were printed in local newspapers, such as the four sons of John Cains of Netchwood,

As part of the psychological pressure on men to join the army, households from which a man had volunteered to fight were given a yellow cardboard shield to place in their window and thus proclaim the fact. When a number of such shields were displayed in a street it must have been difficult for those households with young men who had not volunteered. (Courtesy of Shropshire Museum Services)

The three Griffiths brothers were brought up at 1 Lower Mill Street, Ludlow. George and Charles (Charlie) Francis (seated) were identical twins and between them stands their elder brother William. All were members of G (Ludlow) Company of the Territorial Army attached to the 4th Battalion KSLI and consequently they were waved off from Ludlow station the day after war was declared. October found them on board ship to the Far East. In 1917 they returned to fight on the Western Front, where William met his death in December. George and Charlie were hospitalized with 'trenchfoot' by January 1918. A stepbrother, Arthur (Arty) Griffiths, ran away from home aged 16 to join up. His father brought him back the first time but after a successful second attempt he was wounded on the Western Front and returned home with only one leg. (Courtesy of Shropshire Museum Services)

Faced with the uncertainties of war it was usual for men, after enlisting, to have a photographic portrait taken. No doubt one copy was taken to war with the husband whilst the wife kept another at home. Here 37065 Pte Alfred Taylor, Royal North Lancs. Regiment, poses proudly with his wife Gertrude née Powell and sons George and Sydney. Before enlistment Alfred, who lived in Richard's Castle, was an estate worker at Moor Park. (Courtesy of Jean Giles)

John Boulton, the landlord of the Stokesay Castle Hotel in Craven Arms, proudly poses with his family. Pride of place goes to his son Harry, who had enlisted in the army. John himself had also volunteered to do 'his bit' by joining his local Volunteer Training Corps (VTC). (Courtesy of Craven Arms Local History Society)

Ditton Priors, or the five Palmer brothers of Stottesdon. A William Evans of Woodhouse Fields, Bourton, Much Wenlock, who had seven sons serving, was reported to have received a letter of congratulation from the King, as had Charles Lewis of Fishmoor, Ludlow, who had six sons in the Army. A similar letter was received by the Phillips family of Lydbury North when four brothers joined up, and it became 'a cherished framed memento' hanging on the wall of their parents' home. But pride of place was given to the enlistment of John Davies, a farm wagoner of Gretton, near Church Stretton. His enlistment meant that all 17 of his mother's sons from two marriages were serving in the army.[7]

However, these many ploys to encourage enlistment were not successful enough. As a result, the central authorities organised a number of speaking tours, many of the talks being given by men who had served with distinction at the front. One of these rallies was held during a performance at the Picture House in Ludlow. A Private Hitchins of the Canadian Expeditionary Force came to appeal for more recruits. He had been one of only 300 men, out of 1,100, who had gone into action against the Germans on the Western Front and had returned, albeit wounded and gassed. His speech reiterated two of the most common exhortations used to encourage enlistment. The first was an emphasis on the brutality inflicted by German forces against defenceless civilians adding that 'if the Germans were to land here ... Heaven help the women and children'. The second common appeal that he made was to the local women who must 'urge their husbands and sweethearts to go'.[8]

A speaker for the Imperial Maritime League stood on a platform in Ludlow's market place to appeal for recruits. He too dwelt on the cruelty of the Germans towards the women and children of France and Belgium. He even went further and claimed that these 'damnable devils' had threatened 'to perpetrate greater cruelties on the [British] population'. Just like other speakers he also encouraged women to 'do their best to get the men to enlist', adding that if the men only went after conscription had been forced to be introduced then they 'would be despised by those who had volunteered'.[9]

So worried were the Government about the low recruitment figures that a national Recruitment Day was announced for 2 October 1915. At Bishop's Castle, as posters advertising the event were placed around the town, two buglers from the local Scout troop blew a prolonged blast as each one was put up. On the Saturday that it was held the Scout band paraded around the town to remind the populace. The day, however, proved a failure in the town. No outside speaker could be found so the Mayor had to make the patriotic plea. Sadly, his 'forceful and eloquent appeal for recruits' was mainly ignored, 'only one coming forward, a married man with a numerous family', even though 'there were a goodly number of eligible men present'.[10]

It was the same in Ludlow. Their rally was held at 7pm in Castle Square in drizzling rain. Two lorries were used as platforms for the speakers but only a 'fair crowd' turned up. Not a single man was tempted to volunteer and it was duly noted that

To persuade men to volunteer for the forces the manhood of those who failed to join the forces was questioned. As part of this onslaught, posters were displayed portraying the pride felt by women whose men had answered their country's call.
(Author's collection)

'eligible men were conspicuous by their absence from the meeting'. The equivalent rally at Bridgnorth, held in the High Street outside the Crown Hotel, was also an abject failure. Here a motor dray was used as a platform for the speakers and the Alveley Brass band provided martial music. The Mayor used the occasion to wax lyrical about the barbarism aimed at the women of France and Belgium and the need 'to give a good thrashing to the brutal Germans'.

> Young girls were carried off to the trenches by licentious German soldiery and there abused by hordes of savage and licentious men. People hiding in the cellars of houses have heard the voices of women in the hands of German soldiers crying all night until death or stupor ended their agonies.

Just as happened in other parts of south Shropshire, his eloquence apparently fell on deaf ears since no mention in the report of the rally referred to any man being

The pride, tinged no doubt with concern, felt by many parents whose sons volunteered has to be acknowledged. In the early months of the war, Thomas and Mary Lowe, landlord and landlady of the Queen's Arms (now the Bridge) in Lower Corve Street, Ludlow pose with their children for a family portrait. Their eldest son William wears his new KSLI uniform. (Courtesy of Gareth Thomas)

moved enough to volunteer.[11] It appeared that the recruitment well had virtually dried up.

One other method chosen to bolster recruitment was the parading of captured German guns. A 77mm field gun, captured at the Battle of Loos, drawn by six horses, arrived in Bridgnorth from Ironbridge. The local Volunteer Training Corps (VTC), the Grammar School Cadets and the Scout band met the contingent and took them on a tour of the town. The gun was then kept on view at the end of the High Street for a week. From Bridgnorth it wended its way around the south of the county until it arrived at Ludlow where it again toured the town. It then remained on display for a few days before the escort returned to take it on its next stage to Leominster, being sent on its way by cheering crowds. Similarly, a field gun captured by the Cheshire Regiment was put on display in front of the Town Hall at Bishop's Castle complete with its shattered muzzle, and two machine guns captured by the KSLI were exhibited alongside it arousing 'considerable interest' on market day.[12]

One of the main reasons that men no longer came forward to enlist in enough numbers was the detrimental effect that stories of the conditions suffered by the men at the front were having. No longer did men dream of exciting adventures that they would soon be at home retelling to their loved ones by the fireside. The fact that the war would not be short was now obvious to all and, in addition, the reality of the horrors of a new type of war, trench warfare, were being relayed back in letters home. A number of these, which described aspects of the conflict in graphic detail, were being printed in the local newspapers for all to read and digest during the first months of the war.

Former school friends and neighbours were soon describing the apparently interminable day-to-day life in the trenches in very spartan surroundings, spent under constant fire from an unseen enemy. The over-riding message being relayed back was of the cold and wet conditions they had to endure. Edward Preece of Ludlow complained to his mother that 'it is awfully cold at night in the trenches; we get no blanket and the cold ground seems to strike straight to the bone'.[13] It also

As the war became static, letters began arriving home describing the terrible conditions in which soldiers lived and fought. The dreams of heroic charges that young men left Shropshire to take part in turned into a nightmare of survival. As early as the winter of 1914/15 the casualty lists not only men killed or wounded but also those who were in hospital due to frostbite. It is little wonder that the number of men volunteering to serve began falling after Christmas 1914. (Author's collection)

did nothing to help that after rain the ground turned into a quagmire as Colour Sergeant Frank Foxall from Bridgnorth described:

> We have had more mud than we could possibly put up with, for as fast as we get the trenches something like habitable, so the rain washes the mud in again ... At the present time I am wearing a pair of gum boots, overcoat and mack but the mud hangs on to the bottom of the coat and mack, making them feel a ton weight, to say nothing of our feet sticking in the mud, which makes getting about one continual hard struggle.[14]

A Corporal Jenkins from Church Stretton underlined the consequences of living in such conditions:

> It has been raining nearly every day for about five weeks and we are doing our work in about a foot of mud and no earthly chance of getting a pair of dry boots. The country is nothing else than a quagmire. As regards the war it appears to be at a standstill. Both armies seem to be living underground like a lot of rabbits, only coming out when necessary ... Some of the poor fellows can hardly walk through standing in the mud and water for days at a time, with a bitter wind that seems to freeze one through to the bone.[15]

Living in such conditions affected the general health of the troops as Franklin Lavender, who had worked in Bishop's Castle, soon found:

> We are in the trenches again. Bad ones this time. There is thick mud up to our knees and we are wet to the skin up our legs. I fell on my back in the mud last night. ... Two of our company came out of the trenches last week all crocked up with rheumatism and one or two with paralysis.[16]

When the weather dropped below freezing, frostbite became prevalent amongst men surviving in such conditions. When Gill Griffiths of Ludlow arrived in France at the end of January 1915 to join his battalion he found many of them in hospital suffering from the effects of cold. Even the weekly casualty lists reproduced in the local newspapers began to list not only those killed or wounded but those who had to be removed from the front line due to frostbite. Lewis Hoskins of Bishop's Castle summed up the feelings of the men at the front when he wrote to his wife in January 1915 that 'it was very cold, wet and freezing in the trenches. I wish to God the war was over'. Sadly, it soon was for him as he was killed in a poison gas attack five months later.[17]

It was the same on other fronts. From the mountains of northern Greece Albert Bright of Bishop's Castle wrote that:

We are still under canvas and the place is up to our knees in mud and water. A lot of our chaps are sick ... There are hundreds down the line suffering from frostbite.[18]

It is not surprising that after reading of such conditions being suffered by their family and friends, their compatriots in south Shropshire would think twice before volunteering. In addition, it was soon realised that death tended not to be 'glorious'; it mainly came from an unseen enemy via a shell or a sniper's bullet.

Private Gough, formerly in service at Downton Hall, had first-hand knowledge of the terrible effects of shellfire. He was interviewed in a hospital in Llandrindod Wells suffering from wounds received in action, and recalled an incident when a shell landed in his trench in the middle of himself and six of his chums. Of the seven of them he was the only one to remain unscathed, with two killed immediately and the other four badly maimed.[19]

One of the greatest fears associated with shelling was not of being hit by splinters but of being buried alive by the earth that was dislodged in the explosion. Such a story was relayed back by George Davies of Bishop's Castle:

Well, dear mother, I uttered a prayer this morning. About 4.00 o'clock I was sitting in the trench when a large quantity of earth fell on me and buried me. My first thoughts turned to you all at home for I felt myself going fast. About eight men dug as hard as they could and succeeded in uncovering my head, letting air into me, whilst others dug around my body. Had they delayed another minute I should have been dead.[20]

For Bombardier R.G. Duck, writing to his former employer in Clun, being buried alive was an experience not of minutes but of many hours:

Well, here I come to my misfortune. I had got to the German trenches which we had captured when lo and behold the Germans began to pour shells of all sizes into it. All I can remember is about a ton of earth and sandbags falling on top of me and a terrific explosion and about fourteen Cameronians and myself included were buried alive, in which position we remained for 24½ hours. At last some fellows of the Territorial Black Watch found us and got three of us out of it, the rest being beyond aid ... I can tell you it was an awful experience.[21]

Sniper fire was another ever-present danger. As Albert Dyke of Ludlow warned, being hit by a sniper was a threat not just to those in the front trenches:

Sniper Joe is a nasty customer to deal with. We have gone through the mill this last time – two officers killed and four wounded, and, of course, the men in the firing line suffered as well.[22]

Death from an unseen enemy was the same in all areas of conflict, and similar stories were later read in letters sent home from Gallipoli. Ernest Kershaw described how close to death he came whilst just resting:

> I was talking to some infantrymen one morning when a shell came over. It took one man's head clean off and killed two more besides injuring several. I happened to bob down in the trench and this saved me from certain death.

As regards the danger of snipers he pointed out that the Turks were 'watching all the wells and many of our fellows go under while fetching water'.[23]

The stories of heavy casualties whenever one side attacked the other must also have had a massive detrimental effect on any thought of volunteering. Charles Francis of Ludlow tried to convey the horror of modern warfare to his old headmaster.

> It is a terrible war. Only those engaged know of the terrible things seen and done. In places it has not been war but wholesale slaughter. I, myself, with a party, buried over one hundred in one small field. When one looks at the fact that the whole line for miles were doing the same thing, only then can one realise the great loss of life.[24]

George Davies of Bishop's Castle wrote to his parents that 'the Huns are poisoning us by blowing deadly gas across our trenches. Oh to witness the poor fellows writhing about like drunken men under its effects.' He also described the aftermath of a British attack on the German lines that again showed those at home that there was no glamour in this war:

> We, in our charge the other night, were nearly all cut up. I never saw such a thing. The roads and fields were covered with the dead and dying. Oh the people of England do not know what we are going through out here, but God was with me and kept me safe. ... Oh dear parents I cannot tell you what it is like out here, it is the most awful thing ever known. ... We went up to the trenches about 1,100 strong and doubt that there is five hundred left.[25]

To add to the picture that these letters were painting in the minds of those back in south Shropshire were the descriptions of the wounded and the unburied dead. Bert Robinson of Bishop's Castle, who was a driver behind the lines, saw the constant stream of wounded being taken to the rear:

> Sometimes we were held up for two or three hours for troops to pass and ambulance cars coming down from the trenches with wounded. It is a pitiful sight to see some of our poor fellows writhing with pain, some of them asking to be killed out of their misery.[26]

Letters published in local papers described in detail the terrible conditions at the front. Men wrote home about horrific sights such as the many unburied soldiers that littered the battlefields and the consequent stench from them as their bodies rotted. Such descriptions must have played a part in dissuading many at home from enlisting. (Author's collection)

As for the dead, it was often impossible to get to them in order to bury them. But even if this were possible, being once buried did not mean that you remained so as future shelling often brought the bodies back to the surface. Charles Francis graphically painted the scene:

> It is terrible where we are at present as there are so many unburied bodies and the stench is unbearable in this hot weather. Close behind our lines the Germans have shelled a cemetery and turned the bodies up and the human bones lie all over the place. The stench is almost more than one can stand and plenty of dead horses lie about unburied. There are also hundreds of bodies barely covered by soil ... the country all around is just one large burial ground.[27]

Arthur Steadman from near Bridgnorth looked out after the Battle of Loos on the unburied men littering no-mans-land seeing 'dead men all over the place. It was an awfully gruesome sight'. A week later he wrote that 'we can still see any amount of dead men in front but cannot get out to bury them'.[28] Sometimes, as Franklin Lavender told his aunt, the dead could not be avoided as trench systems were improved and added to:

> In the reserve trenches behind us, which were very shallow, they tried to deepen them but whichever direction they tried they came across bodies (there were 1,200 French buried round about here). It was the same in some parts of our trench.

The result was a plague of rats. After a while the soldiers just lived side by side with them as Eric Burton explained to his parents in Bridgnorth:

> In answer to your question about vermin, we certainly have plenty, but I am sure if they were taken away some would feel quite lonely, as they give us plenty of occupation and many hours of hunting in the billets and also in the trenches.[29]

With recruitment falling, in 1916 the government tightened the rules on censorship to prevent such letters from being published in the local press.

In the meantime there was growing frustration and bitterness felt by those who had volunteered to fight for their country towards those who had stayed safely at home. Such feelings were being freely expressed in their letters back to family and friends. Thomas Woodhouse of Ludlow, who sent an open letter via his old headmaster, wrote:

> I hope any of the young men who read this will think about it and come and give us a lift. There are men who have been out here since the commencement and could do with a rest. Well, come and relieve your pal or perhaps a relation. I hope you will forgive me for writing a letter of this type, but feelings get the better of men sometimes and they like to say what they think.[30]

John Preece, also of Ludlow, recovering from a wound in a Sheffield hospital, was another who wrote of the strong views held by himself and his comrades regarding those who had failed to join the colours:

> They are also very bitter against the slackers, ... and I have heard some very bitter remarks passed about the young unmarried men who have not joined to do their bit, and what some of our boys would do with them if they had the chance.[31]

Lance Corporal Geoffrey Roden from Claverley, who had had to write to the wife of a fellow comrade informing her of the death of her husband, posed the following question to his mother:

> Are there any single young fellows who dare stop in England and shirk when men with families are giving their lives for their countries sake?[32]

Another soldier, Thomas Jacks of Stanton Lacy, put his view very plainly when he wrote, 'I hope if there are any young men left, they will come and not let it be said that their mother raised a jibber'.[33]

Herbert Tipton, of Lydham, confirmed how important this issue was to the ordinary soldier:

> The main topic out here is the conscription business. The majority of the fellows are in favour of it. As far as we can see it will take every jack man to polish the Kaiser off, and it is of no use underestimating the enemy as they can always give as much as they take ... Now if the young men of Bishop's Castle could only realise what it would mean for us if the Huns came to England they would join at once like men and not wait to be fetched.[34]

Something clearly had to be done to stimulate recruitment, not only to help restore morale amongst those at the front, but to raise the reinforcements that were considered necessary to further the war effort. As early as the spring of 1915 it was becoming recognised that voluntary recruitment was not going to be enough to provide the numbers of men that it was now estimated would be needed to success-fully prosecute the war.

The first change of strategy came with the passing of the National Registration Act on 15 July 1915. Though essentially an information-gathering exercise on the basis of which further decisions could be made, it was also another way of exerting moral pressure on young men to enlist. All men and women aged between 15 and 65 had to register, but men of military age had to complete their own special pink forms. The day stipulated for completion was 15 August 1915. Each local council appointed voluntary enumerators and assistants – middle class ladies in the main – who would deliver the relevant forms to each household and then collect them, helping people answer questions if required. In Clun it was noted that:

> As elsewhere, more time was apparently spent on answering those relating to employment and whether the person was skilled in anything else other than that engaged in at the present time.[35]

The reason for this was that one way to avoid compulsory conscription, if and when it was later brought in, would be to have a skill that could be used in what was deemed an 'essential occupation', so much thought had to be given in completing this section. The possibility of conscription certainly did not appeal in south Shropshire. At a recruitment rally in Cleobury Mortimer those attending voted by 'a vast majority' to keep to voluntary enlistment though their cause was not helped by the fact that 'not one recruit offered himself for the service of his country'.[36]

The results of the registration process were published in September. They showed that nationally, there were just below five million men of military age who had not yet volunteered to fight and that only 1.6 million of these were in 'starred' protected jobs. As a result, on 11 October Lord Derby was appointed Director General of Recruiting and within five days introduced a scheme that was a last attempt to stimulate voluntary enlistment and forestall the growing pressure for compulsory conscription.

This 'Derby Scheme', as it became known, allowed men aged between 18 and 40 to attest that they were available to be called up if and when they were needed. The men who attested would be divided up into married and single and into 23 age groups. For example, group 1 would be for single 18-year-olds whilst group 46 would be for married men aged 40. The men who attested would be told to return to their homes and jobs until they might be called upon in the future. They were issued with a brown armband bearing a red crown and it was claimed that men could be seen sporting these in the streets of south Shropshire by the end of the year.[37] It was promised that no married man would be called up until all single men had been called up. Local tribunals were set up within each council authority so that men could ask to be listed as in an 'essential' occupation, which would hopefully mean that they would never be called upon. The tribunal that was appointed on 4 November 1915 in Ludlow was typical of all those set up in south Shropshire. It was made up of the minimum five members allowed by law and comprised the Mayor, Councillor Valentine; the Deputy Mayor, Councillor Ernest Evans, an insurance agent; Councillor Henry Green, a solicitor; Henry Lloyd, a local businessman who was also a magistrate; and George Randles, the Secretary of the Railway Union, who it was hoped would add expertise regarding certain essential occupations. The first decision that the tribunal made was to sit behind closed doors.[38] It only sat a few times before further legislation overtook it.

Under the Derby Scheme, out of the 2.17 million single men on the National Register who were eligible for the Army, only 1.15 million men attested, and after those in essential occupations were deducted only 343,000 remained. As regards married men, of the 2.83 million on the National Register only 1.5 million attested, and again those in protected occupations had to be deducted from that figure. Even though all single men aged between 19 and 23 who had attested were told to report for duty on 20 January 1916, the scheme was judged to have been a failure, and compulsory conscription was introduced.

The Military Service Act was passed on 27 January 1916. This made compulsory the enlistment, when called upon, of all single men between and including the ages of 19 and 40. In May 1916 the Act was extended to include married men. By April 1918 the age limit had risen to 50 and lowered to 18. The only men exempted from the Act were those who held a certificate of exemption through being in a protected or reserved occupation, and those who were in Holy Orders or were ministers of any religious denomination. A number of the latter still volunteered and the Bishop of Hereford supported them, asking that they choose to serve as army chaplains or in the Royal Army Medical Corps.[39] The Revd Ralph Guy of Claverley was one who volunteered to be an army chaplain as did Canon Tyrwitt, the rector of Rolleston Church. He even suffered a wound, coming home in the summer of 1915 to recuperate before returning to the front. The Revd George Bishop, vicar of Cardington, was another churchman who chose to become an army chaplain, a decision that cost him his life in the bombardment that preceded the third battle of the Aisne in May 1918.[40]

For those within the bounds of the Act it was still possible to claim an exemption from military service. There were four grounds for this: ill health or infirmity; that your work was important to the national interest; that serious hardship would ensue to your business or domestic situation; or that you held a conscientious objection to war service. Military Tribunals were set up in each local authority to hear and pass judgement on such claims.

The composition of these tribunals appears to have followed a pattern throughout south Shropshire. The gentlemen (there is no record of any woman ever being chosen) already appointed to serve on the Derby Scheme tribunals were now transferred to the new military tribunals, with the addition of a military representative who was also a local man. At Ludlow he was the recruiting officer and solicitor Edmund Marsden, whilst at Bishop's Castle it was an alderman, Dr Selwyn Hale Puckle. In the boroughs the president was always the local mayor, whilst in the rural areas it was the chairman of the rural district council who was often a leading member of the gentry, such as Sir William Rouse Boughton in the Ludlow District. As for the other members of the tribunal, they were mainly local councillors. In the boroughs these were often major tradesmen of the town, a shopocracy of drapers, grocers and their like, whilst in the countryside they tended to be gentleman farmers. These rather narrow cliques were leavened in the boroughs by the odd representative of the professions and in the countryside by one of the local parish vicars. In the boroughs, after pressure was exerted from above, token working class representation was introduced with the addition of a trade union representative. This was done in Bridgnorth after three months had elapsed, whilst in Ludlow it was done from the start with the appointment of George Randles of the Railway Union and William Nash of the Carpenters Union, though both were nominated by the councillors themselves and not by their trade union members. Because the main employment was agriculture, joining the tribunal that met at the Guildhall, Much Wenlock, as well as that at Cleobury Mortimer, was a representative of the Board of Agriculture to add expertise and advice.[41]

Because 1916 saw conscription for the first time, a small part of the duties of local tribunals was to adjudicate on appeals on the grounds of conscientious objection. In the vicinity of Bridgnorth this was not difficult because, as one military visitor to the town noted 'there was not such a thing as a conscientious objector in the area'.[42] Elsewhere in south Shropshire this was not the case. The tribunal in Ludlow, in particular, had to interview a number of objectors, as members of the Christadelphian Church and of the Plymouth Brethren lived in the town. From the tenor of their questions and other remarks, there is no doubt where the sympathies of the tribunal members lay. George Randall was especially annoyed by those whom he saw as trying to avoid their responsibilities. This can perhaps be understood, as within days of being appointed to the tribunal he had heard that his 20-year-old son had been killed in action. Questions such as 'Would you protect your sister against the ravages of Germans?' were commonplace. The Rural District Tribunal used the same type of questioning against a Cardington man. 'Suppose I met you in the road and gave you a right good hit in the face. What would you do?' Such questioning of conscientious objectors brought an immediate rebuke from the Bishop of Hereford.

> Many members of Tribunals seem to misunderstand their function and duty and need to remember that their sole business is to find out whether a so-called conscientious objection is really honest and put forward *bona fide*. If so, the plain duty of the Tribunal is to exempt the objector. Even if, in their judgement, he is misguided or prejudiced, their duty is to respect his conscience.[43]

After this admonition the tribunals exempted such objectors but still attempted to punish them by insisting that any non-combatant work that they carried out would not be in the local area. A Ludlow fishmonger who had found work at Sheet Farm on the outskirts of the town was told to find war work further away so that he could not go home at night. He then found farm work at Priors Halton. The tribunal was not happy with this either, but they were overruled when the man appealed and, to local chagrin, was given full exemption on religious grounds and allowed to return to his shop. The tribunal met another defeat when they tried to stop a local painter and decorator from carrying out his war work felling timber at nearby High Vennals. The military representative had to warn his fellow members that the central authorities would support the employer against the tribunal.[44]

Further evidence of local animosity towards conscientious objectors can be seen at Ditton Priors. After 73 objectors died in various prisons due to maltreatment, the Home Office decided upon a scheme whereby objectors could instead labour for ten hours a day. The first such scheme was set up at Dice near Aberdeen in the summer of 1916, and it was quickly followed by others – including one at Ditton Priors. Here conscientious objectors were housed in three wooden huts and during the day they worked at a local quarry. In June 1918 one of the huts, housing 25 men, was burnt to the ground. An investigation concluded that this was the result of arson almost certainly carried out by locals.[45]

The major workload of the tribunals, however, was in regard to hearing the appeals against being conscripted on hardship grounds. This could be linked either to a man's domestic situation or to his employment. Hearing such applications began immediately as both individuals and employers began to appeal against either their own or their employee's conscription. The sheer numbers of people appealing to avoid conscription is quite staggering and it has to be borne in mind that the number of cases heard often seriously underestimates the number of men applying since an employer could ask for exemptions for a group of employees. For example, at the first meeting of the Ludlow rural district committee, where thirteen cases were heard, one case was from a local stone company in the Clee Hill area who were

The camp established outside Ditton Priors for conscientious objectors, had three wooden huts constructed alongside each other. The one on the right of the picture, on top of the railway embankment, was almost certainly the one that was burnt to the ground in an arson attack in June 1918; luckily no one died. (Courtesy of Alfred Hinton)

In early 1917 the first batch of 35 conscientious objectors arrived at Ditton Priors to begin work at a local quarry. Many of them were Quakers from the Birmingham area; others came from the north-west of England. Pictured here on a snowy day in March, outside one of the wooden huts erected to accommodate them, are 28 of the group, together with a woman and a smartly dressed man who had probably come to inspect the conditions in which the men were being held. (Courtesy of Alfred Hinton)

This group photograph of conscientious objectors outside one of their accommodation huts near Ditton Priors shows the young Albert Henry Hinton of Smethwick on the far left. (Courtesy of Alfred Hinton)

applying for the exemption of 22 of their employees. These quarrymen, all young, single and physically fit, worked at the dangerous face of the quarry where, it was argued, men needed to be agile to avoid falling rocks. The firm claimed that 97 of their original workforce of 220 had enlisted and that this had reduced their output considerably even though the military had increased their demands for stone for road building on the western front. At the tribunal's second meeting the number of cases increased to 70 and they were forced to sit in the boardroom of Ludlow Workhouse from 10.30 in the morning until 4.45 in the afternoon without a break. The number of such appeals did not decline, with 80 being heard at one meeting in December 1916 and 66 at the first meeting in January 1917. It was the same in the Clun rural district where, at the workhouse in Bishop's Castle, an average of 50 cases were heard each week, In the Bridgnorth rural district, where the tribunal also met at the workhouse, the average was nearer 60.[46] There were fewer appeals in the boroughs, but they still averaged about 30 a week.

One important difference to the Derby Scheme tribunals was that all the military tribunals in south Shropshire agreed that journalists should be allowed in to report the proceedings, on the proviso that the names of the appellants were not printed.

This allows us to gain an insight into the flavour of the arguments put forward to avoid serving. The first cases that came before the Ludlow tribunal included an assistant schoolmaster who asked to be exempted on the grounds that his enlistment would affect the education of children. Another was a local corn merchant who pleaded on behalf of one of his drivers, claiming that he was the only support for his invalided, widowed mother. A motor engineer, again said to have a dependent widowed mother, claimed that he was also the only skilled man at the garage, the other two being apprentices. A haulier working in his father's business argued that, as he ran the haulage department, this section would have to close if he was enlisted. Finally a motor driver employed by a grocer and provisions dealer claimed that he was the sole support for his mother and deaf and dumb sister.[47] At the first meeting of the Bishop's Castle tribunal, held in the Town Hall, a local chemist was given an absolute exemption with the remark that 'We could not possibly do without you'. The owner of a local bakery and confectioners appealed on behalf of his only baker on the grounds that he, the proprietor, had asthma and could no longer bake. The baker was given three months' exemption to allow his employer to find another worker, though he could apply again then if no suitable replacement had been found. A scrap dealer claimed that his son was indispensable to the business, but that appeal was rejected.[48]

Many of those appealing, especially employers, began to ensure that a solicitor put forward their case, to add greater expertise and weight. At the Bridgnorth tribunal solicitors from outside the borough tended to be hired, perhaps local solicitors might have connections, either politically or socially, with tribunal members. A local pork and bacon curer was successfully represented by a Wolverhampton solicitor who argued that since his employees had already enlisted, his business would fold if he had to enlist as well. Total exemption was granted. At the same tribunal a master baker, represented by a firm of solicitors from Stourbridge, also won full exemption. The greater expertise in putting forward a case exhibited by these professionals so frustrated one of the tribunal members at Ludlow that he told one solicitor that 'you must not make a speech. You are not allowed to do so by the regulations'. The solicitor then calmly said that instead he would make a detailed statement – and duly obtained an exemption for his client.[49]

Whenever anyone was dissatisfied with a decision, they were allowed to appeal to the county tribunal that would sit in their local area at regular intervals. The success rate enjoyed by some who appealed against rulings of the Bridgnorth tribunal so annoyed the members of the tribunal that they considered it 'disgraceful', especially when they who were better acquainted with the local facts than those lodging the appeal. At one point, they even threatened to resign if this continued.[50]

Another difficulty that the local tribunals had was with the changing advice that was handed down from central authorities, especially as regards the protected occupations. In south Shropshire this concerned the railways, quarrying, mining and agriculture. State-controlled industries could exempt any worker they wished; the military tribunals could only rubber-stamp any such decision, much to the annoyance of some of their members. One of the tribunal's military representatives explained to an irate member that 'they are quite helpless in the case of railway servants. Like coalmines, they dealt with exemptions themselves.'[51]

However, it was decisions relating to agricultural workers that took up most time in south Shropshire. In such cases the tribunals had to balance the need for keeping the nation's food supplies flowing whilst attempting to ensure that the army was fed with recruits. Matters were made even more difficult by the changing advice and instructions received from above. For example, in July 1916 the Local Government Board issued guidelines that advised that one man was required for every 200 sheep on enclosed land. In addition the employment of one man for every 50 stall or yard stock cattle should be allowed, and also one man for each team of horses needed to cultivate the land. Then, three months later, tribunals were told to adjourn all cases involving farm workers and then, two weeks later, all tribunal chairmen were called to a meeting at Shrewsbury to be told that as from 1 January 1917 all men under 30 should be conscripted. They were informed that:

> A scheme had been drawn up for finding substitutes for farm workers taken before that date but after that date every man under thirty would be taken, substitute or no substitute.[52]

It was then decided that half of all exempted men on farms, whatever their age, married or single, should join the army if possible. It was envisaged that men graded medically as C3 would replace them.[53] But this instruction was amended yet again when it was realised what the effect would be on food production since virtually all C3 men would have little or no experience of farm work. As a result, until a suitable replacement was actually found, it was usual for local tribunals to grant farmhands exemption. In agricultural areas such as south Shropshire this meant that hundreds of able-bodied young men avoided conscription.

In June 1916, another circular from the Local Government Board advised the tribunals that they could make service with the Volunteer Training Corps (VTC), a condition of exemption. The Church Stretton tribunal took the decision to implement this for nearly all their cases, whilst the Ludlow one would do so only where the exemption was for six months or over. Then problems began to arise when a number of men, after accepting the condition, failed to abide fully by it. When attendance at the Ludlow VTC was checked in September it was found that though many had attended all the programmed drills, others had not. A number had only attended a handful of times, one man just twice and two men only once.

The tribunal decided to recall these men to ask for an explanation and threatened to withdraw their exemptions if they were not satisfied. They then introduced a rule whereby a man had to present a record of attendance at VTC drills when he next came before the tribunal to ask for a further extension of his exemption. The same problem was encountered at Bridgnorth. Here, not only were some men not turning up to drill with the VTC but a few were said to be actively trying to persuade others not to go either. The tribunal asked for a list of the 40 men whose attendance record was poor and summoned the worst six of them back to the tribunal. Five were given a stern warning as to their future conduct but only one had his exemption rescinded.[54]

In November 1917 the tribunals were relieved of dealing with such problems when it was decided that absence from the VTC would be the subject of military discipline. Then in January 1918 the Local Government Board allowed the tribunals to make it a condition of exemption for those not deemed fit enough for the VTC that they had to undertake to help the war effort via some other form of public service such as the Red Cross Society, the St John's Ambulance Brigade or even by working on the land in their spare time.[55]

Being a tribunal member and making unpopular decisions meant that some received abuse both first and second hand. One man who had criticised what he saw as the virtual automatic exemptions given to all railway employees admitted that:

> He had got himself into very hot water over this matter. He did not mind himself, but to have his wife and family shouted at in the street was very disagreeable.

It was especially hard on the working-class members, whom some saw as class traitors. Of the two union men on the Ludlow tribunal, William Nash 'complained that since the previous sitting he had been cursed in the street by certain people'. The other, George Randles, said 'that he had had one or two threatening letters with no name on them' which he had put on the fire.[56]

From the very beginning the tribunals had come under outside scrutiny mainly because of their apparently incestuous links to the local councils and the ruling local elites. Accusations of bias were levelled from the very beginning. At the very first meeting of the Ludlow rural district tribunal it was claimed that an employer sat on the panel when an appeal from one of his own workers was heard. In addition it was claimed that the Ludlow borough tribunal, which included the mayor, the deputy mayor and a further councillor, was due to hear exemption appeals for many of the council's own workers. Feelings were so strong that an editorial in the *Ludlow Advertiser* warned the tribunal that the newspaper would be carefully watching all decisions:

The instructions issued by the LGB with respect to the National Service Act explicitly state that when a member of a Tribunal is an interested party to an application being made he shall retire during the hearing, and take no part in the deliberation of the Tribunal on that case. We hope that this reminder may prove sufficient, and that it will not be necessary for us to enter into details, which we will not hesitate to do if the official instructions are set at defiance.[57]

The same warnings were being given to the tribunals in and around Bridgnorth. Here the issue was even raised in the House of Commons. It was stated that of the five members on the Bridgnorth tribunal three of them, including the chairman, were in the boot and shoe trade and that they had sat on the panel when the appeals of two other boot and shoe competitors were heard and refused, with the consequence that their businesses were closed down to the trade advantage of those making the decision. Smarting from this public censure, the tribunal increased their membership and added representatives of other trades to their numbers. However, at the very next meeting another boot and shoe retailer, aged 35, married and a sole trader, submitted an appeal. Though the members of his trade stood down whilst the case was heard, the result was still that he was given just three months to put his affairs in order so that he could then report for duty.[58]

At Bishop's Castle an engine fitter and agricultural mechanic went as far as to accuse his local tribunal to its face, claiming 'that the majority of the tribunal was interested in him being cleared out of the town', and he challenged them to administer the law without bias. His outburst did not help; he too was given three months to arrange his affairs before reporting to the army.[59]

Another member of that same tribunal, Alderman Dr Selwyn Hale Puckle, twice successfully appealed on behalf of his chauffeur, stating that he needed a driver if he was to carry out his duties effectively and that the three applicants who had applied for the post were not suitable to drive the quality of car that he owned. His appeals were won even though a fellow member, Councillor Edwards, claimed that the chauffeur had wanted to attest under the Derby Scheme but that Dr Hale Puckle had contacted his friend Captain Marsden at the Ludlow Recruiting Office to ask that he did not accept him.[60]

Sir Rouse Boughton of Downton Hall, the chairman of his local tribunal, also successfully appealed for the exemption of his fully fit gamekeeper on the grounds that he occasionally helped out as a farm labourer on the estate at a time when workers on the land were in short supply and more food production was sorely needed. Though he stood down for this case he was very happy when his fellow tribunal members upheld the appeal. This decision was in contrast to another at the same tribunal meeting when a farmer from Ditton Priors asked that his son be exempted since he was the only worker on the 75-acre farm two other workers having already joined the Army. Unlike the gamekeeper his request was refused, with the unsympathetic remark that 'the farmer took the farm with his eyes open'.[61]

Accusations of favouritism persisted over the coming months. Ludlow tribunal which, as we have seen, was chaired by a grocer who also happened to be the mayor, laid itself open to question when other grocers had their exemptions refused after the chairman had won exemptions for his own employees:

> As a case in point, some weeks ago a local firm of grocers obtained exemptions for three assistants, one single and two married, while last week you reported that a local grocer, married, running a rising one man business, unassisted, also as far as possible taking the place in his father's business of a brother who is fighting, was given only one month. This illustration of my meaning could be augmented by dozens of similar decisions and I think you will agree it is time some explanation of their policy is due from the powers that be.[62]

A similar complaint was volubly aired regarding the butcher trade:

> It still rings in the air about the unfair and most unjust way in which the butchers' cases in Ludlow were dealt with. ... Does not the disgrace seem to grow more when one can see two young, strong A men still in the same shop? The two B1 men are to join up on Monday next ... knowing that they are the victims of a most unjust decision. ... It is little to be wondered at that the question is asked 'Is it the military or is there some influence being used from other sources?'[63]

A pattern of young, up and coming new businesses being forced to close down whilst more established local businesses, represented by many on the local councils, traded on with apparently little inconvenience was the subject of much disquiet in letters to local newspapers:

> How is it that our tribunals seem to be determined to ruin the tradesmen of the town; a young fellow commences business and is getting on, gets married, and the tribunal lays its iron hand upon him, sweeps him into its net, and his business is destroyed![64]

In Bishop's Castle alone six small local businesses were forced to close down within months of conscription being introduced. It appears that for many of the local elite who sat on the tribunals, sending your sons off to war was a patriotic duty, but keeping your key workers at home whilst sending your competitors to the front was an economic duty.

The reputation of the tribunals was not enhanced when their members successfully appealed for their own exemption. Alderman E.S. Davies, the Mayor of Bishop's Castle, appealed against his own call-up to the army on a number of grounds. One was that he had a business that would have to close down if he went, but others were of a more tenuous nature: that he had a wife and two children to support; that he was one of the largest ratepayers in the town; and that he was a 'considerable taxpayer'. His fellow tribunal members and friends listened sympathetically and granted his exemption.[65]

Eyebrows were also raised when close friends of tribunal members successfully applied for exemptions for their employees. Mrs Elizabeth Garnett-Botfield, a lady of social standing in Bishop's Castle, asked for an exemption for her chauffeur and was granted it. A Miss Whittaker, the lady master of the local United Hunt, successfully appealed at the Clun military tribunal for her whipper-in. As she could not attend in person, she even asked the chairman of the tribunal to speak on her behalf since he was the Hon. Secretary and Treasurer of the Hunt.[66]

Favouritism to hunt members also occurred in the Ludlow and Bridgnorth areas. The kennel men for both local hunts were exempted, though the decision at the Ludlow district tribunal provoked a spate of irate letters to the local newspaper. The decision was not helped by the fact that two of the tribunal members were hunt members: one the joint master and the other the Hon. Secretary. Though they stood down for the case their presence must have been felt. One letter compared the tribunal's decision to that of another at the same meeting:

> The poor man's business may go bang but hands off the rich man's sport. I refer to the crying scandal of the repeated period of exemption granted by the Rural District Council's Tribunal to the kennel man of the Ludlow Hounds. They send a draper (aged 35 – Class B3) into the army but exempt for another three months the kennel man of the Ludlow Hunt (aged 31 – Class A). It was stated that a substitute could not be obtained. Then here's a chance for rich gents to practice a bit of the patriotism they are so fond of preaching to the 'lower orders'. Let them take their coats off and do the necessary work themselves if it is of such vital importance to the nation that the Ludlow Hunt should be kept up. But is it? The writer will be convinced when he sees a follower or two who have never done a day's productive work in their lives release their servant for the Army and buckle down to his job themselves.[67]

The apparent hypocrisy of some influential local men and women was the topic of an editorial in the *Ludlow Advertiser*.

> The majority of people have long ago been fed up with would be teachers who themselves decline to comply with the demands they wish to force

upon others. We refer to the previous recruiting campaign, of course. Much has happened since those days and we imagine many people must not only [have had] their eyes opened, but have used strong words at the spectacle of men pressing others into the Army, but who, when the time came that they thought their own businesses were likely to be inconvenienced by more men being called up, took instant advantage of every loophole the Military Service Act afforded.[68]

Tribunal favouritism provoked so much anger that even an ex town councillor of Ludlow felt obliged to write about the scandal of it in the strongest terms:

> We were told in the early stages of the war in the town hall, Ludlow, that our boys should go and uphold the tradition of this ancient borough. The majority of them have gone; some have returned maimed for life; some will never return. Yet we see the favoured few who swank around the town, as if there was no war on. As a father and brother of two of the boys at the front, I speak the sentiments of many fathers and mothers of this and other districts, that we can trace the work of the 'Hidden Hand' that has played SUCH a part in the war. The boys have endured untold hardships and misery, while a favoured few have been packing their parcels and not their kitbag.[69]

Tribunals also saw unsuccessful attempts to sway their judgement. Because of blatant attempts to influence members of the Clun tribunal the military representative publicly warned appellants that any further attempt to canvass any individual member would be reported to the full tribunal. Others appearing before tribunals to ask for exemptions lied or, at the very least, were prone to bend the truth. A grocer asked for his 'indispensable' assistant not to be called for service, as female labour 'could not be employed with any prospect of success'. It was then discovered that he already employed girls in two of his other branches. On another occasion, at what must have been at the risk of losing his job, one employee wrote to the *Church Stretton Advertiser* that his employer had not told the truth to his local tribunal. It appears that the employer claimed that his chauffeur also worked as a gardener. However the head gardener publicly contradicted this, saying that he could certainly agree that though a 'chauffeur he certainly is ... I wish to contradict that he is a gardener ... Excuse me interfering, but I do like justice'.[70]

No doubt to the embarrassment of some tribunal members, even fellow councillors were accused of misleading tribunals. At Ludlow, Councillor Edward Rickards, who ran an established ironmongers, was accused of lying in a letter to the local newspaper signed 'Justice':

Will the military authorities move and test the evidence given by Mr Rickards as the clause in the Act is still in force dealing with a person or persons making wrongful statements before any of the tribunals. Or is it a case of a law for the rich and one for the poor? I question if Mr Rickards would be able to find room and work for his seven or eight assistants which he states he had before the war.[71]

It appears the writer's fear was justified since his letter of complaint was apparently ignored.

The sheer numbers of men appealing for exemption rather than accepting conscription and going off to fight understandably angered those already serving. John Penny of Ludford wrote to his local newspaper expressing his bitterness:

As a result of your paper, which I have had every week since I have been out on active service with the BEF, I am quite shocked to see so many young fellows belonging to the outlying districts of Ludlow applying for exemption in cases where they are not necessary. What are they afraid of? Being shot or are they afraid to leave the peaceful country where they belong? If I had my way I would put them in the front line of trenches where far better men belonging to the old town have given their lives for the sake of the country.[72]

Such bitterness was seen back in Shropshire. A saddened vicar of Lydham wrote to Frederick Green, one of his parishioners serving at the front, describing how village life had been fractured due to a number of men successfully applying to their local military tribunal for exemption from conscription whilst other villagers daily risked their lives in the trenches:

I can't say as much for the friendliness of the people in Lydham. Some next door neighbours don't speak to one another and others only when they are obliged to. It is all sad and very unchristian but so long as people let their temper and pride have full swing and don't curb their spiteful remarks, so long will unfriendly feeling go on.[73]

Not all letters to or about the tribunal were complaints. Others gave information that it was felt the tribunal should hear. Many, especially those who had family members at the front, found a sense of bitterness growing because so many men were successfully avoiding being conscripted, and felt compelled to inform on them. 'Bo Peep' was advised by her local newspaper to contact the Recruiting Officer with her information. Clun's tribunal received two letters, one anonymous, citing two examples of able-bodied young men of military age not in the Army whilst those in their own family were. Angered that only a temporary exemption had been given to a married traction engine driver at Clee Hill who had four children, another anonymous writer drew the tribunal's attention to two other young men:

> If the Military Representative would just have a look on two traction engines round Ludlow he would find two single young men, both Class A, younger than the above man, who rushed into the job and have got off military service; and should be found something better to do than joy riding on Sundays with their motor bikes.[74]

Other accusations were less specific:

> There are families in Ludlow whose sons have known the horrors of three winters in the trenches but there are families of two or three sons whose chief anxiety is that they will not be exempted by the Local Tribunal.

Another letter signed 'Disgruntled of Bishop's Castle,' penned after reading about a local family where six brothers were all in the Army, stated that:

> I know of a family of seven brothers and not one is in the army, most of them of military age and A men. I want to know the reason why these men should shirk the army. ... When conscription came out they were soon after a horse of some sort to jog about on and get a certificate or badge to keep them out of it.[75]

Tribunal members sometimes asked that specific people be investigated. George Randles, incensed at the number of single young men still in Ludlow, gave the military advisor to his tribunal a list of names. When told that all of them were either medically unfit, exempted, or had been badged as doing work of national importance, he promptly gave him another list of names.[76]

There were attempts to catch men who had not been exempted or badged. One tribunal member, after saying that it was a matter of comment in Ludlow that a lot of single young men could be seen on the streets, especially on a Saturday night, was informed that the police had the power to stop any man and demand to see his exemption certificate. If he failed to show one he could be arrested. In August 1916 a number of men from Ludlow, Clee Hill, Cleobury Mortimer, Craven Arms, Bishop's Castle, Clun and Minsterley who had been called up into the armed forces failed to report on the day stipulated. An official list of these men was then placed in the local newspapers with the message that any informant who told the authorities where any of them were could remain anonymous. In addition, all employers not only had to supply a monthly list to their local recruiting officer of all workers but also had to inform him within 24 hours if any man between the ages of 18 and 42 was taken on as an employee. Employers also had to display a list of all workers of military age in a prominent public place and could be fined, as was a farmer near Bridgnorth, if they did not. After one spot check on a farm near Bourton, Much Wenlock a 33-year-old man who had never registered was arrested, fined and then handed over to the military authorities.[77]

Though many men voluntarily answered the call to join the armed forces, it is clear that many did not, and subsequently sought to avoid conscription. The reasons for the latter were varied, ranging from a fear of the conditions and casualty rates in the new trench warfare, to the worry of leaving their families destitute without a wage earner or the possibility of not having a job on their return. Many sought to stay at home by working in a protected industry and being 'badged'. Very few men who were conscripted went without a struggle. But it still remains a fact that many men donned khaki. In the borough of Ludlow alone, where a population of 5,923 was recorded in the census of 1911, 1,025 men had served in the armed forces by the end of the war in 1918. Virtually every family had sent at least one member to the trenches, and many families far more.

3 Helping on the Home Front

Even if they could not serve their country in the armed forces, many men and women throughout south Shropshire wanted to help the war effort in some way or other and to be seen to 'do their bit'. The upper and middle classes, who had the organising ability, social connections and spare time available, tended to take the lead and as a result committees sprang up everywhere to co-ordinate activities and collections for numerous causes. These ranged from sending woollen mittens to keep the hands of the troops warm in the trenches to collecting vegetables to help keep sailors healthy at sea. People also offered places of safety for refugees and some their houses for the care of the wounded. Others sent parcels of what they deemed 'necessaries' to individual soldiers whom they had never met. In towns and villages throughout the area patriotism was soon expressed in a myriad of flag days and a plethora of sewing and knitting workshops.

One of the first causes to be taken up was that of offering a home to Belgian refugees, who were seen as plucky defenders against Germanic militarism. The call went out from a central committee in London for councils to persuade their local communities to offer hospitality to as many Belgian refugees as they could. As early as September 1914 a committee to take this forward was formed in Bridgnorth at the instigation of the Revd Harry Victor Davies, the headmaster of the grammar school, who became its secretary; the mayor was its chairman. The social make-up of this committee, and the one established in Ludlow a month later, comprised the great and the good, setting the tone for the many committees that followed. In Ludlow it was the mayor, Samuel Valentine, who became chairman; Reginald Threlfall, the grammar school headmaster, was secretary; and George France, manager of the Capital and Counties Bank, was treasurer. A similar committee came into existence in Church Stretton in late October whilst the Mayor of Bishop's Castle became chairman of one in his town in November.[1]

Speed was of the essence, for refugees began to arrive before properties to house them were obtained and prepared. In Bridgnorth three families and a single man, totalling seven adults and seven children, were met at Bridgnorth railway station. The single man, an artist, was given shelter by the Reverend Davies whilst the remainder were offered temporary accommodation at St Leonard's Church House and the children's ward at the workhouse. Soon after, at Ludlow station, fifteen refugees arrived from Tilbury via Shrewsbury. Met by the mayor, they were driven in four cars to the town hall for a civic reception before being taken to temporary homes offered by townspeople who were paid between 10/- and 12/- a week for each refugee. This was pending a permanent home being made available.[2]

Such homes were often gained by accepting the offer of empty properties rent free, as was the case at Culmington, Ashford Carbonel, Stoke St Milborough and Elsich House, a farmhouse at Seifton near Craven Arms that could house 14 people. This latter property was offered by a Mr Holder of nearby Corfton Hall, whilst the Earl of Powis made a similar offer of a cottage in the parish of Lydbury North. Others offered rent-free housing in Bridgnorth, such as at Innage Gardens, and a house for two families was made available at Brampton Bryan. Other homes were provided where generous benefactors offered to pay the rent. An anonymous donor in Ludlow, for example, paid the rent for a house at 12 Dinham, whilst a Mrs Catterall of Church Stretton paid for rooms at Tower Buildings to house 18 Belgian refugees. In Bishop's Castle the De Bakaar family stayed in a rent-free property on Union Street, and another family were found a home in Welsh Street. A few families were placed in lodgings in family homes, as happened in Ashford Bowdler and Brimfield. As for furnishings, they were sometimes rented, as done at 12 Dinham, Ludlow at £5 per month – once again paid for by an anonymous benefactor – or supplied as gifts or loans by local people, as occurred in Church Stretton, Bridgnorth and Brampton Bryan. The total housed can be judged by the fact that by the end of January 1915, 88 Belgian refugees had been given a home in the area covered by Ludlow Borough and Ludlow Rural District Council.[3]

As regards day-to-day living expenses, these were covered in a variety of ways and sometimes depended on the class of person being helped. At Bridgnorth a plea went out to surrounding villages for help in maintaining the refugees given shelter in their area. The villages of Claverley and Glazeley responded by collecting and sending clothes, whilst the villages of Chelmarsh, Chetton, Burwarton, Cleobury North, Sidbury, Worfield and Morville sent weekly hampers of food. To raise money, concerts were put on and auctions held. A Percy Reynolds of Snitton gave a pig to be auctioned and it was bought, given back and sold yet again a total of 44 times, raising £25. Throughout south Shropshire weekly subscription funds were set up to ensure a steady stream of income both to pay some of the rents and to allow weekly allowances to be paid to the housed families. In Bishop's Castle each adult was given 5/- per week and each child 2/6d. In the Ludlow area the decision as to the amount of the weekly allowance was delegated to a ladies committee, which recommended 6/6d per week per person. Then the different needs of those in different social classes reared its head. The full Refugee Committee decided that those housed at

12 Dinham, who included a wine merchant, a restaurateur, an owner of a ladies' outfitters and the owner of an import/export business, required a higher income to cater for their needs. The committee voted that they should receive an extra shilling a week per person compared to those housed at Elsich House, who were described as of the artisanal class. The difference in the allowance for clothing, again based upon a decision made by the ladies' committee, was even greater. Those deemed to belong to the middle classes were awarded a clothing allowance of 10/- per month per person, whilst those further down the social scale received half that amount. To help reduce such clothing allowances, the people in and around Bridgnorth were soon asked to donate sewing machines so that the refugees could make their own clothes.[4]

Weekly allowances were not meant to be permanent because it was expected that the refugees would try to find work to support themselves. To encourage this, in Bishop's Castle it was agreed that once any of the refugees obtained employment then half their weekly wage would be deducted from that family's allowance. One refugee, a metalworker, was employed in making the memorial gates for the park at Church Stretton. As the weeks passed, the patience of the middle class committees began to run short with those who failed to look for work or otherwise appeared undeserving of charity. Ten of the working-class Belgian refugees given shelter at Elsich House near Craven Arms were declared 'undesirables' and returned in December 1914 to the central committee that had sent them. One of those who replaced them only lasted a few weeks for it was claimed that 'this refugee wished to lie in bed most of the time and would do nothing outside'. By October 1915 all at Elsich House had either been evicted or had obtained work elsewhere, two in the mines at Billingsley. The property was then used to house Belgian soldiers on leave from the front whose homes were in areas occupied by German forces. By February 1916 the subscription fund covering the Ludlow area was closed since all refugees had either left the area or were working and could maintain themselves. A number of the middle-class families returned to the Continent.[5]

Meanwhile, numerous flag days and house-to-house collections were held in towns and villages. Such events raised money not only for British or Empire needs, but also for French, Serbian and Russian civilians and troops. As the years passed and the cumulative cost of prosecuting the war grew, the call went out for men and women to invest in War Bonds. War Savings Committees sprang up nearly everywhere and one of the earliest, formed in October 1916, was that in Ludlow. An office was opened at 17 King Street and war trophies and relics were exhibited in the window to catch the public's attention. These included what was claimed to be a German cat o' nine tails said to have been used to punish their troops, five German bullets and a piece of shell fragment that had been extracted from wounded local soldier Sergeant David Kellock. Staffed by ladies, the office accepted weekly savings. A similar committee was set up in Bridgnorth in January 1917 and savings clubs were also set up in many villages. At Lydbury North the local vicar proudly announced that 'a flourishing War Savings Association has been formed' of which he was the president.[6]

Following the lead from London, local people also took part in national savings campaigns, including a Victory War Loan Week in early 1917 and two War Weapons Weeks in 1918. In the first War Weapons week the Bridgnorth committee aimed to raise £15,000 in order to purchase six aeroplanes. This figure was not only reached but exceeded to the tune of £55,000. In nearby Highley the more modest target of £5,000 was set to purchase two aircraft, and this too was overtaken, with £6,500 raised. The Ludlow committee, like the Bridgnorth one, set itself to raise £15,000 for six aircraft. To encourage the purchase of bonds, ladders were erected on the town hall, the Buttercross and at the top of Corve Street on which the total raised would be posted and updated daily. As part of the accompanying publicity, an aeroplane landed in a large field near

Throughout the war local people would take part in events such as fetes, parades and concerts in order to raise funds for many causes. Here, in 1916, John Fury, a Boer War veteran who lived in Tower Street, Ludlow, shows off his cavalryman's fancy dress outfit to his neighbours after presumably taking part in a war effort event. (Courtesy of Gareth Thomas)

Whitcliffe Wood before taking off to give a flying display over the town. It then landed again in Ludford Park where it 'ran into a ditch in the field, where its nose struck the ground and broke the propeller'. Notwithstanding this mishap, a final total of nearly £42,000 was raised. At the second War Weapons Week in June, three aeroplanes showed off their paces in the skies above the castle, generating much excitement on the ground.[7]

However, from the very early weeks of the war the main aim of those left behind was to ensure that the men who had gone to fight were supplied with 'comforts' in the form of clothing, food and day-to-day necessities. One of the main organisations to provide clothing 'comforts' for the troops was HM Queen Mary's Needlework Guild, which was set up centrally on 10 August 1914. It was hoped that towns and cities

One of the new sights that the war brought to Shropshire was that of the new flying machines. A number of aircraft were forced to land in various parts of the county due to mechanical failure or merely to ask where they were after becoming lost. This plane was being used to advertise the purchase of War Bonds during a national War Weapons Week in March 1918. After taking off from a field near Whitcliffe Wood, it came to grief when it attempted a landing in Ludford Park following a flying display over Ludlow. An inquisitive crowd soon surrounded it. (Courtesy of Gareth Thomas)

throughout the land would organise sewing and knitting circles under the umbrella organisation. Within days this was happening, formed mainly from the middle classes. In Bishop's Castle the mayoress, Mrs Annie Mary Hale Puckle, set up a circle that met weekly in the local parish room. Showing amazing industry, this branch had soon made and sent off its first batch of 20 shirts, 31 nightshirts, 8 pairs of pyjamas, 6 bed-jackets, 36 handkerchiefs, 6 pairs of socks and 36 small cushions to Netley Military Hospital near Southampton. In Ludlow the mayoress, Mrs Catherine Valentine, set up a branch which by Christmas 1918 had produced and sent to the Guild's headquarters just under 7,000 articles of clothing. In addition, many other items had been delivered to local hospitals looking after wounded soldiers and to local men serving at the front. The Mayoress of Bridgnorth organised a group in her town that met every Thursday in the Drill Hall. Here between 20 and 30 ladies met, and by early 1915 had made 1,103 'comforts'. Similar bands of women formed in villages far and wide including Hopesay, Chelmarsh, Culmington, Deuxhill, Stoke St Milborough and Claverley. Money to purchase materials was collected in a number of ways including donations, fund raising events such as teas and concerts and even by placing boxes in local village shops as at Clungunford.[8]

As news filtered home from the western front about the lack of suitable clothing to survive the winter conditions, there was a further expansion of groups making 'comforts'. By mid 1915, groups set up in Clee Hill village and Knowbury in November 1914 had made over 600 shirts and pairs of socks. These were mainly sent direct to local servicemen. In Bridgnorth a Voluntary Workers Association was

One member of the Cheshire Regiment keeps watch whilst his comrades try to sleep on ledges or holes cut into the sides of the trench, covering themselves as best as they could from the wet and the cold. It was because their menfolk daily suffered from conditions such as these that local women set up sewing and knitting groups in virtually every town and village to make 'comforts' for the troops. Even schoolchildren joined in the effort to provide items such as balaclavas, scarves and mittens. (Author's collection)

organised and by 1917 it was annually turning out a staggering variety of items, including 1,200 pairs of mittens, 779 pairs of socks, 195 towels, 229 sun shields, 11 dressing gowns, 154 handkerchiefs, 25 mosquito nets, 22 helmets, 110 hospital bags, 237 anti-vermin vests, 55 pairs of bed socks, 574 mufflers, 521 shirts, 55 pairs of operation stockings and 8 bed-jackets. In Church Stretton a Miss Louisa Jane Crump organised another group of volunteers, while the town's schoolchildren decided to try and make the plight of the common soldier more comfortable. Pupils at the local elementary school knitted sweaters, scarves, mittens and mufflers. Thirty-four parcels were sent to local servicemen, and a large box to a base hospital in France. They then embarked on making further items to be sent to the Royal Navy and to troops fighting in Salonika, Greece.[9]

It appears that local servicemen truly appreciated these gifts and many sent back personal replies. George Rogers of Ludlow wrote to say: 'Will you please thank Mrs

Barker, Mrs Cliff and all the members of the sewing class for me. Shirts and socks arrived safely.'[10] Arthur Phillips of Lydbury North thanked all the women carrying out such work when he returned on leave. Speaking for himself and his comrades he said that:

> We out there all admire the way the brave English women are working for us at home. Words cannot adequately express our appreciation of their kindly efforts on our behalf.[11]

Knitting and sewing clubs proliferated in order to make 'comforts' for the troops both in the trenches and in hospitals. As a result, a small industry developed to produce patterns – for a few pence instructions could be purchased to show how to knit mittens, socks and balaclavas, to crochet sleeping caps or to cut out and make pyjamas or bed jackets. (Courtesy of Shropshire Museum Services)

One particularly poignant example of such work occurred at Claverley. In the last letter sent home by Captain George Gatacre, and received by his mother on the day that he was killed, he asked for winter socks for his men. The ladies of the parish immediately set to work and fulfilled his last request.[12]

Various bodies wishing to play their part in making the lives of servicemen just a little easier sent 'comforts' other than clothes. The Ludlow Evening Club provided a chess set, three sets of dominos, two sets of draughts and a table quoits set for the local territorials. A Patriotic Concert was held at Ludlow town hall for which 'most of the leading townspeople took tickets' and entered through a guard of honour provided by the Boy Scouts. The money raised purchased 108 blankets from local tradesmen of which 54 were sent to the Territorials and 54 to local men serving in Kitchener's New Army. Similar fund raising concerts were held throughout the area including small villages such as Bitterley, where a concert was held in the schoolroom.[13]

Individuals also organised the sending of gifts. Under the national Smokes For Soldiers and Sailors Fund, the owner of

J.H. Grant and Son, tobacconists of the Bull Ring, Ludlow, collected cigarettes from customers who donated them from the packets they bought at his shop. In the first week they collected 625. Then, in addition to cigarettes, gifts of chocolate, tinder lighters and pipe tobacco were collected, packaged and sent off. On one day alone seven postcards were received at the shop from soldiers at the front thanking the firm and their customers for their gifts. In yet another national campaign taken up locally, gifts of razors for servicemen could be given to any postman or handed in over any post office counter.[14]

Foreign soldiers and the Royal Navy were not forgotten. Local people were asked to bring donations of groceries to their town halls to be sent to Belgian soldiers both in the trenches and in hospitals. As for the Navy, an ongoing campaign to collect fresh fruit and vegetables to be sent to the fleet via the naval base at Aberdeen was initially run from the Recruiting Office on Corve Street, Ludlow before moving to 5 King Street where a depot was set up. The first batch of four hampers was despatched in June 1915, and by September an average of 4-5 cwt of produce was being sent weekly. The officers and crews of *HMS Superb* and *HMS Hercules* sent their heartfelt thanks, whilst those of *HMS Cyclops* relayed the news that 'the rhubarb, cucumber and gooseberries were particularly appreciated'. Other groups also helped, with the boys of Ludlow Grammar School collecting jars of jam for sailors.[15]

The odd begging letter was also received. An officer of a paddle minesweeper that was built and launched at Goole in 1916 and named *HMS Ludlow* wrote the following to the Town Clerk in September that year:

> I have the pleasure to inform you that the above named ship of HM Navy, which was commissioned last month, has been named after your town and on behalf of the crew I wish to convey to you the fact that we have been presented with a very nice gramophone by the shipbuilder, but unfortunately the number of records for same are very few.

He then went on to ask if the town could possibly send them some records and also 'any warm comforts such as sweaters, gloves etc. or smoking material at your disposal'; a request that was granted, though the gifts did not bring the crew much luck since the ship was sunk within weeks off the Suffolk coast in December 1916 by a mine that it had failed to detect.[16]

It appears that those in the trenches especially appreciated gifts of food since these alleviated the boredom of the usual daily rations, and special requests to families would be made. Private W. Painter wrote to his stepbrother in Church Street, Bishop's Castle saying that as regards clothing he was fairly well supplied but that 'a small cake would be very acceptable'.[17] The typical contents of parcels sent by a soldier's family can be seen in a letter to his sister in Ludlow from an Ernest Ovens. He listed the contents of a parcel that she had sent him in order to check if any item had been pilfered on its journey.

> It contained two pots of ham and chicken paste, one tin of coffee and milk, two bottles of lemon tablets, soap, sponge, notepaper and the coke, so you will know if anything has been taken out.[18]

Parcels were especially appreciated at Christmas time. In 1914 it was mainly family and friends that sent such gifts, but with each passing year more were paid for with money raised by community events and sent off in the name of the community. Such communal efforts occurred at Lydbury North, Clungunford, Bedstone and Clunbury for Christmas 1915. At Church Stretton a whist drive and a dance were held to collect funds to send seasonal gifts to local men at the front, whilst the pupils of Ludlow Grammar School sent 62 parcels to serving 'old boys'. Again in Ludlow, a concert was held to help pay for presents for other local servicemen. John Lucas received his whilst serving in Greece and though it arrived late it was still received with gratitude.

> The bulk of our Xmas mails are still arriving and amongst my recent share of the good things has been a pleasant surprise afforded by a gift of the parcel sent by Mr O'Connor's concert fund. The contents have given great pleasure to myself and my comrades and I trust you will convey my heartiest thanks to all concerned for such a kindly and generous thought.[19]

By Christmas 1916, many local councils began to take on the responsibility of ensuring that each serviceman from their area received a seasonal parcel. In Ludlow it began with the mayor placing an advertisement in the local newspaper asking for donations in order to send gifts to Ludlovians serving in the Far East with the 4th Battalion KSLI. At the next council meeting, fellow aldermen and councillors asked why such gifts could not be forwarded to all Ludlovians serving on the western and other fronts. As a result a committee was immediately formed to organise this. It was decided that cash would be sent out to those in the Far East whilst the rest would receive gifts in kind. At the same time the council in Bishop's Castle raised £40 to pay for parcels for its 160 local servicemen. Those serving in France and Belgium received a tin of sardines, a tin of salmon, soup tablets, Oxo cubes, toilet soap, tea cubes, chocolate, cigarettes and a box of trench ointment which was supposed to help alleviate frostbite. Rural parishes, both large and small, carried out the same task for their parishioners in the armed forces. Winstantow Parish, just north of Craven Arms, sent out over 120 parcels, whilst at Hope Bowdler the vicar's wife, Mrs Mary Matthews, oversaw the sending off of 18 parcels.[20]

Throughout the area auctions were held in aid of the war effort, many of them organised by local branches of the National Farmers Union. On a warm September day in 1915 a crowd gathered in a farmyard near Clun to bid for various donated items, some of which would be purchased and then offered for sale again. In the lower photograph, of the opening of the event, a young girl is presenting the Countess of Powis with a bouquet of flowers whilst the Revd Richard Machen looks benevolently on. (Courtesy of A.T.D. Evans)

Ludlow Borough Council's efforts threatened to become a scandal when it appeared that the money sent to the troops in the Far East failed to arrive. This led to questions as to the possibility of local councillors and their friends profiteering from the sending of the Christmas parcels to other theatres of war. The editor of the local newspaper duly wanted to know what was the total amount of money collected? How was the money spent? And finally, since the mayor and a number his fellow councillors owned shops, what were the names of the tradesmen to whom the orders for the gifts in kind were placed, together with the amounts spent with each? It appears the questions were never publicly answered. The council at Bishop's Castle avoided such suspicion of profiteering by declaring that local tradesmen supplied all the goods at cost price.[21]

Partly to avoid any repetition of such embarrassing questions, Ludlow Council decided that for Christmas 1917 each of the 543 Ludlow men serving overseas would be given a gift of a 5/- postal order. The funds were raised mainly from a house-to-house collection.[22] This change certainly appears to have been welcomed by the recipients. George Brown received his postal order on Christmas morning and immediately used it to purchase 'a lot of tasty things from the canteen which otherwise we would have had to do without; the boys who helped to eat them gave three cheers for the Mayor and the borough of Ludlow'.[23] Spending a postal order was not always easy, however. William Munns of Mill Street stated that he 'had to walk about eight miles last night to change it but to a soldier out here [France] that was only a detail.'[24] The advantages appeared to outweigh the disadvantages as George Chapman of Bell Lane, Ludlow, explained:

> I have read the *Advertiser* each week with interest since being out here, and was pleased to note that it was finally decided to send the boys postal orders in place of parcels, which I am sure, in nine cases out of ten, will be more appreciated. The BEF canteens, the YMCA and Church Army Huts cater so well for the boys that the 5/- postal orders will, out here, go further than it will in England especially in the purchase of cigarettes and tobacco and in fact the majority of little odds and ends needed by a soldier out here.[25]

The hundred servicemen from the parish of Clun had received a 5/- postal order since Christmas 1916, but not all switched to this system. Bishop's Castle council still preferred to send a parcel to their serving men in 1917. The contents had subtly changed and now held a number of more practical items, though who advised on this is not known. They still contained a tin of salmon and a tin of sardines, cigarettes and cocoa tablets but now, in addition, to trench ointment to combat frostbite they also held Keating's flea repellent powder and a heating lamp. The council finally did switch in Christmas 1918 to the sending of postal orders: one of 10/- for men overseas, and 5/- for those on Home Service. This was slightly more generous than that sent that year by Ludlow, who had increased the amount to 7/6d for the 442 men serving abroad.[26] The gifts certainly travelled, as Charles Amphlett of Ludlow recalled:

> I have just received my third Christmas gift from the borough. My first – in 1916 – I received in the shape of a parcel near the foot of Mount Olympus in Greece, where my unit was on outpost. The second one I received while in Bethany, on the Jericho Road, near the Holy City.

The 1918 gift found him in camp at Heliopolis near Cairo awaiting transport home.[27]

Parcels of food and 'comforts' were also sent to local men who had been taken as prisoners of war. In the first months of the war, once news of their capture was received and the address of the camp in which they were held was known, it was left to family members to send clothes, toiletries, food or any other small luxury such as cigarettes, but this was difficult for poorer families. The result was a number of

At the behest of Lady Catherine Gaskell, Albert Brazier and Richard Davies, employed as gardeners at Much Wenlock Abbey, prepare plants for sale to raise money for wounded soldiers. A wide variety of fund raising activities to help the war effort took place throughout south Shropshire. (Courtesy of Ina Taylor)

what can only be called 'begging' letters sent by prisoners to anyone of local social standing that they knew.

Captain E. Richard Marsden, the recruiting officer in Ludlow, received a letter dated 1 April 1915 from a POW camp at Gottingen in Lower Saxony. It was from two men who had previously served under him in the old Ludlow Company of Volunteers: Alfred (Fred) Jones, whose parents lived in Lower Broad Street and Herbert Handley who had been brought up in Mill Street but then lived with his wife in Craven Arms:

> We were both taken prisoner at Ypres in Belgium last November [1914] and Pte Handley has had the misfortune to lose his left eye. I believe we are the only two Shropshire men in a camp of some thousands.

They went on to ask whether it was possible for parcels containing food, clothes and tobacco to be sent to them since other prisoners were receiving such items from their local area. As a result, Marsden asked the local newspaper to publish their

In 1915, girls attending the preparatory school at Brockhurst House, Church Stretton, hold a small sale of toys, probably in aid of the Red Cross. (Courtesy of A.T.D. Evans)

letter, giving the addresses of the two men and asking if any local person would like to help by sending parcels direct to them.[28] At news that yet another local man, James Bishop from Clee St Margaret, had been taken prisoner, Marsden said that he was happy to receive gifts for the prisoners and see that they were parcelled out to be sent to all local POWs that he had been informed about. Some people heeded the call and within six weeks a postcard was received from Handley thanking the inhabitants of Ludlow for sending three parcels for himself and Jones.[29]

The Revd H.V. Davies, headmaster of Bridgnorth Grammar School, received a letter from Leonard Lythall, one of the school's old boys, who was also in a POW camp at Gottingen. His request was similar to that received in Ludlow:

> I hope you will excuse me asking this favour. ... It is rather hard for me to see so many parcels and food come into this camp and my name is never mentioned, so I thought I would write to see if you could help me. If you could send a box of bread and treacle, a bit of cheese, milk, tea or anything eatable to make up a box, you will hardly realise the kindness you are doing to me.[30]

The receipt of warm clothing from home including underwear, socks and foot-wear was also important and came as a blessing to the men in the camps, as Herbert Handley explained:

> You must remember that some of our fellows had no coats, no shirts or boots ... From the time of my going to the camp till April 1st 1915 ... I myself had no clean linen. ... Our beds were wood shavings in something like sugar bags and two very light blankets. It was so bitterly cold that some of our chaps tore them up to wrap round their feet to keep them from being frostbitten.[31]

Once the parcels began to arrive, requests for specific items, either to be sent or not sent, were often made in the return letter of thanks. James Bishop explained that 'it is advised to send either biscuits or Quaker Oats instead of bread as the latter is mostly bad when it reaches here'. He then added a request for 'one or two mouth organs ... to help cheer the boys up'. A Geoff Bridges, a scholar at James's old school, soon sent one. Herbert Handley and Fred Jones, after saying thanks for their jacket and waistcoat, asked 'may we have mufflers and bread a day old before packing and hard baked?'[32]

The appreciation for these gifts, which arrived nearly once a fortnight, cannot be over-emphasised. Herbert Handley, in a letter to Captain Marston, promised that 'if we reach home safely, Jones and myself will make it our duty to call and thank you personally'. In fact Handley explained the need for such parcels after he had been repatriated home to Craven Arms via Switzerland in 1917 due to his wounds. He recalled that on his arrival at the POW camp at Gottingen 'we had coffee and dry bread for breakfast; soup, no meat in it, for dinner; tea and boiled barley for tea. That was all the meals we had.' This meagre diet changed when the parcels began arriving:

> The first parcel of food I received was on 1 March 1915. I can tell you that the only thing that kept me alive were the parcels of food so kindly sent by my wife and friends in Ludlow and Craven Arms. How can I thank them all for their kindness to me?

Even with these extras, when Herbert Handley was sent to Switzerland in August 1916, he weighed less than seven stone.

Sergeant William Ashwood, of Bridgnorth, at a public dinner given to celebrate the return of local prisoners, also spoke of the gratitude felt by all South Shropshire POWs: 'The men out there could never have lived on the food given to them.'[33]

Belatedly, a system began to be set up so that local POWs would no longer have to rely on just family help and the charity of a few kind individuals. In June 1915 the KSLI set up a fund to help its men who had been taken prisoner. At first the only extra help that the fund provided, in addition to the support given by the family and their local town, was an extra supply of bread, clothing and tobacco. Then in December 1916 the War Office set out a new scheme under which the sending of parcels would become the responsibility of each prisoner's regiment. One reason for this was that the authorities were worried that German spies were sending information back to Germany in private parcels purporting to be for a POW. Another was that many parcels were not arriving because they were either badly packed or incorrectly addressed, or both. Starting in early 1917 only authorized committees with their own known and supervised packers could post parcels to POWs.[34]

At first the packing for the KSLI was carried out at 7 Castle Street, Shrewsbury by four packers under the control of a Mr and Mrs Thomas Butcher. Three parcels a fortnight were sent to each man at an initial cost of 6/- a parcel. Each contained two tins of meat or fish, oatmeal or other dry grain, jam or syrup, margarine or dripping, chocolate, soups, tea or cocoa, sugar, condensed milk, soap, salt, pepper, tinned vegetables, tobacco and cigarettes. Cake or some other extra was then added when possible. Books were sent occasionally. In addition bread was baked and sent in winter from Berne, Switzerland or Copenhagen, Denmark to ensure that it was fresh on arrival. In summer a 'substantial biscuit' replaced bread. The family could still send parcels but these were limited to one every three months and had to be sent via the Shrewsbury depot. The weight of these could not exceed 11lbs and they were not to contain food. Recommended were such items as mufflers, mittens, toothbrushes and hairbrushes, shaving soap and games such as dominoes and draughts.

A postcard was placed in each parcel for the recipient to sign and return to show that the parcel had arrived safely. If a Shropshire prisoner was a member of another regiment, details were forwarded to their depot for them to organise the posting of parcels.

The system worked well at first since the number of prisoners being looked after was relatively small and each local community were able to help raise the necessary funds. In early 1918, with six Ludlow men known to be captive and only two of those with the KSLI, a £10 donation from the borough council was deemed sufficient.[35] The problems began to mount after the German offensive in the spring of 1918. On 1 January 1918, 34 KSLI POWs were receiving parcels, a number that had risen to 96 by 1 March and 973 by the time of the armistice in November. Not all lived in Shropshire, and fewer in south Shropshire, but to this figure must be added the local POWs in other regiments. In Bridgnorth and the surrounding villages the number of POWs who had returned by January 1919 totalled over 80.[36]

Due to the massive increase in the number of men in captivity after the spring offensive, the original workroom in Shrewsbury and the number of packers employed could no longer handle the parcels. In July 1918 larger premises at St Alkmund's Rooms were leased and the voluntary staff rose from four to 112. The main problem, however, was raising the money needed to pay for all the parcels, especially since the cost of each parcel was increasing in line with the rising cost of food: from 6/- to 8/- and then to 10/- per parcel. A massive fund raising effort was therefore set in motion throughout the hamlets, villages and towns of Shropshire.

Each small parish helped in any way that it could. As soon as news came through to Lydbury that three of its parishioners – Arthur Phillips, Thomas Meyrick and Charles Wilcox – had been captured, the Earl of Powis called a special meeting of the parish council to set up a committee to collect the funds to enable the Shrewsbury depot to send out its three parcels a fortnight to each man. The estimated cost for one year was £40 per man: a total of £120. With generous donations from the main families in the area and a house-to-house collection throughout the entire parish, the amount was more than raised. In Lydham parish the local parishioners quickly raised the money required to pay for parcels to be sent to Harry Harries from Church Stoke. Other small parishes raised what they could even if none of their parishioners were incarcerated. A dance at Deuxhill raised £8 whilst at Morville and Aston Eyre £22 was collected.[37] Fund-raising events were widespread. At Overton Lodge, near Ludlow, a sale of work was held in a large marquee with stalls selling fancy goods, clothing, vegetables and plants whilst the depot band of the KSLI played a programme of music. This was followed by an auction and the whole day raised £82. By Armistice Day the KSLI Prisoners Fund had received payments totalling nearly £26,000.

There were other problems too, not least the lack of up-to-date information as to the specific whereabouts of individual prisoners. Official channels sometimes worked more slowly than unofficial ones, the first news of a transfer to a new camp often coming in a letter to a family from the prisoner or one of his comrades. In such cases the next of kin were asked to inform the local POW committee in Ludlow or a Mr Willis at 27 St. Leonard's, Bridgnorth, who was presumably a member of that town's local POW committee. They would then pass on the details to Shrewsbury.[38] This happened to the mother of John Powell of Bell Lane, Ludlow. John had been taken prisoner in March 1918 but after news of him in June from a prison camp his whereabouts suddenly became unknown. Then in late September a letter arrived from a camp on the German/Polish border which stated that he was still 'poorly and weak' after having spent two months in hospital and had not received any parcels for many weeks. Immediately his mother informed the local POW committee and they quickly arranged that an emergency parcel be sent to him.[39] A number of others failed to receive parcels because they were not held in camps but were members of labour gangs just behind the front line that were continually on the move. This happened to Arthur Phillips of Lydbury North, who was captured on 22 March 1918 and set to work on the German railways. Consequently, he had no fixed address and by the time a parcel was sent to the address on any letter or postcard he managed to send home, he had once again been moved on.[40]

Local people also put their hands in their pockets to help soldiers reach their homes when coming back on leave, though sadly this was not until the last year of the war. Since 1914 soldiers in the rural areas had had to walk home from the nearest railway station, carrying their kitbags. It was only just before Christmas 1917 that stories began to circulate about the treks a number of returning servicemen had to make. George Hamer, in order to visit his parents who lived in Bishop's Castle, had to walk from Shrewsbury station. This story was made even more poignant when the news came back that he was killed just after his return to the front.[41] The editor of the *Ludlow Advertiser* decided to highlight the issue:

> They are often dumped down at Ludlow railway station after an all night journey at 8am and have to carry their kit to their homes in the country. We heard of one man who had to carry his between eight to nine miles last Monday.[42]

He then took up the issue of trying to provide transport for these men. He broached the matter with the Mayor of Ludlow but was rebuffed, being told that as the men lived in the villages they were the responsibility of the rural district council. The chairman of this council, Mr Richard de Courney Peele, was then contacted, and he:

... when approached, entered heart and soul into the matter, and by Tuesday he had completed temporary arrangements for the next fortnight by which soldiers arriving in Ludlow on leave, whose homes are over three miles distant from the town, will be conveyed thither by motor car no matter by what train they arrive in Ludlow.

The stationmaster would contact R.H. Wood of Corve Street Garage, who would take them 'at an exceedingly moderate charge'. To pay for this service the newspaper started a subscription, putting in 50/- itself. £42 was soon collected and within the first ten days eight men had been driven home, including a sailor who had already been travelling for three days and nights.[43] The mother of one of them wrote to the newspaper enclosing a small donation to express her heartfelt thanks:

> Will you please accept this towards your fund with gratitude for kindness my son received on reaching Ludlow Tuesday night 8.45. He started from the Cambrai front on Saturday – was held up by air raid in cattle trucks for hours – and therefore didn't reach England till Tuesday night. Can you imagine what a relief it was to find he hadn't to tramp two and a half miles whilst dirty and worn out.[44]

A similar scheme was soon organised at Craven Arms station covering the area to Bishop's Castle, Shipton, Onibury and Wistanstow. The operation remained in force until July 1919 when nearly all men had been demobbed.

For some time before this local people had been helping soldiers and munition workers by raising money for the Young Men's Christian Association (YMCA). From the beginning of the war this organisation had been running rest centres for troops near major railway stations in Britain and for war workers at factories. By mid 1915 the people of Bishop's Castle had raised the £50 needed to build a hut for munition workers called 'The Bishop's Castle Worker's Hut' and were soon collecting for a second one. That same year the YMCA began building rest centres just behind the front lines, and both Ludlow and Bridgnorth decided to raise money to build and equip a hut that would be named after their towns. Bridgnorth started their fund in May 1917. The South Shropshire Farmers Union also financed the building of one that was erected in the summer of 1917 in the centre of Arras after the town had been recaptured at Easter. It was situated within the grounds of the ruins of the Hotel de Ville. At first it was used to hold 'numerous lectures and concerts and entertainment of various kinds ... Every hour it was open the hut was crowded with troops.' It was soon refurbished as a rest hut 'for all men who wish to rest awhile in chairs more comfortable than usual, to read, whether it be the London papers in goodly selection but one day late or literature according to their special inclination or taste which they may borrow and take up to the trenches with them.' Light refreshments and tobacco were also available in the hut.[45]

Once Ludlow had decided to raise £600 for its own named YMCA hut it embarked on a series of fund-raising events mainly based around a 'Hut Week' that began on 1 October 1917. A 'clock' erected on the YMCA headquarters on Corve Street displayed the growing amount collected. The Picture Hall donated the proceeds from one of its performances, and two flag days were held, as was a house-to-house collection. In addition a jumble sale and concert were arranged in the town hall for both of which the local Girl Guides distributed advertising literature. There were even school collections.[46] Local servicemen truly appreciated this local effort as William Munns of Mill Street explained:

> After spending several weeks in the danger zone, the first time I went into a YMCA hut was to me a real haven of refuge, and to a good many more who had been roughing it ... I write this in sound of guns and shell fire and in a dug-out named after our castle ... May we soon see a Ludlow hut out here.[47]

His wish soon came true for within a month £716 had been raised, more than enough to build the 'Ludlow and District' hut at Achiet-Le-Grand in northern France. Sadly, it did not last long, for it was lost during the German spring offensive in 1918. When the land was retaken a few months later, Wilfred Packer, a YMCA volunteer from Ludlow, wrote home to his sister to say that all that remained of the hut was two bolts that he would bring home. The local branch of the YMCA also became directly involved in helping to keep up the morale of local servicemen by organising the free photographing of their families so that photographs could be sent to them at the front.[48]

The Church Army, an Anglican evangelical movement set up in 1882, also provided rest centres behind the lines. Funds for a hut named after Bridgnorth and District were successfully collected by February 1918, the hut being erected in the Calais area, whilst at Ludlow the mayor began collecting £300 for a Church Army tent in that same February.[49]

A few of the men who had not joined the regular forces, either because they were too old or because they had been exempted due to their employment, had joined their local Volunteer Training Corps (VTC) as their contribution to the war effort. As we saw in chapter one, these units were set up as part of a home defence force in case of invasion. In 1916 it was decided to amalgamate them all into a new county regiment. It was hoped that this would consist of two battalions, each with 1,300 men. At first it was proposed that members who transferred to the new regiment would be asked to swear a fresh volunteer's oath that included the promise to serve in the regular forces if called upon by the war office. This proved a massive stumbling block to the formation of the new corps since it was stated that any refusing the oath would not be able to join. In Ludlow, out of the then 50 members of the local VTC only six agreed to take the oath and even after various exhortations the number only rose to 17. At Church Stretton it was noted that 'there seemed some reluctance to take the oath', whilst at a recruitment meeting held at the town hall in Bridgnorth there were 'very few present'. The mayor tried to set an example by taking the oath, but very few followed him. A compromise had to be found and was. When the men were told that they would only be called up if this country were invaded, then the numbers agreeing to transfer swelled.[50]

The numbers hoped for, however, were never reached. Bridgnorth had the second largest contingent after Shrewsbury and boasted 200 members, but Ludlow never exceeded 100, whilst the Bishop's Castle detachment at first numbered only around 20. Even a year later those enlisted in the 2nd Battalion that covered south Shropshire totalled less than 900 as opposed to the planned 1,300.[51] A call also went out for donations to equip the new force with both uniforms and rifles. It was estimated that £4,000 would be required, but when the force was formed only £900 had been raised. Another call went out for funds but the response was mixed. In Ludlow the council sent out 60 letters to gentlemen of means whom it was hoped would help, but only one solitary £5 note was received. It was November 1917 before the Ludlow contingent was fully equipped with uniforms, rifles and bayonets. Even the small detachments at Bishop's Castle, Clun and Aston on Clun only received their full equipment in May 1917. These men gave up their free time to drill and train each week. This included learning how to dig trenches as well as rifle practice, the latter being carried out by the Clun detachment in the old castle grounds whilst the Ludlow platoons used the rifle range in the Drill Hall. Members also had to attend a one-week camp at Fleetwood, Lancashire whilst a few in the summer of 1918 volunteered to serve for up to three months as part of the defence force on the east coast.[52]

Children also played their part in helping the war effort – especially in food production as will be seen in the next chapter, but they helped in other ways too. In the autumn of 1917 it was agreed between the Board of Education and the Ministry of Food that schoolchildren were to be employed in the collection of horse chestnuts, acorns and blackberries during school hours. The acorns and some of the chestnuts would be used for animal feed since it was estimated that every ton used for fodder would release half a ton of grain for human consumption. In addition it had been discovered that horse chestnuts could be used as a substitute for one of the ingredients in the production of cordite for shells. The village youngsters of Acton Scott managed to collect two cwt. The blackberries were used to make jam for the troops. The following year children were also asked to collect nut shells that were 'immediately required for an urgent war purpose' – to make charcoal for gas mask

Schoolchildren were encouraged to take a full part in helping the war effort. As well as taking part in national efforts, collecting various nuts for use as substitutes in the making of munitions or gas mask filters and picking fruit to make jam for the troops, children also helped to pack and send Christmas parcels to local men serving in the front line. In recognition of her efforts in this respect, Hilda Stinton of Ludlow was proud to receive a certificate thanking her for doing 'her bit'. (Courtesy of Shropshire Museum Services)

filters. Local hotels and boarding houses were also asked to save fruit stones left by guests on the edge of their plates which could be used for the same purpose. Local schoolgirls from Bromfield and Girl Guides from Ludlow collected foxglove leaves and dandelion roots for the manufacture of drugs.[53]

But one of the main ways in which local communities helped the war effort was in the treating and caring for wounded servicemen. At first, to cope with the expected influx of casualties, a number of civil hospitals set aside parts of their buildings for use by the military. This occurred at the Lady Forester Hospital, Much Wenlock where the matron in charge was a Miss Mary Smith and the medical officer Dr Francis Bigley; the Lady Forester Hospital, Broseley whose matron was a Miss C. Morris; and Bridgnorth Infirmary under Matron Miss H.M. Baillie and Drs William Craig and Dixon. The hospitals at Much Wenlock and Broseley at first took up to 50 military patients between them, whilst at Bridgnorth a ward with 20 beds was initially set aside though this capability was soon enlarged to 30. Though Girl Guides at Bridgnorth did the 'pantry work', the nurses were members of the local Voluntary Aid Detachment (VAD) units. The Red Cross VAD detachment

The Lady Forester Hospital at Much Wenlock was built in 1903 as a community hospital. When war was declared, part of the building was set aside to be used for military casualties but, as with the hospital system in general, it was soon found to be inadequate to cope with the numbers of wounded requiring help. However, problems regarding staffing were solved by the use of the local St John VAD detachment. Such units had been formed in 1909 for just such assistance in time of war. (Courtesy of Ina Taylor)

under the command of a Mrs Wood took over military nursing duties at Bridgnorth Infirmary whilst the St John VAD detachment under a Miss H. Potts helped staff the Lady Forester hospitals. Such units had been formed in 1909 to provide medical assistance in time of war. These nurses, usually members of the local gentry families or upper and middle classes, worked part-time in a voluntary capacity. Many were young and had never worked outside of the home before. Local ladies made the initial uniforms of both nurses and patients from standard patterns supplied by the Red Cross Society, that for patients consisting of a blue jacket and trousers with white lapels that was worn with a white shirt and a red tie. At the Bridgnorth Infirmary 717 soldiers were treated in total, whilst the hospital at Much Wenlock saw a total of 963 military admissions.[54]

It was soon realised that these initial plans for dealing with the wounded were totally inadequate due to the number of casualties. As a result, extra auxiliary hospitals had to be opened – over 3,000 of them by 1918 – and south Shropshire had its share. Many were situated in houses lent by local families. A commandant ran each, although the medical side was wholly the responsibility of a local doctor who gave his time free on top of looking after his usual practice. A matron or sister directed the work of the nursing staff that again was provided by local VAD detachments.

Essex House at Church Stretton was opened in the early months of the war as an Auxilliary Hospital. This was loaned by Mrs Catherine Treasure and staffed mainly by nurses from the local St John's detachment. Nineteen of the convalescing soldiers have been brought outside to have their photograph taken with their carers.
(Courtesy of A.T.D. Evans)

As 1915 dawned, Essex House, in Sandford Avenue, Church Stretton, loaned by a Mrs Catherine Treasure, was already open and occupied. At first it offered 15 beds but this was later increased to 36. The first commandant was a Miss Mary Urry, the daughter of a retired solicitor, and Nurse Harvey, the local district nurse, was the sister in charge before being replaced after her transfer to a Sheffield Hospital in 1915 by a Mrs Henrietta Auden. Local St John's VADs from a detachment set up just prior to the start of the war by Mary Urry carried out the bulk of the nursing, with other local ladies coming in as ward maids. The medical officer was a Dr Horatio Barnett, whose wife Elizabeth was the quartermaster before later becoming the commandant. Over 600 men passed through the hospital before it closed in May 1919 at a ceremony attended by over 500 local people.[55]

Three other properties, converted into auxiliary hospitals, were opened at the same time. These were Broadway House, Churchstoke; Hightrees House, Leintwardine (now Leintwardine Manor); and the Recreation Room at Worfield. Broadway House was lent to the Red Cross by a Mrs Price-Davies and took up to 25 patients. The commandant was a Miss Norah Montfield and most of the nursing staff was recruited from the VAD detachment at Bishop's Castle, whose quartermaster was a Miss Whittaker, whose parents lived at Totterton Hall. These women worked at the hospital for two weeks before returning home for a break.[56]

Miss Gertrude Helen Crawshay converted Hightrees House in Leintwardine into a convalescent hospital for wounded servicemen. Staffed by the local Red Cross unit, this house was made ready to accept its first twelve patients in January 1915. Later it could cater for 39. The building provided an isolation ward, five general wards, a small operating theatre and two recreation rooms. (Courtesy of the Leintwardine Historical Society)

Mrs G.M. Jebb of Leintwardine House was responsible for setting up a local detachment of the Red Cross before 1914, recruiting women from the surrounding area. When Hightrees House was opened as an auxiliary hospital she took on the post of commandant and her Red Cross nurses took over all nursing duties. They worked in shifts, with six nurses being on duty at any one time. (Courtesy of John Williams and the Leintwardine Historical Society)

Hightrees House was the home of Miss Gertrude Helen Crawshay, who stayed to take on the role of hospital superintendent. Mrs G.M. Jebb of Leintwardine House, who had set up the local Red Cross VAD detachment, took on the post

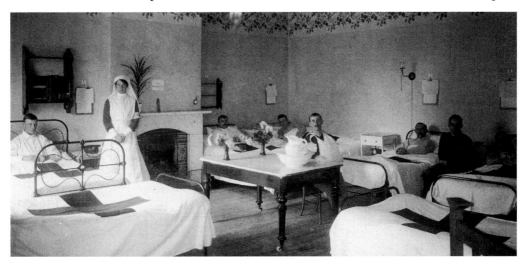

This rather austere yet spotlessly clean ward at Hightrees House displays only one plant, the patient's medical record on the wall over their heads and a No Smoking sign above the fireplace. Local ladies had sewn the very large Red Cross design on each top sheet. (Courtesy of John Williams and Leintwardine Historical Society)

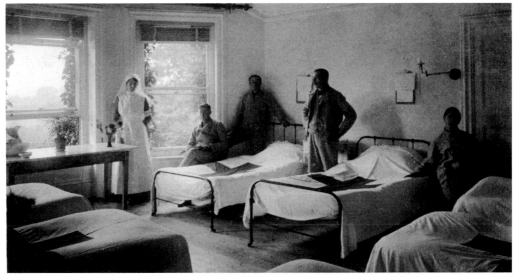

The number of beds that have been placed in this ward at Hightrees House gives an indication of the crowded conditions that the staff and patients had to endure as the numbers it catered for increased. However, the view of the many trees is a reminder that for men who came from poor housing conditions in inner cities their stay in such country homes must have seemed an idyllic interlude. (Courtesy of the Leintwardine Historical Society)

Taken in October 1915, this group photograph of patients, who were some of the earliest to arrive at Leintwardine VAD Hospital at Hightrees House, shows two points of interest. One is the clothing they wore. Many appear to be wearing rather hastily, locally made jackets and trousers with extra-long legs which could be turned up at the bottom so that they could be worn by men of mixed heights. The second point is the varied nationality of the troops catered for. The patient on the extreme left appears to be an Australian soldier, whilst standing just to the left of the nurses and wearing a cardigan there appears to be yet another of the many troops recruited from the Empire. (Courtesy of the Leintwardine Historical Society)

In this group photograph, also taken outside the VAD hospital at Hightrees House, patients can be seen both in the early uniforms made from whatever material was available and the later correct uniforms. These latter ones were still made locally by volunteer labour. (Courtesy of the Leintwardine Historical Society)

of commandant and Dr William Darroll was appointed medical officer. The first patients arrived in January 1915 to fill the initial twelve beds, which later increased to 39. The VADs worked in shifts with six nurses being on duty at any one time and three kitchen staff. The hospital provided an isolation ward and five general

The auxiliary hospital at Worfield was opened in the village recreation room. The building was divided into two main sections: a convalescent ward and a recreation area. This photograph was taken just before the soldiers shown were taken out for a car ride in the surrounding countryside. On the right is their chauffeur and second from the left appears to be the car's owner. (Courtesy of Jane Smith)

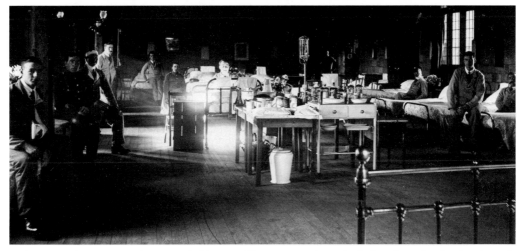

The convalescent ward at Worfield initially contained 20 beds but later had 34. Though it had gas lighting, this large space must have been very difficult to keep heated in winter. (Courtesy of Worfield Recreation Committee)

This is an early photograph (circa March 1915) of patients and staff at Worfield Auxilliary Hospital as the former are dressed in rather rough uniforms that would have been made locally when the troops' imminent arrival was announced. Their original uniforms would have been taken to be cleaned and deloused. (Courtesy of Jane Smith)

These patients at Worfield, since they are either in khaki uniform or civilian dress, are apparently about to depart after their period of convalescence. Those no longer fit enough for military service would be discharged from the forces. It appears that virtually the entire nursing staff has turned out for the farewell photograph. (Courtesy of Jane Smith)

wards together with two recreation rooms and a small operating theatre. Over 700 patients were treated here before it closed in early 1919. Finally, the Recreation Room at Worfield provided at first 20 beds, later increased to 34, ten of which were designated for emergency use only. It received its first eleven patients from the western front, many suffering from rheumatism and frostbite, in early February. This building had two main sections: the convalescent ward and a recreation room. The commandant was Miss Helen Corbett of Stableford Hall, who was in charge of the local St John VAD detachment. Four nurses were on duty each hour of the day and two throughout the night. Many of the senior staff came from the surrounding area. Mrs Martha E. Eykyn of Ackleton was the sister in charge and a Mrs W.O. Wilson of Norton was appointed quartermaster. The medical officers were Dr L'Oste Brown of Shifnal and Dr Thomas Hewitt of Claverley, who gave their time voluntarily.[57]

Throughout 1915 further local auxiliary hospitals opened. These were to be found at Overmead House, Ludlow; Overton Lodge, near Ludlow; Stokesay Court,

Gaius Smith, grocer and former mayor of Ludlow, handed his property, Overmead House, off Livesey Road, built in 1900, over to the Red Cross to be used as an auxiliary hospital. Here can be seen convalescent soldiers who have been enjoying a game of croquet in the grounds. This was a far cry from the experience of most of these men who had gone to war from damp country cottages or cramped terraced streets in industrial towns and cities. (Courtesy of Gareth Thomas)

Onibury; Aston Hall, Aston-on-Clun; and Walcot Hall near Lydbury North. In Ludlow the auxiliary hospital at Overmead House, off Livesey Road, was a relatively new property that was owned by the local grocer and former mayor Gaius Smith. Miss Dorothy Marston, who had set up the Red Cross VAD detachment in the town, took over as commandant and oversaw 30 beds. The medical officers were Dr Malin Gilkes and Dr William Farmer. Overton Lodge, owned by Lt Colonel Edward D. Kennedy, had eleven convalescent beds, one being in an outside hut, and the commandant was a Colonel E. Cooke, with a Sister Fowler being in charge of nursing. Stokesay Court's owner, Margaret Rotton, opened most of her house in April 1915 to house wounded troops. The patients at this property had a different experience to that elsewhere in the county. Initially offering ten convalescent beds that soon increased to 30, Mrs Rotton, who took on the role of commandant helped by her matron Miss Lilian Weekes, a Sister Alice Williams and the medical officer Dr Edward Greene, opened up nearly all of her house. This meant most patients had a room of their own, a luxury that some would never have experienced in their lives before. At Aston Hall a Miss Helen Garnett-Botfield was appointed commandant before being replaced by her sister Mrs Corbett-Winder.[58]

In Ludlow Miss Dorothy Marston set up a Red Cross detachment just before the war. Here they can be seen parading on ground outside the Drill Hall with Portcullis Lane behind them. It was they who provided the nursing care at Overmead House, off Livesey Road, for up to 30 convalescent soldiers. (Courtesy of Shropshire Museum Services)

In 1916 Helen Garnett-Botfield became commandant at Walcot Hall, near Lydbury North, the home of the Earl and Countess of Powis, when the last of the area's auxiliary hospitals was opened in a wing of the house in August. It had 15 beds and the medical officer was Dr Selwyn Hale Puckle of Bishop's Castle. The nurses mainly came from the VAD detachment at Bishop's Castle, overseen by the Lydbury North District nurse Sister Fowler. A total of 114 patients were treated at the Hall before it was the first to close down in April 1918, when the Earl and Countess temporarily moved out. The remaining patients were transferred to Aston Hall.[59]

The arrival of the first batch of wounded to Shropshire in the early days of 1915 proved deeply moving:

> Some pathetic scenes were witnessed at the Shrewsbury Railway Station on Thursday when a special Red Cross train arrived with close upon one hundred wounded British soldiers who are to receive care and comfort at the Royal Shrewsbury Hospital and four local hospitals. The arrival of the wounded was witnessed by a large crowd of residents, who were moved to tears in many cases.

The scale of the casualty numbers arriving far exceeded the capacity of the local ambulance service, and as a result about 50 private cars were used to transport the soldiers to the hospitals, though 'a number of the badly wounded had to be carried to the Infirmary on hand ambulances'.[60]

Those awaiting the arrival of the first batch of casualties at Bridgnorth station faced the same problem: how to convey the wounded to the infirmary and local auxiliary hospitals. Given just a few hours' notice of the possible arrival of men from the front, a call was put out for local people to put their private cars with volunteer drivers at the disposal of the Red Cross. Three stretchers were also hurriedly found, one being supplied by a local carpet works. The expected wounded failed to arrive, but the experience forced an organisational rethink. For instance, since the wounded men would be arriving virtually straight from the battlefield it was realised that plans would have to be made to have their uniforms and kit immediately cleaned and disinfected. The example of casualties that arrived in Shropshire in mid March 1915 highlighted this. Arriving in Southampton by boat from France they were quickly put on board a train to Glasgow leaving at 9.30pm. Those to be treated in Shropshire were unloaded at Shrewsbury Station at 3.30am with the 15 destined for Bridgnorth, still with the mud of Flanders on them, arriving by car in the town at 4.45am. Though the problem of dirt was soon solved, that of transport that could cope with all types of casualty was not. Because of this, the first wounded men that arrived in Bridgnorth 'were not of the serious type' since any stretcher cases could not be conveyed in private cars.[61]

The answer was for local tradesmen to convert their delivery vans so that they could accommodate stretchers. This had been done by the time further casualties began to arrive in May 1915. One Saturday night 180 arrived, followed by a further 104 in the early hours of the following Thursday. At the same time 50 were taken off a train at Buildwas station destined for the Lady Forester hospitals at Broseley and Much Wenlock. Yet more arrived in October following the Battle of Loos, but now all types of wounded could be taken and treated at a wider variety of hospitals. The hastily converted motor-van owned by a Mr Frank Roach allowed three stretcher or 'cot' cases of men with serious leg wounds to be brought to Bridgnorth from Shrewsbury. Church Stretton Hospital was now able to take one cot case, ten sitters and ten walkers, whilst at Much Wenlock and Broseley eight cot cases and 29 sitters could now be shared. By the following year the need for the long drive to and from Shrewsbury was reduced as ambulance trains began calling at Bridgnorth station. By this time 'all the conveyances now have canvas covers painted on a white background which shows the errand of mercy they are engaged in'.[62] From well-meaning

Local people did all they could to make the stay of wounded soldiers as pleasant and enjoyable as they could. A few upper- and middle-class car owners allowed their vehicles to be used to take soldiers on trips through the Shropshire countryside and they would often have a picnic on the way. Here at Worfield a small group, proudly back in their khaki uniforms for the day, are about to be taken out for such a trip complete with their own liveried chauffeur. (Courtesy of Jane Smith)

but amateur beginnings the incoming wounded were now greeted, dispersed and cared for with growing efficiency.

Whilst these servicemen were convalescing, many people within the local communities in which the men found themselves did their best to make their stay as pleasant as possible. For Christmas lunch in 1914 the wounded patients at Much Wenlock Hospital dined on twelve rabbits and a brace of pheasants, followed by wine and brandy. In addition they shared a case of oranges, sweets and crackers, all donated by local people. Owners of large country houses invited patients to enjoy their grounds. Twenty soldiers from the military hospital, Holly House, Shrewsbury were picked up at Ludlow station and taken in four cars to Henley Hall. Here they were served luncheon in the orangery, then spent the afternoon playing bowls and other games, listening to the Clee Hill Band, or just walking in the grounds. Finally they joined in a treasure hunt in the maze before being driven to the railway station to catch the 6pm train back to Shrewsbury. Patients from Aston Hall were taken to Bishop's Castle by car to be entertained in the 'picturesque grounds of the Hut', the home of Elizabeth Garnett-Botfield, whilst patients from the Lady Forester Hospital, Much Wenlock were entertained at Tickwood Hall and given 'an abundance of cigarettes'. Margaret Rotton of Stokesay Court, however, decided to bring the entertainment to her patients by opening up the grounds of her house to the general public every Sunday from 2.30 to 8pm. Mrs Rotton provided the tea and organised talks but asked her visitors to bring their own sugar and food. In this way she hoped to bring companionship to the 'boys in blue'. Other well-to-do people organised car trip tours. Wounded soldiers from Broadway House, Churchstoke were taken in four cars on a tour of Bishop's Castle and the Clun Valley to 'enjoy the invigorating and brilliant sunshine'.[63]

The middle classes were not to be entirely outdone by the gentry. Patients from Overmead and Overton hospitals in Ludlow were often invited by the Castle Tennis and Bowls Club to their Linney pavilion, and after matches were served tea on the green. Once, on leaving, they were all given a box of cigarettes and the mayor distributed cigars. Whitcliffe Bowling Club vied with their near neighbour in offering similar hospitality to local convalescents. Bishop's Castle Bowling Club entertained patients from Broadway House Hospital, also serving them tea on the green after a game of bowls.[64]

The men also found themselves invited to concerts. At Church Stretton patients from the local convalescent hospital were taken to the Barn Theatre to be musically entertained, followed by tea and a gift of cigarettes as they left. To celebrate Christmas and New Year in 1918 a concert party was brought over from Bridgnorth to Worfield Hospital to deliver a musical programme for the patients, whilst local schoolchildren put on a play. On Christmas Day a party from the village of Badger came to sing carols in a ward that was festooned with wreaths of evergreens and flags.[65]

When a death occurred in one of the hospitals all sections of the community came together to pay their respects. The coffins, draped in the Union Jack and escorted by members of the local Volunteer Corps, were conveyed to the railway station, usually on a hand-held bier, to be taken home for burial. The populace would line the streets in silence as the coffin passed. When, as once occurred in Ludlow, it was a Canadian soldier who had died, the oak coffin was transported for burial to Langholm, Dumfriesshire where he had been born and brought up before emigrating.[66]

The relationship between the convalescent servicemen and the local people was not always problem-free, especially in Ludlow where the Overmead Hospital was situated in an expanding middle-class suburb. It appears that some of the nearby residents were far from happy with the noise that some soldiers made when returning to their beds after a night out at a public house. A complaint must have been made to the staff and patients at the hospital since a letter from one convalescent soon appeared in the local newspaper:

> The wounded Tommies of Overmead Hospital were greatly surprised to be informed that they were creating a disturbance in the town, some unkindly civilian complained. It is very hard to think, after having the misfortune to be wounded, that we should be insulted after serving our King and Country as we have done. If you could see your way to put this in your local paper we will be greatly indebted to you.

The middle-class complainant received short shrift from other citizens in the letter page the following week. One was signed by 'A Soldier's Father':

> Let them do as they like, they have done more than those who made the complaint, faced death, so that a select few could live in comfort in Ludlow. Nothing we can do should be too good for them, but let us give the people who complained of them a real taste of what they have gone through, to bring them to their proper senses.

A second letter was also blunt and to the point:

> Bye the bye did you swear when in action? Never mind! Our impeccables didn't hear you. They were on the right side of the Channel. The great majority of Ludlow people appreciate what you have done, so please don't worry if one or two of the Pecksniffian breed do complain.[67]

Overall, however, most men convalescing in south Shropshire enjoyed their time here. For many from the industrial towns, inner city slums or even country cottages, their stay in a large country house and being able to wander the often-spacious grounds must have been an experience of a lifetime. Private E. Humphries of the Essex Regiment, who stayed at Stokesay Court, said that 'he spent the best time of his life there'.[68]

A Canadian convalescent at the hospital in Church Stretton wrote home that:

> The hospital here is fine. It is run by the St. John's Ambulance Society and all the work is done by volunteers, doctors and nurses, too, and they are all fine people and do everything they can to make us comfortable. Also the people of the village are very good to us and invite us out to teas at every opportunity and send all kinds of good things to the hospital.'[69]

To show their appreciation for local hospitality, patients often put on concerts to entertain the local people. A Private Hampson, who had been a professional music hall artiste, organised such a show at Worfield, whilst patients at Walcot Hall entertained an appreciative audience in the schoolroom at Lydbury North.[70]

Ensuring that patients had as enjoyable a time as possible was not the only task local communities undertook, for they also helped raise money towards the running costs of the hospitals. The War Office paid an allowance for each patient, but it was never enough to cover all the expenditure incurred, even though most of the staff were unpaid volunteers. For example, at Hightrees House, Leintwardine, the running costs for one year exceeded the government allowance by £421. A similar annual shortfall was suffered at Essex House, Church Stretton, in 1916. The costs incurred that year were £800 whilst only half that sum was received from London.[71]

Fêtes were often held, ranging from small ones, such as those held in the grounds of Alston Hall and of Broadway House, the latter raising £165 to the background music of the Bishop's Castle Brass Band, to large ones such as those held in the grounds of Ludlow Castle, which attracted 4,000 and 5,000 people respectively in 1917 and 1918. Half the money raised at these went to the Red Cross. The South Shropshire Farmers Union held auctions of donated animals and agricultural equipment. A number of these auctions were held in 1915. One, in a meadow just outside Church Stretton, raised £220, another at Ludlow £147, whilst similar auctions were held at Clun and Much Wenlock.[72] In Bridgnorth a joint Sales and Flag Day held in late May 1916 raised £900. Even schoolchildren played their part. Those at Eaton School sold 4cwt of potatoes that they had grown in the school grounds. Schoolchildren were again involved in picking 15,000 bunches of primroses in the spring of 1915 to be sold by the Conservative Party's Primrose League. The £70 collected from their sale went to local Red Cross hospitals. Not all the money raised was to help pay running costs. The £159 amassed from a bazaar held in Ludlow town hall was used to supplement the 2/- a day that each convalescent received at the Overmead Hospital.[73]

Local communities also helped the local VAD hospitals with gifts in kind. Egg collections were organised in most areas and local hospitals were the first to be supplied, with the excess being sent to a central Red Cross depot to help feed the wounded countrywide. The eggs were often collected by local schoolchildren and Boy Scouts, though in some villages collecting points were established. In Bitterley and Middleton baskets were placed in the two churches, whilst at Clee St Margaret one was placed in the local post office. In the rural deanery of Bridgnorth every parish organised a collection and by mid May 1915 Claverley alone had amassed and sent off nearly 2,000 eggs. At Bishop's Castle they had collected 14,000 eggs by the end of April 1916. A sewing group at the Hope Bowdler Parish room, set up by the vicar's wife, made pillow cases for the use of the local auxiliary hospital, whilst at Bishop's Castle thistle-down gathering was organised with which to stuff such pillows.[74]

Egg collecting in order to help feed the wounded in hospitals both in France and the United Kingdom was carried on in towns and villages throughout the county. Nearly always organised by ladies in the upper or middle classes, collecting points could be found in schools, church porches and even local post offices. At a stall in Much Wenlock, Lady Catherine Milnes Gaskell of Wenlock Abbey, Mrs Armstrong of Ashfield Hall and a Mrs Patty Haynes publicise the scheme. (Courtesy of Ina Taylor)

Medical supplies were also made locally. The workroom of the Ludlow Branch of the Red Cross, at 5a Old Street, saw 11,480 articles made in just the first six months of 1916. Once again local hospitals were supplied before the remainder was sent off to Red Cross depots. One such depot was at Church Stretton. The brainchild of a Miss L. Lefroy, who later became head of the bandage section, the embryonic depot was transferred in 1916 to the Horne Institute, where a Mrs Swire took command and, with the help of a number of volunteers, supplied local hospitals. They made and stored items such as various types of bandages, swabs of all kinds, fomentation pads, pneumonia jackets, sphagnum moss dressings that were collected locally, splints and pressure pads. When the Countess of Powis, the President of the Shropshire VAD, and her daughter inspected the depot in February 1918, it had nearly 18,000 items in stock.[75]

As the scale of the war became far larger than any had anticipated, in south Shropshire, 'Doing your bit' through voluntary work almost took on the form of an industry. This was especially so amongst the middle classes, who had the time to spare to devote to it, and the organisational ability, allied to the social and political standing, to make things happen. Their efforts were prodigious and appreciated not only by the government but also by the troops serving both at home and abroad,

In order to raise money for the care of the wounded, many communities held events and flag days. At Cleobury Mortimer, a parade was organised for the Red Cross and the local part-time nurses proudly took part dressed in their uniforms. Gertie Giles, the landlady of the Bell Inn, is photographed outside her public house driving a donkey cart and ready to take her place in the procession.

by the wounded recovering in hospitals and convalescent homes and by prisoners of war incarcerated in Germany. More than any that went before, this war was one in which many of those at home were not only needed to play a part but wanted to, and did.

4   SURVIVING ON THE HOME FRONT

In many ways life on the home front was a dress rehearsal for what was to be experienced some 25 years later during the Second World War. We have already seen how fears of possible sabotage or invasion had led to the formation of a 'Home Guard' but, in addition, the local population were also to experience air raid precautions, including blackout regulations, and the rationing of food and other essential items.

At first, however, everyday life in south Shropshire mainly carried on as usual, especially as regards leisure pursuits. Some did question whether sporting activities should continue whilst local men risked and gave their lives for their country, the vicar of Stanton Lacy, for example, calling for 'no football in Ludlow and the neighbourhood this year'. As a result he found himself accused of class bias:

Everyday life still went on locally, as did some sporting activities, but with so many young men going off to fight many cricket clubs cancelled their fixtures for the duration of the war. However, in some places, especially farming communities where some labourers escaped conscription due to the need to increase food production, matches resumed but with a difference. This photograph of Clun Cricket Club illustrates the wide range of ages now needed to put out a team. (Courtesy of A.T.D. Evans)

No doubt the reverend gentleman is now enjoying some good grayling fishing and shooting, in fact enjoying recreation, and what is football, hockey etc. but recreation. Does he want one law for the rich, another for the poor?[1]

The start of the new year in Ludlow in 1915 was 'ushered in with the customary al fresco revels in the town, a large crowd gathering in the vicinity of the Buttercross, dancing to the strains of a band',[2] and life largely carried on as normal. In May:

> Tennis commenced on the Burway ground last weekend and bowling, which commenced in April, has been enjoyed at the various greens in the town. Details of the opening of the new Castle Bowls and Tennis Club will be found in another column. Swimming enthusiasts have been out early in the mornings indulging in their pastime in the river, while the boats were in great demand.[3]

Local hunts carried on throughout the area and Church Stretton saw its usual influx of visitors to enjoy the sights, local walks and scenery, as did the town of Bridgnorth.

But in other respects everyday life did change. In order to preserve their stock of gold bullion, the Bank of England issued the first ever 10/- and £1 notes within days of war being declared. The fear of attack from the air also brought a call for lighting restrictions, although these were ignored in south Shropshire for the first 18 months. Zeppelin raids began in 1914 but at first were limited to the east coast. A visiting auctioneer to Clun expressed some surprise that electric lighting there was not switched off after sunset, and locals were amused when he asked if they were not afraid of an air attack.[4] Home Office instructions regarding the protection of buildings such as hospitals, museums, historic monuments and churches were also ignored at first. Local councils were advised to place a large rectangular panel on their roofs divided diagonally into two triangular portions, the upper one black and the lower white, the then internationally recognized symbol marking out a building that should not be bombed. In south Shropshire this was considered unnecessary in 1915 when the advice was received.[5]

This complacent attitude appears to have been general locally until January 1916 when Zeppelins started to drop bombs on various northern and midlands towns and cities including Liverpool, Birmingham and Burton-upon-Trent. Councils throughout the country then began to enact lighting restrictions and air raid precautions. Street lamps, where they existed, were to be totally extinguished in the smaller populated areas such as Bishop's Castle, Clun and Church Stretton, whilst in the larger towns of Bridgnorth and Ludlow the number lit was to be reduced to a minimum. In Ludlow this was to be just five out of a total of 150 and even the light from these was reduced with each lamp 'being obscured about ⅔rds down with green paint and so shaded as to prevent direct light being visible from the air'. Similar lighting restrictions were introduced in Bridgnorth. Housing and businesses had to install blackout curtains or shutters so that no light could be seen from the outside. In Ludlow the rector and churchwardens of St Laurence's Church agreed to sound a curfew bell five minutes before such regulations came into effect each evening as a warning to the inhabitants. Public warning of an air attack would be signalled by 'three depressions in the gas and three depressions in the electric light'.[6]

The loss of street lighting caused a number of difficulties, and as problems arose, temporary safeguards were found and implemented. With cattle and sheep markets still held in towns, Bridgnorth council stipulated that any more than four animals being herded along a street between sunset and sunrise had to have a white light at the front and another at the rear. Four or fewer animals just needed a light at the front. At the approach of any vehicle the light had to be swung from side to side as a warning.[7] In Ludlow a concern was the danger of people walking into unlit lamp-posts. One councillor stated that 'one boy was rather seriously hurt from running into a lamppost at the corner of Corve Street and the Station Drive'. Action to counter such a danger was taken in January 1917 when permission was given for 20 specifically chosen lampposts to be painted white. The white paint was replaced with luminous paint the following winter.[8]

Within days of the lighting restrictions being imposed, members of the public found themselves in court as a result of breaching them. By June 1916 eleven people had been convicted and fined in Ludlow, most of them shopkeepers. The first was a typical case. William Portlock, who ran a fruiterer's business in the Bull Ring, was found guilty of having two uncovered gas lamps lit within the shop and no dark blind in use. It was the same in Bridgnorth, with most of those convicted having shops on the High Street. Only a few householders were charged, though that did not mean that they always complied with the law, as the police superintendent in Ludlow knew. He warned the general public of their 'gross carelessness' and claimed that 'one could go outside the town and see a great number of bright lights, but it was very difficult to discover them when one got back into town'.[9]

Complaints against the restrictions began to grow as the months passed and no air attack came. Demands grew for councillors to relax the rules, especially as regards street lighting:

> A stranger visiting Ludlow after dark would be justified in asking whether those in charge of the lighting arrangements are suffering from delusions re air raids, or whether they really 'love darkness rather than light'. ... It is absolutely absurd when towns such as Birmingham, Bristol etc. are decently lighted that a town like Ludlow, far removed from all such things as air raids, should be without light of any kind.[10]

Soon some councils began to respond. For the winter of 1917/18 six lampposts were relit, though shaded, in Bishop's Castle. Two shaded lamps were allowed to be lit in Clun, and in Church Stretton it was decided that shaded lampposts could be lit one hour after sunset until 9.30pm. Ludlow was more conservative. Only one extra shaded lamp was to be allowed, and even as winter began in 1918 the number only rose to nine out of a total of 150. One reason cited was a fuel shortage since coal was needed to produce the necessary gas. Even the few lamps lit were extinguished if a night was deemed to be moonlit.[11]

The war also brought a few new exciting experiences to south Shropshire. One of these was the sight of flying machines. Ludford Park, near Ludlow, saw military aircraft making forced landings at least five times. One of the pilots, after his aircraft was repaired, gave the townsfolk a display by flying over the town and completing 'a number of somersaults'. Due to poor weather, another plane landed in a field of wheat at Whittimere Farm, Halfpenny Green to the east of Bridgnorth. The farmer kindly cut an airstrip through the crop to allow him to take off again.[12]

News of escaped German prisoners also caused occasional flutters of excitement. Warnings to look out for escapees were given out from two camps: one at Shrewsbury and one at Kerry to the east of Newtown. Two prisoners who had escaped from the Kerry camp were discovered hiding in a garden in Craven Arms, whilst two more escapees, members of a U-boat crew, were caught by police on the winberry grounds on the slopes of the Black Hill near Clun and taken to Bishop's Castle:

> The news quickly spread and an eager and expectant crowd soon gathered in the vicinity of the police station where, after about an hour's waiting, they were rewarded by the spectacle of the two Huns, handcuffed, emerging from the police station under military escort to the car.[13]

Another German prisoner, who, as will be seen later, was one of those working on the land for local farmers, broke out of Bishop's Castle workhouse where he was housed but was seen, challenged and caught when crossing surrounding gardens. In addition the people of Ludlow were warned that two German aliens, one fluent in English, who had fled from their internment camp at Wigmore were believed to be travelling in their direction.[14]

It was the cost of food, however, that was of the greatest concern to the populace of south Shropshire. We have already seen how prices increased as soon as war began due to fears of shortages to come and the hoarding of food by those with the money to buy in bulk. Basic food price rises did not fall back and indeed carried on rising as the months passed. Compared to August 1914 the price of bread had nearly doubled by January 1916 and had done so by the next year. The cost of milk rose 78% by 1917, whilst butter and bacon had also doubled in price, and beef and mutton were 10d per lb dearer.[15]

The cause of this was essentially threefold. Much of Britain's food was imported, but shipping space was now needed to transport war materials. In addition, German submarines attacked and sank British merchantmen from February 1915 and then, in January 1917, unrestricted submarine warfare was announced which meant that all neutral ships trading with Britain were now also subject to attack. Thirdly, Britain's own ability to produce food was severely hit by a shortage of labour on farms caused by so many young farm labourers leaving the land to fight for their country. This latter problem was tackled in a number of ways that impacted on rural Shropshire.

One solution was to encourage more women to work on the land and to carry out jobs that men had usually done. In early 1915 talks were given in local town halls in an attempt to persuade young, single women to fill many of the jobs vacated by men not just in agriculture but also in engineering factories. One speaker declared that:

> She had heard it on extremely good authority that women of ordinary intelligence could learn the work of machinery, chiefly filling shells, in two or three weeks and after that time could earn 18/- to 25/- per week.[16]

In an area dominated by farming this was a man's wage and a number of young women jumped at the opportunity, although in conservative south Shropshire single women leaving home for cities such as Birmingham often faced opposition, as one letter writer explained:

> When we left Ludlow we were laughed at and jeered at by other girls and told, amongst other things, that we were going to work for nothing; others said that we were going for our own pleasure etc. We wish to say to the numerous girls in Ludlow, who at this time of national crisis are simply idling their time in doing nothing, that we are quite satisfied with the work we have to do; that the wages are good; and that we are found good lodgings; and that, moreover, we are possessed of a clear conscience in the fact that we are doing our bit for our King and Country.[17]

Many locally believed that allowing young women to leave home to carry out men's work in a man's environment would be a nail in the coffin of future family life. They asked: 'Can our future generations go on without a domesticated motherhood?', whilst ladies in large houses lamented the loss of a number of their servants as well as hinting that these girls would probably be led sexually astray:

To entice domestics away from comfortable berths in the country by painting such a deceptive picture of factory life is little short of a crime. There are other things of vital importance to be considered apart from an extra few pence per week, and credit is due to those parents who take into consideration the moral welfare of their children.[18]

Although a number of girls did decide to leave home to work in factories, many chose to remain and work in agriculture. To help them learn the necessary skills, in 1915 the Harper Adams Agricultural College near Newport agreed to take 60 women, 30 each week, and give them two weeks' training. Fees and travel expenses would be paid for by the local labour exchange. Four women from the

One of the skills women were taught at Harper Adams Agricultural College in north Shropshire was how to manage various types of agricultural machinery, including how to drive the new tractors that very few farms in Shropshire had as yet seen. (Courtesy of Harper Adams University College)

Much Wenlock area were among the first to attend. The following year the courses were increased to four weeks in length. Skills taught included working horses, ploughing, milking and hand hoeing. Farmers were encouraged to go and see their training as a first step in persuading them to employ such women. Local agricultural committees also did their best to convince farmers of the benefits that could accrue. This did not always work. When one farmer, giving evidence to the military tribunal at Much Wenlock, was asked why he did not employ trained women on his farm, replied that his 'cows would not stand a woman'.[19]

Strategies were set out to persuade more women to consider work on the land even if only part-time. The Bridgnorth War Agricultural Committee (WAC) arranged meetings in each parish to persuade them face to face to do so, whilst the Much Wenlock WAC called upon the Board of Education to adopt fresh methods of training women to carry out farm work and also organised a house-to-house canvas to find those willing to work on a local farm. Such women, after working for 30 days, would then be given an armband to wear to publicly display their patriotism. Meetings were also held in Town Halls calling upon women to consider farm work as part of the war effort.[20] At Alveley and Tuck Hill a list was compiled of 48 women who were prepared to work on the land. Local farmers were asked to apply for this extra labour when required. Local efforts, however, were still not enough and in 1917 the government set up the Women's Land Army. Harper Adams College trained 92 Land Army girls and began offering six-week-long practical courses on the use of tractors. Once trained, members were paid £1 1/- for a 50-hour week, plus food and lodgings. Some lived on the farms at which they worked whilst others lived together in makeshift hostels, often in previously empty cottages. Two of these were to be found near the villages of Kempton and Lydham.[21]

Children were also to be utilised in helping to make up the shortfall of workers on the land. The Board of

In 1916 the Board of Trade had to send out agricultural organisers to persuade farmers to employ women in what they saw as traditional male roles. By 1917 nearly 26,000 women worked on the land and of these 20,000 were members of the Land Army. Photographed in her uniform, Mary Corfield (later Howard), who was brought up on her parents' farm at Halford near Craven Arms, was sent to work on a farm at Cheney Longville. (Courtesy of Winifrid Howard)

These four Land Army girls in their distinctive coats and hats, who almost certainly trained at Harper Adams College, help a farmer bring in his harvest just over the border in Wales. (Courtesy of A.T.D. Evans)

Education agreed in March 1915 to instruct all Local Education Authorities (LEAs) to allow pupils in elementary schools to be allowed to leave to work on the land from the age of 12. The Bridgnorth WAC encouraged this, as did the Much Wenlock WAC, whilst the Ludlow committee went further and pleaded with the Board of Education to lower the age limit to 11.[22] Since it was expected in rural areas such as south Shropshire that virtually all boys in elementary schools would take up manual labouring jobs such as farm work on leaving school, it was felt that missing up to two years formal education would not be that harmful and might even be of benefit since they would be learning practical skills.

This was not the view for those boys who attended grammar or independent schools. The relaxed regulations did not allow them to miss education to work on the land; this they could only do in their holidays and they had to be at least 16 years of age. During the summers of 1917 and 1918, 16 boys from Shrewsbury School stayed at The Grove, the home of Mr and Mrs Henry Greene near Craven Arms, and worked on local farms. A further 44 sixth-form boys camped for six weeks at Walcot Park helping out with the harvest and general farm work throughout the district during the summer of 1918. The Boy Scout movement also volunteered to help gather in the harvest. Farmers could request their aid and a camp of not less than 25 boys would be established with canvas and equipment supplied by the War Office.[23]

Servicemen were also used as short-term farm workers. In the summer of 1915 advertisements were placed in local newspapers informing farmers that they could request, via their local Labour Exchange, soldiers to help bring in the hay harvest. They would have to meet the men at the railway station and pay them 2/6d per day if providing board and lodging. The men could be employed for a maximum

The labour shortage on farms meant that the War Office allowed soldiers to help farmers. Pte Victor Kidd was one such soldier and for a while he was billeted with the Rudd family at Broome, to whom he later wrote to say that he had worked on farms at Tenbury and Cleobury Mortimer before moving on to Bridgnorth for ten weeks, and then for six weeks at Madeley where he had this photograph taken of himself and his fellow soldiers on agricultural duty. (Courtesy of Keith Rudd)

Because of the shortage of labour on the land soldiers on leave often helped out on their family farm or that of their old employer. One such serviceman can be seen here helping bring in the harvest on a farm near Bishop's Castle. (Courtesy of Janet Preshous)

of 14 days. Such a scheme was extended in 1917. Soldiers were now allowed to apply for agricultural furlough in their home localities and they could even stay in their own homes if close to their work. Agnes Ward of Lower Mill Street, Ludlow was pleasantly surprised to have her husband back home for a few weeks whilst he worked for a local farmer. Council workers also helped out, and many of the rural district councils released their roadmen to help bring in the harvest from 1915.[24]

Timber was another industry that suffered from a shortage of labour due to workers joining the armed forces. To combat this the Burwarton Estate, near Ditton Priors, saw, in the summer of 1916, a tented camp that housed stranded Finnish sailors who were employed to cut wood. They returned in the following two years on fresh contracts and even constructed a sauna to refresh themselves after a hard day's work.[25]

But notwithstanding such help, there was a serious labour shortage, especially of skilled labour. The answer was to use German POWs who had the necessary skills. A few had been used in the winter of 1916/17 to grub out heathland near Church Stretton, but their wider use in the countryside had not been considered, since

Convalescent soldiers helping haymaking at Wyken watched over by Sister Oulton. Note the man in the centre holding a shotgun. His job would be to shoot rabbits startled from the field as the hay was cut – his friend by his side is holding one that has just been shot. These would then be used to supplement Worfield Hospital's larder. On the far left the soldier is holding a jug that no doubt contained home-brewed cider, the staple thirst quencher for those working on the land. (Courtesy of Jane Smith)

With the loss of so much male labour, and a growing demand for wood for industrial and paper products at home and for construction purposes in the theatres of war, a Women's Forestry Corps was set up in 1917, controlled by the Timber Supply Department of the Board of Trade. Here at Bucknell, two members of the corps are seen sawing felled timber. (Courtesy of A.T.D. Evans)

it was felt that guarding them would place too great a burden on employers. The summer of 1917 saw the first POWs employed on local farms, but the conditions imposed made it difficult for many WACs to implement a scheme as they would have to be able to house 75 prisoners plus their 35 guards. The major use of them in south Shropshire came in 1918 when it was decided that they could be requested in smaller groups of ten with just two guards. Small agricultural camps, fed by the parent POW camp in Shrewsbury, were formed in convenient places and the prisoners sent from there each day to local farms. The farmers paid the government a full market wage for them and the POWs were given an allowance of 1d per hour or 1½d if they were skilled workers. A working day lasted 8-9 hours and they received double pay for overtime.[26]

One such camp was formed at the Ludlow racecourse at Bromfield where 40 POWs arrived in March 1918, the majority of them skilled ploughmen. As well as being put to work ploughing up part of the nearby golf course for sowing with oats and planting with potatoes, the POWs were taken out to work on local farms

German prisoners tend their vegetable plots in the POW Camp built on land owned by the London and North Western Railway Company next to the abbey at Shrewsbury. It was from here that, later in the war, prisoners were sent to stay in towns and villages throughout south Shropshire from where they would be taken daily to work on local farms. (Courtesy of A.T.D. Evans)

with some being used to plough up a section of Ludford Park. Another group were billeted at Pinkham in Cleobury Mortimer whilst others arrived at Wentnor where, in addition to working on farms around Wentnor and Norbury, they helped construct an overhead railway at the Bog Mines. Yet another group were billeted at Newcastle where they laboured on surrounding farms. Twenty men were also based at Much Wenlock where 'they caused a lot of interest and were the theme of much comment'.[27] Similar excitement, mixed with curiosity, occurred at Bishop's Castle when, on market day, ten POWs arrived at the railway station to be met by a large crowd. Their baggage was loaded onto a lorry whilst they walked behind, down Station Street and Union Street to the Union Workhouse where they were lodged in the casual wards.[28]

Having German soldiers in the area brought some difficulties, since many families still had loved ones fighting, whilst others had had a family member killed or maimed for life. Because of this there were strong views on how the POWs should be treated. Farmers were warned not to allow any prisoner to drink cider on pain of losing their workforce and came under criticism if they were seen to be pampering them in any way. Anger was expressed when some POWs were seen being given a lift back to their billet at Bromfield in a car. The authorities had to explain that prisoners were always taken to and from work by horse and cart except when they worked overtime. In those instances it was the responsibility of the farmer to arrange their return transport. How he did this was up to him.[29]

Fraternisation with local girls was also an issue that angered many. A report that girls were encouraging the prisoners to wink and smile at them brought a flurry of letters of protest:

> It's enough to make any decent woman sick to think that any of her sex could so forget themselves as ever to look in the direction of a Hun, let alone smile or salute them in any way. The pillory or the ducking stool should be the portion of these fools who, for the sake of the splendid fellows who have laid down their lives for us, ought to be ashamed of themselves.

Another letter raised the memory of the belief that many Belgian and French women had been raped by the Germans:

> If the girls looked the other way, the Fritz would have nothing to snigger at and chaps who have been over there, through it, must feel raw when they see the fuss and flatter that is made everywhere of the Germans. I don't think any really nice girl would so forget themselves and their men folk after all they have suffered and to give the 'glad eye' to men who would certainly, granted opportunity, serve them in the same way they did their less fortunate sisters in Belgium and France.[30]

Part of the need for POW labour was the growing pressure to plough up as much land as possible in order to increase the production of staple foods. It was hoped that for the harvest of 1918 an extra 100,000 acres of pastureland in Shropshire would fall under the plough – 25% of the total pastureland in the county. In the Bridgnorth district the local WAC organised local volunteers to survey all farms as to possible future land use and give advice. The incumbent of the rectory in Hope Bowdler offered his land of just over an acre and allowed a government team to plough it up and sow oats. He hoped that such an example would inspire other landowners to offer their grassland.[31] For the farmers willing to plough up pasture, help was at hand via their local War Agricultural Committee. Firstly, there was the offer of horses for hire, since the Army had requisitioned many, together with skilled ploughmen if necessary, and secondly an offer of tractors that could also be hired, complete with drivers. These machines, never seen before in parts of south Shropshire, provided a fresh spectacle for many of the populace such as those in the vicinity of Bishop's Castle:

Considerable public interest is manifested in this modern labour saving device and its capabilities ... Messrs Kilvert have engaged the services of two expert Army Service Corps drivers in charge of their tractor which is being requisitioned by many farmers in the district.[32]

To ease the general food shortages, the general public also had a part to play. Householders were asked to turn their gardens over to vegetable production. But whilst councillors at Bishop's Castle were congratulating their fellow citizens for doing just that, in Ludlow a councillor was publicly castigating his fellow townsfolk:

There are in the borough an enormous number of gardens which have never been cultivated; practically allowed to run wild. At the same time these particular people are complaining about the high price of potatoes, whereas if they had exerted themselves they would have been able to produce potatoes themselves.[33]

The council attempted to do its bit by encouraging the keeping of pigs, amending by-laws and providing swill tubs around the borough to collect food waste to help feed them. At the same time a Food Production Committee was set up though

To help farmers produce the food that the nation required the local war agricultural committees (WAC) could call upon the Army to help. Here, on the Welsh/Shropshire border, members of the Army Service Corps instruct local farmers on the use of one of their tractors to help in ploughing. In bowler hats, two members of the local WAC oversee the training. (Courtesy of A.T.D. Evans)

the mayor, Councillor Valentine, decided for once not to take the chair. This was perhaps because that week he had been convicted in court on two charges of selling potatoes in his shop in Broad Street at above the maximum price after 'many families in the town had to go without potatoes with their dinner last Sunday caused by a great shortage of supplies coming into the town'. The committee's first action was to purchase two tons of seed potatoes and distribute them to householders and allotment holders. A similar scheme was carried out in Bridgnorth. In addition, towns both large and small all over south Shropshire obtained land to be converted into allotments.[34]

Parallel with all of these actions to increase food production were many to encourage a change in eating habits. After a Ministry of Food was set up in December 1916 new meal regulations were introduced for hotels, restaurants and other eating

Due to the shortage of labour on the land the War Department provided aid especially at harvest time. At a farm at Espley, near Cound, a threshing machine and a stationary baler, both powered by a traction engine and with servicemen to work them, help a local farmer. As well as grain to feed the nation, hay and straw were needed in abundance by the Army to help feed their many horses. (Courtesy of Robin Hill and Paul Stamper)

establishments. No more than three courses could be served between 6 and 9pm and only two courses at any other time. In the following February Lord Devonport was appointed Food Controller and he attempted to introduce voluntary rationing. He asked that each household should limit itself to 4lb bread, 2½lb meat and ¾lb sugar per person per week. Then in April he asked for one meatless day to be observed per week. The royal family, it was claimed, was setting such an example. Committees were formed all over south Shropshire to encourage adherence to this voluntary code. Cardboard shields, for display in windows, were issued to willing households inscribed 'In honour bound, we accept the national scale of voluntary rations'. At Bishop's Castle the local Food Economy Committee also asked all local organisations to refrain from serving refreshments at meetings. In Ludlow they went further. Here ladies carried out a house-to-house canvass. A total of 230 houses in the Corve Street Ward were visited and the households asked if they were following the King's example. Unsurprisingly, 225 of the households claimed that they were keeping to the prescribed rations, but it is illuminating that only 109 were willing to sign a pledge card that they would continue to do so.[35]

In late 1916 the Ministry of Food brought in fresh regulations regarding the amount of wheat flour that could be used when making bread. Substitute flour

Since most small tenant farmers could not afford farm machinery the War Department supplied travelling agricultural machinery. On application to the local War Agricultural Committee such help would be supplied. Here, a convoy of machinery, pulled by a traction engine, is leaving a farm near Cound bound for one of its neighbours after completing its work. (Courtesy of Robin Hill and Paul Stamper)

made from other grain had to be substituted, and brought comments in the local papers:

> Bread baked in accordance with the new Government regulations made its appearance in the town last weekend. The difference in the appearance of the 'war loaf' is not so marked as most people were led to expect.[36]

Within a month the amount of wheat flour per loaf was reduced by a further 10%. The Ministry also banned sugar and chocolate from being used to decorate cakes. Three months later, in April 1917, confectioners could no longer 'make for sale, crumpets, muffins, tea cakes or fancy bread or any light or fancy pastries or any other like article'.[37]

It was, however, the failure of voluntary food rationing that led to the Ministry of Food giving instructions to all local authorities to set up Food Control Committees in 1917. These committees had the power to set maximum prices and ensure fair distribution, and were to prepare for compulsory rationing if this was deemed necessary. Complaints that some local traders were taking advantage of the shortages to carry out profiteering had been bubbling under the surface for some time. In the autumn of 1916, for example, there were claims that a 'ring of dairymen' were setting the local price of milk in the Ludlow area and that, as a result, the price of a quart of milk was 25% higher than in nearby Bishop's Castle. In another case, someone contacted the *Ludlow Advertiser* to say that he understood that the town's small bakers had been instructed by the large bakers' firms to put up the price of their bread to one shilling in order to garner larger profits.[38]

Qualms about the possible effectiveness of these Food Control Committees were voiced when the make-up of them was announced. The Ministry of Food had recommended that the twelve committee members should reflect a cross-section of society and include women and members of the working classes, but they appeared to be packed with the same councillor shopkeepers who were already under suspicion of profiteering. In south Shropshire mere lip service was paid to the request for the committees to include women and working men, and when such membership was granted it might be done with a tinge of bitterness. In Ludlow, Heber John Goodall, a railway signalman who had been appointed a Justice of the Peace against the recommendation of the council, was appointed to the committee with the remark that 'They have just conferred an honour on him; let him do some of the work' and cries of 'Hear, Hear'.[39] But it was the remainder of the membership who made up the bulk of the committee that worried many. A letter in the *Bridgnorth Journal* from a 'Housewife' pointed out that 'it would be some satisfaction to the public to know the reason why so many traders have been appointed on the Food Committee for this district'.[40]

Yet a further worry was that some of the committees decided to hold their meetings in secret and refuse entry either to the general public or to the press. The reason given in Ludlow was that 'matters that come before them were to be treated as strictly confidential'. Such a decision soon gave rise to growing suspicions as to what was or was not being discussed or done:

> I see in your last issue [of the *Ludlow Advertiser*] that the Shrewsbury Food Control Committee acted well and wisely in what looked very much like profiteering in milk. We are constantly reading that other towns are doing the same, notably among them Wrexham, so that we in Ludlow are beginning to think it is about time the same thing was done in Ludlow and as we never see any report of the committee meetings we should very much like to know if they ever hold any, and what it is they do, and where to apply for the information the public require.[41]

When the committee did report to the full council as to their deliberations and actions, evidence indeed surfaced of an apparent tradesmen's cabal. An order for local butchers to display a list of the maximum prices of various cuts of meat was only made at the insistence of an outside inspector. As for dealing with the breaking of regulations by local bakers, 'several tradesmen in the town were warned as to their technical breaches of the Cake and Pastries Order, doubtless committed in ignorance'. This sympathetic and understanding attitude taken by the committee members meant that not one baker was prosecuted. In fact, the only prosecution enforced by the Food Control Committee was that of an outsider: a wholesale butter dealer who visited Ludlow market.[42] The few prosecutions that did take place in Ludlow were as a result of police undercover shoppers. A blitz on stores selling jam at above the maximum price resulted in six people being charged. The same police undercover work led to the conviction of a shopkeeper in Ashford Carbonel together with her supplier George Stead and Co. in Ludlow.[43]

The same lenient attitude by a Food Control Committee towards fellow traders seems to have taken place in Bridgnorth. Edward Allen, a butcher, after selling meat at above the maximum price was 'warned and allowed to escape conviction'. Only when he persisted in continuing to sell at 17% above the maximum price and, in addition, to sell meat at that price over and above the ration limits when they were introduced, was the committee forced to act.[44] As a result of such lack of action, suspicions that the Food Control Committee members in Bridgnorth were using their position to feather the financial nests of both themselves and their friends were voiced openly. A letter to the local newspaper compared maximum meat prices in Birmingham, where it was pointed out that higher transport costs had to be borne, to those in the town. Many were 40% higher. As the letter writer bitterly pointed out, 'I should imagine the Bridgnorth butchers will all very soon be able to retire.'[45]

The committee in Bishop's Castle also came under criticism because of their apparent lack of action in stopping profiteering. Here, it was claimed, the committee failed to stop local cheese from being sent to the midlands towns and cities by rail where better prices could be had, leaving 'some justifiable grumbling locally, supplies for private consumption being considerably below requirements'. Complaints were also aired about dairy farmers who were not being stopped from selling their milk to wholesalers outside the locality where they could find a better price. Because of this there was a severe shortage of local milk and butter. This in turn led to Clun RDC having to ask their Food Controller to make arrangements to ensure that nursing mothers and infants did not go short, and local doctors and parish nurses were asked to give a list of such individuals to the committee. There was also disquiet in Bishop's Castle over the fact that the committee set the maximum price for a quart of milk at 7d whilst one small producer claimed that he was still making a fair profit at 4d a quart.[46]

It has to be noted, however, that Food Control Committees could face difficulties when attempting to set what they saw as fair maximum prices. At Clun, when there was a failure to come to an agreement with butchers regarding prices and maximum ones were imposed, the traders banded together and closed their doors, refusing to say when they would open again. Faced with this lockout of the public the committee had to start negotiating again and the shops only opened two weeks later when the butchers were satisfied with the prices agreed.[47]

Even with all this action being taken, food shortages continued to grow, especially of meat. In January 1918, due to lack of supplies, butchers in Bishop's Castle were forced to close from Monday to Thursday, in Clun on Mondays and Wednesdays and in Ludlow on Tuesdays and Wednesdays. At times committees did attempt to intervene in the market to try to alleviate such shortages. In Bridgnorth they commandeered one third of the rabbit supply brought to the town's market that would have almost certainly been purchased by dealers to sell elsewhere. The 500 rabbits were then sold off to local people.[48]

The increased food shortages gave rise to another voluntary activity organised by local ladies. This was the opening of War Kitchens. The first one appears to have been started by Mrs Harriet Greene of The Grove, Wistanstow in June 1917. The idea was to serve a 'wholesome and satisfying midday meal' of 'meat, vegetables, herbs, milk and suet pudding' to local schoolchildren at 1½d per head. The meal was served in a room at the Rectory. Within three weeks of opening, 1,200 two-course meals had been consumed. Whilst villagers donated many of the vegetables, Mrs Greene covered any deficit. The point of the scheme, other than ensuring at least one healthy meal for the children, was to reduce the demand for wheat, since the staple food provided by most working class parents for their children was bread. It was estimated that by April 1918 the scheme had saved 15cwt of grain.[49]

Soon after, a few ladies opened a similar kitchen at 2 Old Street, Ludlow. At first, 60 meals a day were served out in the front portion of the shop premises whilst cooking was carried out on two large gas cookers in the rear behind a canvas screen. Once again, as well as giving children a nutritious meal, the main aim was to reduce the local consumption of bread. Meal tickets were sold on a Monday evening at 2d each. Then on meal days:

> Each ticket holder passed in with his or her jug, basin or can by the side door up to the counter where the Mayoress, Mrs Rickards and Mrs Tyrell ladled out the portions, which were carried out through the main door.

Members of the Food Production Committee and their friends generously covered the initial expense of setting up the kitchen. By April 1918 an average of 122 meals a day were being provided, with the record standing at 164.[50] The 'War Kitchen' movement spread. One opened next to Bromfield School in July 1917 followed by another in Culmington in September. The same month saw one opened in the Parish Hall, Church Stretton where 80 meals a day, rising to 100, were served five days a week. Then in November yet another opened in Diddlebury. In Bridgnorth one was set up at Bishop Percy's House, Cartway, though this was for both children and adults.[51]

Despite such voluntary efforts the growing shortages grew so severe that, finally, the Ministry of Food was forced to bring in compulsory rationing. The first item to be rationed was sugar on 31 December 1917. Local Food Control Committees sent out application forms to all households, who then had to take them to a chosen supplier of their choice, who would fill in, sign and return the bottom half to the Food Office, which then issued the ration book.

Rumours began to circulate about which other food items might soon be rationed with the result that hoarding, last seen when war broke out in August 1914, began once more. Yet again the main culprits appear to have been the upper and middle classes who had the disposable income at their command to invest in stocking up with certain foods. From April 1917 such hoarding was illegal and local Food Control Committees warned local residents of this and allowed a period of grace for any guilty household to give up hoarded items. It appears that such an amnesty was a failure in Ludlow and the surrounding area:

> We understand there have been no voluntary surrenders of excessive stocks of food by residents in the town or rural district during the week's grace allowed by the Food Controller which expired on Monday last. Rumour has been so busy of late as to large quantities of food stuffs going to certain large residences – names had even been freely mentioned – that we expected to hear of local hospitals benefitting materially by voluntary surrenders.[52]

Though this escape route of making a charitable donation was spurned, no prosecutions followed even though names were at hand. The most plausible reason for this is that the guilty were members of the same social circle in which the Food Control Committee members mingled. As a consequence, there is evidence of only one prosecution being brought and, once again, this was at the instigation of an external body:

> There was much excitement in the centre of town on Monday afternoon. The cause was the execution by the police of a search warrant at a local residence, said to have been taken out by officials of the Ministry of Food at Birmingham.[53]

As a result of this raid William Henry Sharp of Castle Lodge was charged with 'acquiring quantities of sugar in excess of the ordinary requirements of his household' and his wife of aiding and abetting. They were found to have 129½lb of sugar in their house. In addition 56lb of tea was also found that led to yet further charges. All of it had been hidden, with the couple at first denying that they were hoarding anything. Appearing before the local magistrates, the couple were found guilty on five charges though those against the local firm of Gaius Smith and Co., who sold the couple the tea and sugar, were surprisingly dismissed through, it was claimed, lack of evidence. Complaints were also aired that the total fines of £16 (including costs) were far less than the costs of prosecution. Even the chairman of the Food Control Committee had to agree that the fines appeared lenient.[54]

Fears that the rationing of sugar was just a prelude to further rationing were soon justified. Both cooked and uncooked meat became rationed in April 1918 and, at the same time and in the same envelope as the new ration book, came fresh forms to complete for the future possible rationing of butter, margarine, lard and tea. Except for tea these items joined the ration list in July. Tea was not included but its distribution was controlled on the basis of 2oz per person per week. The rationing of jams and preserves followed in early November with each person allowed 4oz per week. Meat rationing was met with general approval and relief in south Shropshire. Shortages had meant that in Bishop's Castle many families were unable to purchase any meat at all the week before rationing began and, in both Bridgnorth and Ludlow, butchers had had to close on weekdays, causing massive queues at the weekend where people were treated on a first come first served basis with many families, therefore, missing out.[55]

In addition to increasing food restrictions, a growing shortage of fuel caused further problems. Because of the reliance on imports and the increased demands of the armed forces, petrol was in short supply, though at the dawn of the motor age this was mainly an inconvenience for the better off. The growing coal shortage, however, was of far more importance to the overwhelming majority of the population. Coal was the major source of domestic heating for most whilst for the working classes it was also their main power source for cooking since they used kitchen ranges. In addition, coal was needed to produce electricity and gas.

The earliest warnings came in the autumn of 1915 when the government, due to so many miners volunteering for the armed forces, advised local authorities that there could be a shortage of domestic coal in the coming winter and asked that they stock up to ensure that public buildings and schools could be heated.[56] The experience of Bishop's Castle was typical of most places in south Shropshire. In the spring of 1917 the town's coal dealers were already experiencing many days without deliveries and by October of that year there was a serious shortage of coal in their yards. One firm was entirely emptied of stock whilst the other had only part of a truckload remaining. Residents were informed that each household would be limited to 1cwt and that would have to be fetched 'in a wheelbarrow at present'.[57]

Due to the rising prices that accompanied the growing shortages, and the danger of the poorest households being unable to afford the coal they needed, local authorities were given permission to set maximum prices in September 1917. The struggle to do this amicably with the coal merchants and dealers in Ludlow was typical of the problems encountered elsewhere. It took six weeks of negotiations because, as in the words of one councillor, 'the merchants were rather inclined to ride a high horse and assumed a rather threatening attitude'. In Bishop's Castle, while the coal dealers there were arguing with the local council over the maximum prices to be set, they exerted pressure by suspending all deliveries, though they did agree to open for just two hours on a Saturday as a good-will gesture to the local people. Households were also advised to put firebricks in their grates to help save fuel, but once again the attempts to alleviate shortages by voluntary means failed and compulsory rationing was decided on. In August 1918 local Fuel Committees and a Fuel Overseer had to be appointed. The committees were to be made up of 50% council appointees and 50% people who were nominated by the local coal dealers and merchants and the local gas and electric companies.[58] In Ludlow it was decided that households could initially claim for one ton per grate but asked that since most bedrooms had a grate that those living in large houses with bedrooms that were not always used should refrain from claiming the maximum allowed. Sadly this request for fairness fell on so many deaf ears that the mayor felt it necessary to intervene:

> He could not help saying ... some words perhaps he ought not to say, but he did know for a fact that a great many people in the town, in filling up their forms for the Fuel Overseer, had asked for a considerable amount more than was absolutely necessary.[59]

It did not help that the Fuel Committee was yet another group that met in secret and would allow no member of the public or the press to listen to proceedings. This led a local newspaper editor to ask:

> What are they going to do about those extensive stocks of coal one hears so much about in the cellars of certain residencies? Is the Fuel Overseer going to commandeer all excessive stocks and publish the names of those persons he had forced to disgorge?[60]

It appears that the answer was no.

One further way that Fuel Committees tried to reduce fuel consumption was to attempt to reach an agreement with local shopkeepers on earlier closing to save on gas and electricity. Since this would hit sales, such agreements were hard to negotiate. Patriotism and 'doing your bit' to help your country was one thing, loss of income was another. In Ludlow, when a meeting to discuss early closing was called, only 15 shopkeepers turned up. Asked to close on most weekdays at 5pm instead of 7pm and at 6pm on Mondays and Saturdays, the answer was no. They finally agreed to 6pm on all weekdays and 8pm on Saturdays. It was hoped that all traders who missed the meeting would fall in line behind the decision but there was no compulsion on them to do so.[61]

Shortages, with its concomitant rise in prices, would have been a strain on most household budgets, especially working class ones, at any time. For many families, however, this came when the main breadwinner was away in the armed forces or had returned unfit to work or would never return again. For these families life was especially hard. When the war began, the separation allowance for the wives and children of privates, corporals and sergeants when they went away to fight was far from generous and, at first, was based on middle-class morality. It was set at 7/7d per week for a wife but a marriage certificate had to be produced in order to claim this, common law wives receiving nothing. For each son under 14 or daughter under 16 the mother received an extra 1/2d per week and again birth certificates had to be produced. No allowance was given for any child conceived out of wedlock, nor for those born within nine months following marriage. In September 1914 allowances were raised to 11/1d for the wife and 1/9d per week for the first three children and 1/2d for all others, but a maximum of 17/6 was imposed whatever the size of the family. Within a month this had changed yet again but in the opposite direction. Allowances were reduced by at least 3/6d per week. To appreciate the hardship this level of allowances caused it is illuminating to compare them to the average weekly wage of £1 8/- for a general labourer in 1914.

Those who felt unable to live on the amount received could apply to the local branch of the Soldiers and Sailors Families Association (SSFA), a semi-charitable body. Their officials could top up the allowances if the case was deemed deserving. However, by December 1914 state allowances could be paid to common law wives and for children born or conceived out of wedlock. In addition to the allowances, soldiers could have up to 5/3d a week deducted from their pay to be sent home to their wife. Since they only received 7/- per week many could only take partial advantage of this whilst others perhaps chose not to send any home.[62]

Then there were disabled fathers or widowed mothers, often with young children, who had relied on their eldest son's earnings to keep the family. Allowances for such dependants were non-existent at first. After pressure a maximum allowance of 12/6d per week could be granted, but 3/6d of this was taken from the serviceman's pay. This was later fixed at 10/- a week for parents and 5/- for siblings but was only paid if the dependants were incapacitated or had no other means of support. In addition, before any payment was sanctioned a local officer of the SSFA would call at the home to ensure that the full facts of each case were verified. One other point to note is that these allowances, together with those for wives and children, did not take into account any increase in the cost of living. As this was a time when prices were continually on the rise this meant that their purchasing power was being constantly eroded.

As more and more soldiers were discharged due to their wounds or ill health brought about by the conditions they had endured in the trenches, pensions for such men became of crucial importance both to them and their families. At first the amounts they were granted were those in force during the South African War. This was 10/6d per week for total disablement, though it could be raised to a maximum of 17/6d with children's allowances. A new scheme was introduced in May 1915 that gave the totally disabled 25/- per week with an extra 2/6d for each child. Partially disabled men would receive an allowance that 'with the wages he was deemed capable of earning' would give an income of 25/- per week. Any future pay increase would be offset by a similar reduction in the pension. For these men children's allowances could be granted but were discretionary. There was no compensation for pain or suffering. Until 1917 there was also no right of appeal.

Financial arrangements were also put in place when a man was killed, and at a time when working class families tended to have many children these were needed. Beatrice Edwards of Much Wenlock discovered at Christmas 1915 that she had been widowed and now had to bring up her nine children, the eldest of which was only 12, alone.[63] At first, however, widow's pensions were also those pertaining for the South African War: 5/- per week for legally married wives plus 1/6d for each legitimate child. Adopted children and stepchildren received nothing. These figures were amended in 1915. A widow under 35 years of age received 10/- per week rising to 15/- if she were over 45. In addition, an allowance for the first child was now 5/-, 3/6d for the second and 2/6d for all others. For a widow to receive such a pension her husband had to have been killed 'wholly and directly due to war service'. This meant that if death was through illness or accident then the payment of a pension was open to question. Common law wives still received no pension, instead continuing to receive the separation allowance for one year and then nothing. The exception was if the woman looked after the children of the dead soldier, in which case she might be allowed their children's allowance, but that too was discretionary. For families whose menfolk had been declared missing the situation was complicated. In such cases the separation allowances were paid for up to 30 weeks or until he was officially declared dead. If he were later found to be a POW, he would be given his back pay and the separation allowance continued.

A glimpse into the hardships suffered by those in receipt of these awards can be discerned in the cases that came before local War Pensions Committees. These were set up in February 1917 after the Ministry of Pensions came into existence in December 1916 and took over the responsibility for military death and disability pensions and allowances. Three of these committees covered most of south Shropshire: the eastern one covered Bridgnorth and the area of the local rural district council, in the west it was the Clun and Purslow Naval and Military War Pensions Committee that sat in Bishop's Castle, whilst a committee that sat in Ludlow dealt with most of the central and southern area. These committees, using the voluntary funds collected to aid the widows, children and dependants of servicemen, looked at each individual case and dispensed long- or short-term funds to those in need. It was up to each committee as to whether their proceedings should be made public. The one in Bridgnorth decided that they should sit in private. The one in Bishop's Castle chose to allow the press to attend but asked them not to give the names of those who applied for help. In Ludlow, however, as it was public money that was being given out it was decided to allow the press in and also to leave it to them as to the amount of detail they put into print. This was in complete contrast to the proceedings of their Food Control Committee. This situation did not last forever. In October 1917, after two ex-soldiers asked for their names not to be made public, it was decided that the press should keep the identities of those granted money anonymous. Finally, in September 1918 the decision was taken that all future proceedings would be totally private.[64] As to the make-up of these committees, once again it was the local councillors and other local worthies who made up the bulk of the membership, leavened with a few churchmen. This too, however, changed in March 1918 when the committees were instructed to take on board at least two discharged soldiers plus a widow or a dependant of a dead serviceman.[65]

One of the main requests for help was from wives or dependants who found themselves in short-term financial difficulties after their husbands or sons joined the armed forces. Allotments deducted from pay came through almost immediately but it could be weeks before the allowances granted by the State were received. For example, a widowed mother living in Craven Arms had been given 10/- a week by her son who had worked as a railway porter. After he had joined the Army, until her separation allowance was agreed and paid, her only income was the 3/6 per week that her son allotted to her from his Army wage. In consequence, her local pensions committee awarded her 3/3d a week until the allowance came through.[66] A widow at Bedstone facing a similar difficulty was also helped. Her son had always handed over his wage of 15/6d to her but after he joined the forces her only initial income was the 4/4d allotment from her son's Army wage. The committee granted her 2/6d a week until the separation allowance arrived. Wives awaiting their State allowance after their husbands had been called up were also helped. A Mrs Jukes of Craven Arms was given a lump sum of 25/- whilst a Mrs Jacks of nearby Withersley was granted £1 per week until the allowance arrived.[67]

Even after the allowances were paid a number of families still found themselves in financial difficulties due to the rapid rise in the cost of living. This was especially so for wives with young children who could not go out to work. When Joseph (Joe) Cornes, Edward Jones and Thomas Holder joined the Army they left behind their wives in Kerry Lane, Bishop's Castle trying to feed 17 children. A number of wives were helped by being given between 1/3d and 3/6d per week towards paying the rent.

One local reason for the increase in rents was the growing demand for rental accommodation caused by rural families being told to leave their tied cottages. As the war dragged on and agricultural production had to be increased, farmers and landowners required back the cottages that had been left by their former farmhands who had volunteered to fight as homes for replacement workers. Sometimes this necessitated court action. One Bromfield farmer successfully obtained an eviction order against the wife of his former cowman and her six children.[68]

George Vaughan, who had answered his country's call, summed up the overall effect on those left at home. He wrote to his local newspaper asking for help for his mother in Colebatch:

> She was dependent on me when I was at home; now she is getting my three shillings and sixpence allotment per week. With the Government allowance of two shillings and five pence making five shillings and eleven pence altogether, this being her sole means of existence, I feel there is some mistake somewhere as it must be impossible to live on it at the present cost of food.

After an application to the Clun and Purslow pensions committee his mother was awarded an additional 3/- per week.[69]

Sometimes it was a sudden change in circumstances that reduced dependants to poverty and forced them to approach the committees for help. A Mrs Hughes

When a husband was killed this often left families, especially working class ones, in financial difficulties. Beatrice Edwards of Sheinton Street, Much Wenlock, received news of the death of her husband Pte Alfred Joseph Edwards at Christmas 1915 just after he had returned from leave when this photograph was taken. A pregnant Beatrice was now left to bring up her nine children, the eldest being just twelve, on her own.
(Courtesy of Ina Taylor)

of Richard's Castle had been receiving 16/- per week (separation allowances for two sons plus allotments of pay), but one son married whilst on leave and was then killed soon after returning to the front. As a consequence it was his new wife who received a pension whilst the mother lost both his allowance and allotment. This meant that her weekly income was more than halved down to 7/1d and her local committee had to award her an emergency grant of 5/- per week. Another mother to see a change in fortune was a Bitterley widow who was already in receipt of the maximum pension following the death of a son and who then lost her second and remaining son and his allotment of pay. Due to her reduced circumstances her local committee voted her an extra 8/3d a week.[70]

Other wives and mothers suddenly found themselves having to give continual nursing care to totally disabled loved ones. The mother of Arthur Williams of Ludlow found herself in this position. At first she was awarded 5/- per week but this was then raised to 10/- after their doctor wrote to the local War Pensions Committee describing her son's condition and requirements.[71] Also, since there was no national health service at this time most medical care had to be paid for and that included consulting a doctor and purchasing medicines. The pension committees often received requests for help when families of servicemen suffered illness. The widow of Thomas Bissell of Ludlow who had been left with four children to bring up on her own was awarded 5/- per week for four weeks to help pay such medical costs. Another Ludlow serviceman's wife was given the 7/- rail fare to take her child to the Eye and Ear Hospital in Shrewsbury.[72] However, the war could also push into poverty families where the father had not joined the services. One woman who was widowed with four children to look after just before the war broke out found herself in the latter months of the war having to plead for financial help to the local Poor Law Guardians. She explained that:

This photograph, possibly taken in the canteen tent at the annual training camp for reservists, shows Robert Price of Ludlow sitting on the left. As the newly married 7341 Cpl Robert Price, Y Company, 2nd Battalion KSLI he landed in France on 19 February 1915. After three months in and out of the front line he was shot in the face at Hooge during the second battle of Ypres on 16 May. After passing through two clearing stations he had what remained of one of his eyes removed at No 3 Canadian Hospital, Boulogne and was then repatriated to England on 25 May. Here, at the Royal Herbert Hospital, Woolwich, he had the bullet removed from where it had lodged behind his jaw. After his recovery Robert was discharged from the army, one of many who now had to learn how to make a living with a disability. (Courtesy of Cecil Price)

I had help from my brothers until they went to the war. They helped me all they could but one is killed and another crippled so I find it all together a struggle to get on in life.[73]

The War Pensions Committee also helped discharged ex-servicemen with medical expenses. Arthur Davies of Ludlow 'had been invalided out of the Army in a helpless condition, the effect of shell shock and rheumatism'. He had a wife and child to support and the committee awarded him 5/- a week for four weeks to help pay for doctors' bills. Other ex-servicemen needed help with the fitting of artificial limbs. One was recompensed with lost wages when he had to travel to Greater London to have one fitted, whilst Gustave Charlton was given the rail fare to Shrewsbury after the joints of his artificial leg broke. Yet another discharged Ludlow soldier had his travel expenses paid when he had to visit Shrewsbury hospital twice to have pieces of shrapnel removed from his face.[74]

The War Pensions Committees also helped discharged servicemen return to the labour market. A few of them managed to find work for themselves but needed help in getting started. Harry Hatfield of Ludlow managed to obtain a position as a chauffeur in Llandrindod Wells. He was granted his rail fare there and the cost of new clothing. Similarly, Edwin Shutt was given money to cover his rail fare to Craven Arms, where he had obtained employment, and the cost of a new pair of working boots. Yet another Ludlow ex-soldier, who had found himself a job as the Range Keeper at a military barracks at Shorncliffe, Kent, was helped with his rail travel costs.[75]

Other ex-servicemen were assisted in training for a new occupation as their wounds or general health made them unable to pursue their previous employment. Thomas Parr asked for help in being trained as a chauffeur at a Ludlow garage. The proprietor was happy to teach him for a fee of five guineas which the committee agreed to pay. Another ex-soldier, William Downes, wished to be apprenticed to a bootmaker. The committee agreed to pay his employer 5/- a week for six months and to pay the man's wages of 10/- a week for the first six months, 15/- a week for the next six months and £1 a week for the following six months.[76] Some men were offered the chance of setting themselves up as hawkers with a grant of 30/- to pay for a licence and to set themselves up with an initial stock. James Bumford, who had been a chimney sweep before losing the use of his right hand, was one of these men as was another Ludlow man who had lost an arm.[77]

One useful consequence of the make-up of the War Pensions Committees was that they had the social connections to find employment for some men. It was the Clun and Purslow Committee that found a young Bishop's Castle soldier, who had been discharged due to the effects of gas poisoning, suitable employment. In another example, a discharged soldier from Stanton Lacy who had formerly been a woodsman on the Oakley Park Estate but was no longer capable of doing the job, was told that a member of his committee would ask the estate manager to take him on as a rabbit catcher.[78]

When the war began those left at home in south Shropshire, though obviously concerned about their loved ones who had gone to fight, did not expect life to be too different. However, as the war dragged on, as zeppelin and later aircraft bombing raids began, and as submarine warfare began to reduce food supplies, life grew gradually harder. Wives and dependants of the ever-growing numbers of men joining the armed forces also began to feel the economic strain of being without breadwinners at a time of ever-rising prices, as did the growing number of widows. In addition, increasing numbers of discharged servicemen had to be re-assimilated into family life and society. By 1918 life on the home front was far harder than it had been in the heady, patriotic days of August 1914.

5 NEWS FROM ABROAD AND THE TRENCHES

For friends, relatives and loved ones waiting in south Shropshire, the arrival of the postman or telegraph boy was a moment when hope mingled with fear. Would the letter be the hoped-for one from the front or would it be a message of sympathy from a fellow soldier or commanding officer relating news of wounding or death? Would the telegram be an official notification that someone had been killed or wounded or was missing in action or just one to say that a son or brother had arrived back in England and would be home on leave within a few hours? This roller coaster of emotions was one that many households had to bear for months and even years.

In October 1914 the territorial members of the 4th Battalion KSLI came home to enjoy embarkation leave prior to sailing for the Far East to allow regular troops to return to fight on the western front. Before beginning their journey to board ship this group paraded outside Ludlow Castle watched by their families and the local populace as they were given a civic farewell. (Courtesy of Shropshire Museum Services)

For many young men the outbreak of war appeared to give them the chance of adventure away from what many saw as a claustrophobic existence in rural south Shropshire. This group of soldiers, belonging to a number of regiments, appear to have come together for a shooting competition. The soldier standing fourth from the right in the back row is Pte Isaiah Marsh. Soon he was to leave with the 4th Battalion KSLI for the Far East. Little did he know that he would remain on the other side of the world until mid 1917 and then be sent direct to the trenches on the Western Front without being allowed to return home to see his wife, whom he married on embarkation leave back in October 1914.
(Courtesy of Malcolm Marsh)

Writing letters was the main way that everyone kept in touch and shared news. Edward Meadmore of Lydbury North wrote home without fail three times a week to his wife and five children right up until his death in April 1918.[1] In fact, one of the first intimations that bad news might soon be forthcoming was when letters stopped arriving, as was the case for the family of George Lucas. He last wrote to his wife and four children in Church Stretton on 23 April 1915. No further letter was received for over a month until an official communication arrived to inform them that he had died in a casualty clearing station.[2]

Many of the first letters home were descriptions of sights, sounds and scenes witnessed by wondrous eyes new to a wider world. This was certainly the case for the members of the local territorial force who had left their homes within hours of the outbreak of war, as they sailed to Rangoon in the Far East in October 1914. Once the Suez Canal was reached, 'here was a sudden change from West to East. By the canal side natives with flowing robes and hundreds of camels; beyond to the East nothing but sand.' Then at sea, 'as we progressed eastwards thousands of fishes would rise from the water and fly for a considerable distance in front of our ship. The sea seemed full of them.' Their adventures then continued. After disembarkation in Bombay, they travelled by train to Calcutta through the Western Ghats. 'We climbed by a wonderful piece of railroad engineering, stage by stage, in a zigzag fashion. At times the scenery was lovely; forest glades alternated with mountain panorama.'[3]

Writing after arriving in Rangoon, Henry Steenton summed up his feelings:

> We were six weeks getting here. We had a good voyage and saw some grand scenery and some lovely places which we would not have seen if we had stopped in Ludlow.[4]

Sgt Benjamin Nicholas of Ludlow, whilst hunting mutineers after the battalion had been sent down to Singapore, wrote of passing through fields planted with pineapples and rubber plantations where women workers would tap the rubber

For some the dream of experiencing adventure far from their homes in rural Shropshire came true as they spent over two years in the Far East. In between bouts of excitement putting down mutinies amongst native contingents, their time was spent in comfortable safety writing home of their novel experiences. Leisure and sport took up much of their time and here the identical twins, Charlie and George Griffiths of Ludlow, display their football trophies. George is in the back row fifth from the left whilst Charlie, who signed as a professional footballer with Coventry City in 1921, can be seen second from the left in the front row. (Courtesy of Fred Griffiths)

from trees. His men lopped off the tops of coconuts to drink the milk to quench their thirst.[5] As William Griffiths, also from Ludlow, pointed out in a letter to his father: 'You can get pineapples and different kinds of fruit for next to nothing.'[6] Before William went to war a tin of pineapple would almost certainly have been an unaffordable luxury. George Kimber from Knowbury wrote home of the abundance of exotic fruits so easily at hand, though noting that 'the monkeys very often do us down for pineapples'.[7] Bernard Turner, a former assistant master at Low Town School, Bridgnorth, penned a letter about the 'thousands of monkeys' he saw and also pointed out that 'flying foxes and chipmunks are very common', though he warned that the reptiles were the most dangerous with 'pythons of enormous size often being frequently met with'.[8]

Then there was the architecture. Frederick Brookes, a former pupil of the National School in Ludlow, wrote in awe from Rangoon to his old headmaster about the beautiful pagodas and temples that he had viewed:

> I have never seen such a sight as in the Shive Dragon Pagoda, one of the wonders of the world. The Burma carvings and engravings in this temple are marvellous; it is really too wonderful to describe.[9]

As yet another soldier recalled:

> We had arrived in a beautiful country. The tinkling pagoda bells could be heard everywhere as the gentle breezes blew. A country in which one could wish to live forever.[10]

For these young men, especially those from the Shropshire countryside who were used to deferring to their 'social betters', an experience they enjoyed was finding themselves in some ways the masters rather than the servants. As Frederick Brookes explained:

> On the whole it is a fine life, full of interest. I am enjoying it really well. I get on fairly well with the natives, although they are a sly lot. Every one of them around the barracks can speak a little English. They do all the work required around the barracks, indeed it is a very lazy life for a soldier.[11]

They could also afford to have many menial and personal tasks carried out for them by the local people at a very affordable cost, as Joseph Davies, also of Ludlow, pointed out:

> We have a 'Knappy' (barber) to shave all the men in the company for which we pay 8d per month, also a 'Dhobie' (washerman) who collects washing once a week and returns it the next for which we pay 1/4d per month.[12]

For men, many of whom had been near the bottom of the social scale in this country, the experience must have been a very pleasant one.

About 50 men were sent on to Australia as an escort to just under 500 Germans from the local internment camp in Singapore. These were mainly civilians but also included the crew of the captured light cruiser *SMS Emden*. After the prisoners were handed over in Sydney the escort was allowed four weeks' sightseeing in the city. They then travelled to Melbourne for a few days, where their sightseeing included a guided tour of the Melbourne Cricket Ground. Only then did they return to Singapore.[13]

The Far Eastern sojourn ended in the summer of 1917 but that led to their experiencing even more sights. On the long journey home they first stopped off at Colombo and stayed two weeks in the central hills of Ceylon (now Sri Lanka) amongst the tea plantations before sailing to spend several weeks in Cape Town. Then came the disappointment. They arrived back at Plymouth on 27 July but instead of being allowed home on leave as expected they embarked immediately for France where they landed still wearing tropical shorts. For many the adventure would end here on the western front, never returning to the homes they had left back in 1914 and never able to tell in person tales of the wondrous sights that they had seen.

Other local men in other battalions or regiments saw different exotic areas of the world and sent excited word of them back home. Frank Maddocks of Bishop's Castle wrote to his old scoutmaster about the sights of Gibraltar, where he was stationed in a hospital, and described the totally different way of life there compared to that lived in the Welsh Marches:

> The natives here have a language of their own. They cultivate fields of toma-toes, Indian corn, lemons, pineapples, apricots, figs, dates etc. procurable very cheaply. A common and amusing feature is the manner in which they sell milk. They take a herd of goats round and as they receive orders at the doors, milk the animals into the jugs or glasses. They use mules out here and have them covered with fancy cloths and the vehicles are very comical things. ... All the buildings, roads, and most of the soil are white or a yellowish colour. There are no hedges, all loose stone walls, the whole place being just like a picture of the Holy Land and the East.[14]

This comparison with the Holy Land was made by others from the county who were sent out to fight the Turks. Another member of the Royal Army Medical Corps (RAMC), Thomas Kyffin Corbishley, wrote to his father in Ludlow when on the verge of entering Palestine:

Enjoying leave in Egypt in 1916, Clement Roberts of Ludlow, Bernard Davies of Wistanstow and David John of Stanton Lacy, members of the Shropshire Yeomanry, pose on camelback before a Sphinx and one of the Great Pyramids.
(Courtesy of Gareth Thomas)

We have after five days marching reached the first stage of our journey into the 'Promised Land' of old times. ... The journey will occupy nine or ten days they say ... the road we are travelling is the identical road from Palestine to Egypt of Bible times.[15]

Nearly two years earlier, on his way out to the Dardanelles, Corbishley had written home to describe the sights he had witnessed on the way. One of his first stops was the island of Malta:

We were in the harbour there where we stopped to coal. The Maltese are so brown as to look like Mulattoes or Lascars; but their general appearance is Italian. The speech too is like Italian but whether it is or not I can't say. The gestures they make, the jabbering and chattering reminds me of the zoo. As soon as we arrived the boat was surrounded by a variety of small craft, which were chiefly miniature shops. We were not supposed to buy from them for fear of catching Malta fever, but we could not resist, things were so cheap, especially tobacco. Now I smoke cigars and Egyptian cigarettes ... Most of the boats were like Venetian gondolas with their high prows and canvas awnings and coloured curtains.

After it was decided to send help to the Serbs who had been attacked by Bulgaria in October 1915, other local men were able to write home and describe the country that saw the birth of democracy and the home of the ancient myths: Greece. William Jones wrote back to Ludlow to paint a picture in words of the skyline of the city of

Trooper T. Gordon Hodnett, seen here in a tent in Egypt, who rode out of Ludlow as part of C Squadron Shropshire Yeomanry, was first posted for coastal defence duties in England. The brigade was then dismounted and sent to Egypt in March 1916. On arrival, they were merged with the South Wales Mounted Brigade to form the 4th Dismounted Brigade. A few, including Trooper Hodnett, preferred to remain mounted and transferred to the Imperial Camel Corps that was set up in that year. (Courtesy of Shropshire Museum Services)

Salonika which 'possesses a rich collection of churches and mosques some of which are truly "joyeaux d'art"'. As for the people, 'there are so many different races here that one sees a real diversity in the styles of apparel; some of the national costumes worn by old women are extremely picturesque'.[16]

Even those initially posted to the western front sometimes saw wonderful sights that they could write home about. One was a Ludlow man belonging to a cycle division who described his transfer in early 1918 from Flanders, where he had spent three years, to the Italian Front. As their train ran parallel to the Mediterranean coast passing through Nice and Monte Carlo, he wrote joyously that 'the scenery here was the most gorgeous' he had ever witnessed and when they rested they bathed and refreshed themselves by swimming in the Mediterranean.[17]

For those sent directly to France and Belgium, the first news sent home often concerned life at the front. Before conscription men could choose the regiment that they wished to join so that friends often served in the same battalion, the same company and even the same platoon. It was thought at the time that this would encourage enlistment. One consequence was that in letters home they could pass on news of other local men that they served with, information that could then be passed on in turn to their families. Such news could be good or bad. Edward Preece wrote to his mother to explain how he was happy to be fighting in the Battle of Armentières alongside his old schoolfriends, but also passed on news of the first local casualty they had suffered:

> At the time of writing we are entrenched a few hundred yards from the Germans and they don't forget to let us know it. They drop a few dozen shells into us three or four times a day just to remind us that they are still there. Sometimes they strike lucky and get a couple of our fellows, but as soon as we hear the report we run to ground like rabbits; you would laugh to see us. I am next to Tiddly Pounds [Francis Pounds]. He is corporal in charge of the next section and Biddy Didlick [John Albert Didlick] is about a dozen yards behind us in another trench. We were all side-by-side in our first scrap and it was all right to have old boy chums with one at one's first issue of fire for I can tell you it is a hellish time. ... They have taken a heavy toll of our ranks. Many of my old mates are gone, but only one Ludlow boy has been killed yet, that is young Cocky Baron [John Henry Baron]. He was shot in the head and died almost instantly close to me. It seemed such a pity for he was only a young boy.[18]

Whether this was the first indication to John Baron's family that their son had been killed is not known, but almost certainly it would be the first news of how he had met his death.

It was a fellow villager at Claverley, home on leave after being wounded, who brought back details as to how another local man, Thomas Bright, had met his

132

death. Owen Owen, acting as a stretcher bearer, told of Thomas being hit in the side of the head by a German bullet as he was in the act of firing his rifle over a trench parapet. He died one hour later.[19]

Since many brothers served alongside each other, news of the death of one often came from his sibling. Such a letter was posted home by William Bishop of Clee St Margaret giving his parents the sad news of the death of his brother Tom, who had been killed during an exchange of fire with a sniper. As William explained:

> I had just gone into the dugout to change my boots and my brother Jem [James Elisha] was getting breakfast, when suddenly I heard him scream out 'Poor Tom is shot'.

When they managed to reach him about half an hour later he was unconscious and soon died.[20]

Similar news was broken to his mother back home in Alveley by Edward France, who recounted that he had just attended the burial of his brother Harry.[21] The same heart-breaking task fell to Sidney Greatwich of Bridgnorth, who wrote home to his parents to tell them that he had just buried his brother Frederick.[22]

Brothers serving together could also bring double tragedy. William and Thomas Francis of Diddlebury were serving alongside each other when the same shell killed

Brothers in the armed forces also kept in touch with each other in order to pass on news. This photograph of Emmanuel Lovekin, together with a group of friends at the No. 2 Royal Flying Corps Cadet Wing at Hastings, was posted to his brother who was serving with the 6th Battalion KSLI. Emmanuel became a dentist in Church Stretton after the war. (Courtesy of Janet Preshous)

them both.[23] Two other brothers, Alfred and Richard Jones of Onibury, were killed, almost certainly by the same shell or trench mortar, when they were serving together in the front line trench.[24] The mother of Edward and Stanley Bowen of Bridgnorth received similar tragic news regarding her sons. Along with five others they were hit by the same trench mortar. All were killed with the exception of her eldest son Edward, who was still alive but had suffered a head wound.[25] The shock felt by parents hearing such news of two children at the same time is difficult to imagine.

But brothers could also send happier news of each other, even if not serving in the same platoon or company. John Lewis of Bedlam wrote to his mother about a meeting at the front with her other son, after he had received news of his whereabouts. 'Yesterday I set off to find him and before long I did find him looking well. He came down to where I am and we spent the afternoon together and he had some tea with me.'[26]

John Oliver of Bridgnorth was serving with his two brothers and he could reassure his father about them after a diversionary attack at Railway Wood on the first day of the Battle of Loos in September 1915, as well as pass on news, sometimes sad, of friends:

> Just a few lines to tell you that Charley, George and me are all in the pink but it is a miracle we are alive and well to tell the tale. ... Mr Beaumont [Captain Samuel George Beaumont], my officer, got killed on the 24th inst. He was having dinner just outside his dugout when a shell burst over us and a piece hit him on the top of the head and knocked his brains out ... I sat next to Mr Beaumont and yet I escaped, but it was luck. Poor Harry Johnson and Alf Bowen got killed but the other Bridgnorth lads are well enough though it is lucky that there are any of us left to come back.[27]

This letter highlights a point that will be explored further later: the wrong news could sometimes be conveyed back to families. Though Harry Johnson's wife was soon officially informed of her husband's death, presumably on the evidence of his comrades who saw him fall or saw his body lying on the ground, he was in fact still alive. Two weeks after the date of his supposed death, his wife received a postcard from her husband informing her that he had been wounded and taken prisoner by the Germans, and was now in one of their hospitals. He asked her to 'remember me to both mother and father. Tell them I shall be all right and not to worry'. One can only try to imagine the joy this postcard must have brought after the days of mourning a lost son and husband.[28]

Sometimes sons would write home with news of brothers they had stumbled across by accident. Harold Kershaw's mother only knew that her son was back in England from Palestine when he wrote to say that he had been invalided home suffering from trench fever and heatstroke. Since embarking for France in August

From the very beginning of the war, mail, to and from soldiers at the front, received top priority in order to keep up morale. Because of this many servicemen corresponded home every week with news not only of themselves but of family and friends.
(Courtesy of Post Office Archive)

1914, he had only been home once in three years and that was on hospital furlough after he had been wounded in 1916. He had then been posted to the Middle East. But as well as easing the worries of his anxious parents about himself he was able to give them news of his brother Ernest. He had taken part in the abortive Dardanelles landings at Suvla Bay before being sent to Palestine. The two had then met by accident on the outskirts of Jerusalem just before Christmas 1917.[29]

Thomas Corbishley of Ludlow was another son who could pass on news of a brother to his parents. Thomas had landed on the Greek island of Lemnos, which was being used as a staging post for the Dardanelles, hoping to meet his brother Frederick Henry, who was also in the RAMC, but:

> Soon after we landed I saw some of the 32nd Field Ambulance and, to my surprise, heard that Harry had been taken back to Alexandria with dysentery. I cannot find out the details but hope he is not very ill.[30]

Letters home could also contain news of friends and neighbours. George Davies of Bishop's Castle wrote back to his parents from France with the good news that 'Bob Morris of Colebatch, Walter Swain, Brockton, and Bert Wright, Bishop's Castle, are all with us' and asking for a message to be passed on to Mrs Smith, a neighbour and mother of Tom:

> I have not seen Tom for over six weeks, but the last time I heard of him was that he was seen in a Red Cross motor van. He had a little gas and he is in a hospital somewhere.[31]

Sadly this latter news was incorrect and could have well have raised false hope since Tom Smith's mother had already been officially informed that her son was missing in action. That something serious had happened to Tom must have filtered down to George Davies, as he soon wrote to ask his father if:

Mr and Mrs Smith [have] heard anything more about Tom? The last I saw of him was when we were in a bayonet charge, Whitsuntide Tuesday morning. If you have heard anything of him do please let me know for he was my greatest pal. He used to come to my trench when we were in the bombardment at Ypres to see if I was alright and I sometimes used to visit him.[32]

One new facet of warfare that grew during the First World War was censorship. This increased in extent and scope to cover not only newspapers but also servicemen's letters home from the front. Envelopes began to warn that mail could be opened, read and censored, whilst each serviceman now had to sign to say that letters contained only private or family matters. This was partly to shore up morale on the home front and partly to ensure that military information was not unwittingly spread. (Courtesy of Jane Smith)

In fact it was not until May 1916, a full year after he was reported missing, that Tom Smith's parents were officially informed that their son had been killed. Up to that point they had clung to the hope that he was a prisoner of war somewhere in Germany.

Stories related from hospitals were another source of unofficial news for anxious relatives at home. When Ernest Drew from the Claverley area was recovering from a wound in his shoulder, incurred when 'going over the top,' he said he was helped into the field ambulance by two other Claverley men: Fred Bright and Cyril Boucher.[33] A worker for the YMCA in France wrote back to his father that when giving blood in a casualty clearing station he had met Edgar Price who had worked at Hucks Barn Farm, Ludford. He was there having bad teeth extracted.[34] Albert Smallman of Bridgnorth received news of his brother Joe, who had emigrated to Australia before the war, from a very unexpected quarter. It appears that Joe had returned to Europe as part of the Australian Army and one of his comrades wrote to Albert from his hospital bed to keep a promise that he had made:

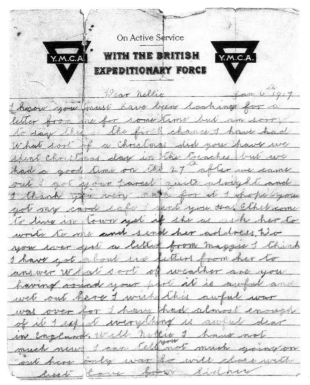

When men came out of the front line they often used YMCA huts to relax in. As well as supplying reading material and games, note-paper was also made available in order for soldiers to write home. Here, on YMCA notepaper, Pte Sidney George Garbett of Netchwood, near Ditton Priors, writes a short letter to his sister Nellie describing his Christmas and New Year 1916/17, and wishing this 'awful' war was over. He was killed in action, aged just 22, the following April. (Courtesy of Margaret Russell).

I was wounded on the Somme. When I was lying down in No Man's Land with my foot off and thinking in my agony it was all up with me, up comes your Joe and says 'What's up kid? Had a knock?' I says 'Only got a knock. You had better be off or you will get one.' Mind you, there were shells dropping round us all the time. Joe says 'No, I will do what I can for you and try and get you back to the trench. We will go together either to Heaven, Hell or Blighty.' So with that he gets me on his back and struggled with me over dead and wounded and through shell holes and mud and slush till he got me to the parapet and over he rolled himself and me into our trench ... The reason I am writing to you is that when they got me on the stretcher Joe said 'Kid, you will be going to Blighty. Here is our Kid's address. When you get there just drop him a line and tell him I am all right and that I will write to him the first chance I get.'[35]

One further conduit of news was via the old school network. A Sergeant R.A. Jones was sent his old school's termly magazine, *The Ludlovian*, which kept him informed as regards the fate of his fellow former school chums. In addition, many headmasters and teachers kept in touch with former pupils. George Rogers wrote to his old headmaster at the British School, Ludlow to bring him up to date with news of old boys at the front, news that would have been passed on to the families concerned:

Back Row l to r: E.G.M. Goodwin, R.J. Melsome, A.N. Scrivener, H. Mantle,
H.W. Warburton.
Middle Row: J.H. Goodall, R.B.S. Munn, H.J. Butters.
Front Row: H.O. Farmer, J. Middle, H.T. Mellings.
A snapshot of the effect that the war had on a generation can be glimpsed in what
happened to the unbeaten Ludlow Grammar School Hockey team of 1913. All joined
the forces with six of them becoming officers whilst the other five remained in the ranks.
Harold Mellings of Bromfield, a flying ace with 15 victories credited to him, was killed
in action and four others also became casualties:
Mantle and Warburton returned to duty after recovering from their wounds whilst
Butters and Melsome were discharged unfit for further service, the latter due to
shellshock. The remainder came through relatively unscathed. Compared to the rest of the
school's old boys their record was good since one in every seven serving former
pupils did not survive. As for former masters, four out of the nine who served died.
(Courtesy of Robert Burns)

I was sorry to hear of Stanley Stead's death. He was killed in the charge I hear was made on the morning of August 9th. It is a day I shall never forget as long as I live, for the amount of shells they sent over on us during the remainder of that day was out of all count. Never through this campaign have I seen the like. But I am glad to say that me and my brother Jack got safely through. Pinches, a postman belonging to Ludlow (one of the men in my platoon) was wounded, but I think is going on well. Ben Price, another Ludlow fellow was wounded, but the remainder as far as I know pulled through safely. ... It was a warm time while it lasted, the Germans fighting to the last. At times the men were so thick that it was impossible to use anything but fists in some parts of the line.[36]

John Diggle, the headmaster of the National School in Ludlow, kept in correspondence with a number of his former pupils who, like Gilbert Griffiths, wrote to let him know what was happening to those he had taught:

At the present I am a short distance behind the firing line but within quite easy reach of a shell ... Tomorrow we are expecting a move again but I do not know where we are going. I expect you know Harold Vale was wounded in the recent fighting and Ernest Lewis was killed. I do not know if any more old boys were in the casualty lists but several Ludlow men were included.[37]

School pals also wrote to each other with news, and this too often filtered home. Joseph Peachey wrote from Salonika, Greece that he had heard from Joe Davies, 'another of the old school K-nuts, in India, yesterday, and I am glad to say he is quite well'.[38] Benjamin Nicholas wrote back from the Far East that he had heard from two old schoolfriends, George Henson and William Minton, who were serving on the Western Front and relayed their descriptions of trench life.[39]

Men also heard news of friends, which they could then relay home, from chance meetings with others at the front. Charles Francis of the 1st Battalion KSLI wrote that:

We passed the 5th Battalion KSLI the other evening. They had just received their baptism having only just returned to billets from a successful advance in which they were supports. They suffered rather heavily I believe ... We also came into contact with the 2nd Battalion, or the remnants of what was the 2nd. They were sadly thinned out, and many were the enquiries that met with the answer 'Gone West' for only the night before, I believe, they charged three times only to get sent back broken but not beaten for they eventually got the trench they were after.[40]

Knowledge that a family member had been wounded brought many worries. Often the news came via an official telegram, but the seriousness and certainly the nature of the wound was often unclear. Greater detail was often gleaned from other sources. This could be from fellow soldiers, medical staff or even the wounded man himself. If a soldier was deemed very seriously wounded then a parent or wife could sometimes be given permission to travel to France or Belgium to visit him. The War Office would then issue a free pass and on arrival on the Continent the YMCA would take the visitor to the relevant hospital by car. Who decided who would be given permission or what level of injury was needed to necessitate a visit appears haphazard – and also rare, since the army did not want too many civilians near the front.

The mother of Edward Cooper was one who was given permission to visit her son, who had been severely wounded by shrapnel, and travelled from Bridgnorth to France in December 1917. He was subsequently transferred to a hospital in Huddersfield where he died nearly three weeks later. His body was brought home to Bridgnorth by train and after being laid out in his parents' front room overnight was buried the next day.[41] Just over two years before, and just a few doors away, the father of Walter Sherry received a telegram that his son was dangerously ill in hospital in Boulogne after suffering a shell wound to the chest. However, the telegram regretted that 'permission to visit him could not be granted'. The next communication he received was a letter from a sister at the hospital saying that his son had died on the evening of 3 July 1915. She wrote that 'he has been very ill ever since he was with us and we were afraid then that there was very little chance for him' and that 'he died very quietly and did not feel much pain at the last'.[42]

Occasionally a visit to Switzerland was arranged for a family member. This was done when a prisoner of war exchange took place to allow seriously wounded men who would never fight again to return for treatment. One of these men was Herbert Handley, whose wife lived in Craven Arms. He had been taken prisoner in 1914 after receiving shrapnel wounds to his leg and losing one eye and the bridge of his nose. This latter injury had become infected whilst he was in a camp and was the reason he was moved to Switzerland in August 1916. His wife was allowed to visit him for two weeks the following January, though it was the late summer of 1917 before he finally came home to Shropshire.[43]

If a wounded man was brought back to this country then it was possible for family members to visit. In August 1918 Colin McMichael suffered severe mustard gas burns that caused both internal and external blistering. After travelling down from Bridgnorth, his mother sat for some days by his bedside at a hospital in Kent until his death two weeks after his gassing.[44] The parents of George Evans of Bishop's Castle had a letter from their son written from his hospital bed in France that, though upsetting, gave cause for hope:

Thomas Llewellyn, from the parish of Forden, was lucky enough, after being shot by a sniper in his left elbow causing severe damage, to be sent for convalescence to Broadway Hall, only a few miles from his home. (Courtesy of Janet Preshous)

I have a bad operation to go through yet as I have got to have shrapnel taken out of my inside. It was a bad wound, it was the next thing to what we call 'a landowner', that's death. It fractured seven ribs. But still I thought myself lucky to get away with that for it might have been worse, so I have finished with fighting for a while.

Nearly two months later a telegram was received from a hospital in Cheltenham to say that their son's condition 'was grave'. Having a car at their disposal, his father and two uncles immediately travelled to visit him and arrived just in time to be by his bedside as he died.[45]

For most on hearing of news of a wounded family member a visit was not possible. This was either because the man was abroad and permission to visit was not given or, if he was in the United Kingdom, travelling to see him was not possible due to the distance, cost, inability to leave family or work commitments or a combination of all three. The majority of relatives could only wait for a news update. In such situations no doubt the worst was always imagined in the face of the unknown.

Harry Sutton wrote to his father in Bishop's Castle a month after being wounded describing what had occurred and giving news as to his present condition. He said that he had been hit in an attack and fell just short of the German front line trench at about 5.30am. He continued that 'I had to stop in a shell hole till 9pm and then I crawled back to our lines. ... I was smothered in blood. Stretcher bearers could not get out to us.' Harry then went on to tell his father that he had just undergone an operation on his thigh though he still had to have a piece of shrapnel removed from under an eye. He had also received a bullet wound to one of his hands.[46]

Harold Armstrong's father in Deuxhill received a letter from his son describing how he had come by his wounds during the early part of the Battle of the Somme that included the loss of part of his leg:

We made a charge across the open and got hung up in the barbed wire. First of all I had a hole through my shoulder and before I knew where I was again a shell caught me sideways from the knee to the foot. I managed to cut the sling off my gas bag and tied it around the remaining part of my poor old leg ... [then] off I went on my elbows and one knee about two hundred yards back under a bank and then the stretcher bearers found me and took me to the dressing station.[47]

His father's relief that his son appeared to be recovering must have been tempered by the fact that he would be disabled for the rest of his life.

Letters from members of the medical staff at hospitals could equally bring relief or pain. The Reverend William H. Thornley of Bishop's Castle was relieved to hear that his son would live, but must have been shocked to be told by the sister in charge of a casualty clearing station that his son 'whilst acting as a stretcher bearer in the first line had, by the bursting of a shell, both arms blown off'.[48]

The mother of George Taylor of Bridgnorth, after receiving an official telegram saying that her son was severely wounded and dangerously ill, then received a letter from a matron serving in a hospital in France warning her that George was in a critical condition. A week later the matron wrote again to give her the sad news that following the amputation of one of her son's legs, 'gas gangrene poisoning set in with fatal results'.[49] Mrs Rhoda Pugh of the King's Head, Bishop's Castle embarked on a roller coaster of emotions when she was first officially informed that her once live-in employee, William Southerton, was in hospital at Abbeville, France with a gunshot wound that necessitated the amputation of a leg at the thigh and that he was dangerously ill. Shortly afterwards a postcard arrived from the matron at the hospital saying 'the leg is broken. I expect you will soon see him

When men died of wounds in a hospital in Britain their bodies were transported back to their hometown or village for burial. Of the 21 men from Ditton Priors who lost their lives during the war Francis (Frank) John Shingler is the only one who is buried in the village churchyard. After enlisting in the KSLI in November 1914 he was wounded by a bayonet thrust to the stomach at the Battle of Loos, ferried across the channel, and admitted to Queen Mary's Naval Hospital, Southend. He died in November 1915 and within four years of burying him both his mother and father also died, never, it is said, having recovered from the shock of their son's death. (Courtesy of Hugh and Di Bryan)

in England'. No doubt greatly relieved at this news, she was soon to be brought back to earth when just two days later the matron wrote again to say that Pte Southerton had died without regaining consciousness after the operation.[50]

After Francis Shingler of Ditton Priors had only served at the front for six weeks, his family, having been informed that he had been badly wounded, then heard from a hospital in Southend that after two weeks he had succumbed to a bayonet wound to the stomach.[51]

One way families heard not only of the extent of their boy's wounds but of how they were obtained was through letters sent by comrades. One corporal wrote to describe how Arthur Wait helped his childhood friend Robert Ward after he had been wounded following an artillery bombardment:

> They blew down the side of our look out in which there were six men including R[obert] Ward and A[rthur] Wait of Ludlow. These two immediately got on their hands and knees and started to rebuild the trench. When they had got it complete Ward noted that the left side had given way. He started work at once, fixing a machine gun plate in the corner. The enemy opened a rapid fire and a bullet glided off the plate and struck Ward on the left side of the forehead. At the same moment a shrapnel shell burst in the trench. Ward fell and said 'I have got it this time.' Wait bandaged him up the best he could and he was sent a small drop of rum and water. Wait bathed his lips and gave him a sup. Fifteen minutes later Ward came round and the first words he said were 'Art, for God's sake keep a good look out or else we shall all have it.' He was in the trench six and a half hours before it was dark enough to shift him and he walked through the slush and water up to his knees until they met the stretcher-bearers. When he was dressed the doctor found that Ward had a bullet wound on the left side of the head, was blind in one eye, had a fractured top jaw at the right side and other shrapnel wounds on the body ... I am pleased to say that after only a week he is going on well and will soon be in England.[52]

It is hard to judge the emotions experienced by Ward's family on reading this story.

The parents of Eric Burton, who was serving in the Canadian forces, also received a letter at their home in Bridgnorth from one of their son's comrades. This informed them that Eric was suffering from shrapnel wounds. It was three weeks later before the official confirmation of his wounding arrived, sadly to be followed a few days later by news of his subsequent death in hospital.[53]

One type of wound that families dreaded was any that led to the amputation of a limb. At a time when the welfare state was virtually non-existent, anything that limited a man's ability to earn a living and bring home a wage would affect either that person's marriage prospects or, if already married, his family's income; it might even force them into poverty. Because of the type of warfare being waged and the prevailing level of medical expertise the loss of limbs became quite common. By 1917 the *Bridgnorth Journal* was reporting stories of local men who had just undergone amputations virtually every week. Consecutive editions reported that the wife of Arthur Mason had been informed that her husband had had his left leg amputated, whilst the wife of Gunner Charles Cornes heard that it had been necessary to remove her husband's right arm. Then the mother of Alfred Higgins was told that her son had lost his left leg.[54]

The Tennant family of Clee Hill is an example of how the loss of limbs affected just one group of brothers. One son, John, had just 'succumbed in a northern hospital to fearful wounds ... one leg having been amputated, whilst the other one and one arm, would have been similarly treated had he survived'. Another of his brothers had lost both legs whilst a third was at that moment in hospital receiving treatment that could result in the amputation of a foot.[55] And there were sometimes side effects when legs were lost. Artificial limbs were in their infancy at this time and were being mass-produced in set sizes. The result was that the *Bridgnorth Journal* reported, with no humour intended, that Eli Jones, who had been 6 feet 2 inches when enlisting in the Coldstream Guards before the loss of both of his legs, now stood on his newly fitted artificial ones at only 5 feet 10 inches.[56]

Charles Cornes of Bridgnorth, a married wagoner with two young children, volunteered in 1915 and joined the Royal Artillery where he was in charge of a team of horses that pulled a howitzer. In 1918 he lost an arm from shellfire and was said to have walked to the nearest casualty clearing station carrying his severed limb. (Courtesy of his grandson Ron Cornes)

Another constant fear that haunted those at home was that of possible facial disfigurement. With shell and shrapnel wounds so common, as were head wounds from sniper fire, this fear was very real. The father of Alfred Reynolds, at his home in Ludlow, was told that his son was back in England 'suffering from severe injuries to the face', whilst the family of George Wilkes learned that he had lost an eye 'and his face had been very much injured'. At Bishop's Castle the father of Llewellyn Bennett received similar news in a letter from the hospital at which his son was being treated. As well as losing the fingers from one hand, he was informed that his son had had 'part of his face blown away'.[57] In Bridgnorth, the parents of Leslie Hughes were informed that their son was in hospital with shrapnel wounds to his face.[58] The extent of the wounds was usually left to the imagination of the recipient of the letter.

Sometimes, usually when the wounds were less disfiguring, the injuries sustained were described in a little detail. At Clee Hill the wife of William Gittens was told that her husband had lost the sight of one eye due to a shell splinter, whilst in Bridgnorth the parents of George Jones read that a bullet had gone through his nose and his right eyelid.[59] In Highley the family of Archie Brown were told that he had been hit in the head by a bullet that had blinded him, though it was hoped that partial sight could be rescued in one eye.[60] But whatever the true extent of the facial injuries sustained, all knew that lives had been changed forever.

The consequences of being affected by poison gas were feared not only by the troops but also by their families at home. This was because it would be they who might have to nurse the returning soldier for the rest of their or his life. The wife of one Ludlow man (probably Archie Smith) was informed that her husband had been blinded in a gas attack and the worry now was whether the condition would be temporary or permanent.[61] Usually the effects were long-term, especially if the lungs were badly damaged. Such men were often discharged from the Army, but many only returned home to die. Phillip Jones of Haytons Bent was discharged in December 1916 as a result of gas poisoning but only survived until the following April.[62] George Brookes was invalided home to his parents' cottage in Oakengates but failed to recover and died after a few months despite constant care and nursing.[63]

Many local men returned home physically or mentally maimed. Thomas Thornley, the son of the Congregational minister in Bishop's Castle, lost both his arms in a shell explosion whilst acting as a stretcher-bearer. Because of the great numbers of men losing limbs there occurred a lot of research and development of prosthetic limbs. Here Thomas is pictured showing his ability to write using his artificial hands.
(Courtesy of Janet Preshous)

Shell shock, a generic term that covered many forms of mental trauma that often took physical form, could be distressing in the extreme and was another concern for those at home. News that his son was suffering from shell shock reached W. Edgell Piper's father in Bridgnorth, and Henry Spink the son of Councillor Albert Spink of Bishop's Castle had succumbed after being buried alive in the trenches from shell fire three times in one month.[64]

The possible effects of shell shock are shown in the ongoing news of the condition of Thomas Taggart of Bridgnorth, who had served in the Dardanelles campaign. The first news his father had of him was that he was in hospital in Cairo and had lost the power of speech. Three months later, after his return to England, Thomas himself contacted home with further clues as to what his true condition had been and still was. His speech had returned and he also said that his 'legs are quite well again' – many suffering from shell shock lost control of the ability to control their muscles, resulting in being unable to stop parts of their body from continually shaking. He also said that his 'nerves are a great deal better'; 'nerves' often affected shell-shocked men, so that they could not stand sudden noises or had trouble sleeping.[65]

Symptoms of shell shock were often missed whilst the men were serving at the front. Thomas Taylor of Highley succumbed whilst home on leave, leading to his arrest for desertion when he failed to return to his unit. He pleaded guilty in the local court, claiming that he was not fit enough to return to the front. The policeman who arrested him appeared to have sympathy since he described Taylor as 'shaking like a leaf' when he encountered him and said that he appeared to be suffering from a nervous debility. The court, though sympathising, had no option but to remand Taylor in custody to await a military escort.[66]

The reception home of those whose wounds were so serious that they were discharged from the Army differed from place to place. In small village communities they tended to be public, with local people coming out to welcome them back as heroes, whilst in the towns, where the numbers returning were greater, it tended to be a private or street affair unless the soldier had won a gallantry medal. William Woosnam of Brockton, near Lydbury North, was discharged from hospital with a leg amputated at the knee. He was met at Craven Arms station and taken home in a motorcycle sidecar:

> On reaching the village, which had been gaily decorated for the event, a vehicle was waiting profusely adorned with flowers, greenery, and flags, with which he was triumphantly drawn by ropes by his admirers to the paternal residence at the head of a procession ... An arch was erected at the entrance gate.[67]

At Churchstoke, Timothy Tipton, who had lost his left leg in August 1917 and had undergone eight operations, was presented on his return home in May 1918 with 12 guineas and a wallet by grateful parishioners, as 'a little recognition to show our gratitude and goodwill towards you for the services you have tendered your country'.[68] Just a month before, Thomas Thornley, who had been awarded the Military Medal for bringing in the wounded under heavy machine gun fire, returned home to a hero's welcome after losing both arms whilst acting once again as a stretcher-bearer. The train he returned on was met by the local troop of Boy Scouts who lined up on the railway platform along with all the town's local dignitaries. Then:

> Amidst the booming of detonators, the salute from the buglers, the roll of drums, the merry peal of the Parish Church bells and the cheering of the large gathering, the hero of the hour entered a vehicle with his father and his wife.

They then drove along a route decorated by flags and streamers to his parents' home, which was also festooned with flags.[69]

As regards wounds, the war had another trick to play. Because of the filthy conditions in which the soldiers passed their daily lives, a small cut or graze could give rise to a serious medical condition. After ten months in the trenches and surviving the battles of Festubert and Neuve Chappelle, Joseph Whittall of Bishop's Castle succumbed to a septic wound originally caused by trying to open a tin with a knife. His condition deteriorated to such an extent that he was invalided back to a hospital in England to face an operation.[70] Charles Davis of Ludlow was not so lucky. After serving at the front for two years, and just after writing home to say that he had been awarded the Military Medal, he suffered a scratched heel which led to blood poisoning and his death in a French hospital of lockjaw just four days before the armistice.[71]

Those at home also often received information that a relative or friend was missing in action. Whilst the probability was that the individual was dead, families would unsurprisingly cling to the hope that he was lying anonymously in a hospital somewhere or that he had been taken a prisoner of war. Naturally such hope would fade over time but, no doubt, would never totally go away.

When a man was posted missing there were two main official channels of discovering what had happened to him, both calling on the help of the Red Cross. After being passed the details of those who had been posted as missing by the government, some 1,500 Red Cross workers toured hospitals both in England and abroad checking on the names of those admitted and interviewing as many patients as they could to try to ascertain what might have happened to the missing men. It is estimated that over five million interviews took place. The other main channel of news came via the Red Cross in Geneva. Through this conduit the German authorities would pass on the names of those taken prisoners of war and those whom they buried and had managed to identify. Such information travelled at varying speeds and was often extensively delayed, especially towards the end of the war when the infrastructure of Germany was showing signs of severe strain.

The Red Cross, scouring the hospitals and hospital records, discovered what happened to a number of local men listed as missing. The mother of Frederick Davies of Astley Abbotts, who had been reported missing in April 1918, was told two months later that it had been discovered that their son had died under medical care within 24 hours of being wounded.[72] The parents of Donald Easthope of Hayton's Bent were told, three months after their son had been reported missing during the Gallipoli campaign at Suvla Bay, that he too had died whilst being treated for wounds.[73]

Other families heard news of their missing men after the Red Cross had interviewed fellow soldiers. Nearly three months after Alfred Stokes of Claverley was listed as 'wounded and missing' on 3 September 1916, it was confirmed by a comrade that he had been killed on that same day.[74] The parents of Fred Brereton of Lydbury North only had to wait one month before similar interviews confirmed

After a battle each side often found itself burying enemy dead. The Germans attempted to keep records of the name and regiment of each man buried. Details were then passed onto the Red Cross in Geneva who in turn relayed the information to the British authorities so that next of kin could be told. In this way many of those listed as missing could now officially be stated as having been killed in action. Unsurprisingly, many families were left in doubt as to what had happened to their loved one for months. (Author's collection)

that their son had been killed on 9 October 1917.[75] Sometimes the information gleaned by the Red Cross workers was not categorical. The parents of Maurice Harley of Alveley were informed in September 1918 that their missing son was 'likely' to have been killed the previous March but that 'it did not consider the evidence conclusive'. This glimmer of hope was later sadly extinguished.[76]

Confirmation of the death of Francis Packer of Ludlow came via the Red Cross in Geneva. He was reported missing during the German spring offensive in March 1918 and then, two months later, news was received that he had been killed and buried by the Germans in a communal grave.[77] Four months after the event, the wife of Albert Johnson from Bridgnorth was told that her husband had died in a German field hospital of wounds suffered to the 'chest and stomach' on 26 March 1918.[78] Almost certainly via the same route came news for the father of Second Lieutenant Arthur Southwell of Oldbury. He had initially been told that Arthur was 'wounded and missing', last being seen wounded but alive in a shell-hole after an attack on German lines during the Battle of Ancre on 13 November 1916. After twelve months of perhaps hoping that Arthur had been taken prisoner came the news that his body had been found and buried by the enemy shortly after the battle.[79] News of the fate of John Husband certainly came via Geneva. His parents in Bishop's Castle had been told that their son had been reported missing during an action at Welch Ridge on 30 December 1917. After what must have seemed a long nine months, they were finally informed that the Germans had reported that John had died in their hands on 15 April, though no details of the cause of death was given.[80] Similar news was heard by the parents of Edward (Ned) Davies at their home in Ludlow, though theirs came after earlier news had given them hope. They were initially told that he was 'missing' in March 1918. They were then relieved to be informed that he was a prisoner of war, but their dreams of one day seeing their son again were shattered when news came that he had died whilst in captivity.[81]

Details of prisoners of the Turks came via the same route and this was how the parents of Jack Harrington of Onibury learned in August 1917 that their son had died back in April, almost certainly of his wounds, whilst in Turkish hands following the first battle of Gaza.[82]

But happier news also came to south Shropshire via Geneva. It took four months before the parents of Ewan Mitchell learned with relief of his incarceration. Listed as missing on 21 March 1918, it was mid July before the notification of his captivity arrived at their farm near Cleobury Mortimer.[83]

A number of families found out unofficially that their son or husband was still alive and in a prison camp. They might receive a letter or postcard from the prisoner himself or sometimes secondhand news from someone with whom he was imprisoned. Clement Deighton's parents, who lived in Bridgnorth, were told that their son was missing with few chances given for his survival after fierce fighting at Sanctuary

Wood. With very little hope to cling to, it is difficult to imagine their feelings when a postcard arrived a month later from Clement to say he was 'very fit and well' though a POW in Cologne. He then explained how fortunate he had been:

> We had a severe cutting up and stuck it out to the last man. As far as I can tell there are only about a dozen of us left, but I am glad to say I came through the thick of it without a scratch. It was hell ... We finished with a corporal in charge.[84]

The parents of Frank Griffiths of Ashford Bowdler had a similar wonderful shock. Their son had been reported missing believed killed in March 1918, but at the beginning of June a postcard from him suddenly landed on the doormat. He was alive and well in a POW camp.[85] Harry Evans' mother in Bridgnorth, whose son was one of thirteen local men still on the 'missing' list at the end of May 1918 after the German spring offensive the previous March, was overjoyed to receive a letter from him on the last day of the month. This informed her that except for a slight wound to the right arm he was safe and well in German hands.[86] A month later, the wife of Fred Lawley, another of the thirteen missing, received a postcard from her husband saying that he was safe though a prisoner.[87] When Albert Edwards wrote to his father in Church Stretton that he was safe and well at a camp in Minden, Westphalia, he also passed on the information that Thomas Shuker of All Stretton was with him, and asked for the news to be passed on to his family.[88]

Good news of 'missing' men sometimes emanated from hospitals where they were patients. Harry Garmston, who had been posted missing in March 1918, sent a postcard in April to his brother Walter in Stanton Lacy, though it did not arrive until early July. This was to tell him that he was in a hospital in Belgium being treated for wounds.[89] The mother of Second Lieutenant John Pugh of Ludlow, who was recorded as missing after his plane failed to return on 4 November 1918, received a postcard from him some two weeks after the armistice to say that he, and his pilot, had been taken prisoner but were now being looked after by a Belgian family 'who are very good to us'.[90]

Fellow soldiers still serving in the trenches also wrote back with news of the missing. Sometimes a letter from one of the last people to see the missing man would try to explain the circumstances around the event. The officer who accompanied a Bridgnorth man, Percy Griffiths, on the foray into no-mans-land in which he went missing, wrote to Percy's mother:

> On the afternoon of the 6th July he and I were on a daylight reconnaissance of the enemy's lines when we came unexpectedly upon an unknown enemy post. Leaving Percy behind, I crawled on ahead to find out more about it, but had to return without the information. Your boy asked me to be allowed

to have a try as he thought he saw a good position from which he could view the ground. I kept him in sight for about ten minutes when he was lost to my view. I never saw him again. A shower of enemy grenades fell near me. I remained crawling about the same spot for nearly half an hour but could find no trace of him. My great and confident belief is that he was spotted by the Hun and allowed to come within close range when he was quietly taken prisoner. Unless he had changed direction none of the bombs fell near him.[91]

Sadly, the hope he gave her proved fruitless. It was later found that Percy was killed after crawling off, but at least his mother knew some of the circumstances of how he met his death. The platoon sergeant of another Bridgnorth man, Horace Jones, wrote to his family to break the news that though officially reported missing he was in fact dead. He explained that Horace had left the dugout to fetch their gun in when a shell struck, wounding him badly, 'and he died within a few hours'.[92] Though the worst news possible, at least for this family the uncertainty was at an end. Such uncertainty ended for the mother of George Lloyd of Bridgnorth when his immediate officer wrote from a POW camp in Germany about her son's death:

He could not have died more nobly being almost the last to retreat in the action of March 26th. He died at my side a few moments before I was captured … One day I would like to tell you heaps that would make many a mother proud.[93]

Many men who were listed as missing were later recovered from the battlefield where they had fallen. This often occurred a number of weeks later when the ground was either retaken or a temporary truce arranged for both sides to collect the decomposing bodies. (Author's own collection)

Other men came off the 'missing' list when their bodies were later found or their burials located. The grave of Arthur Vaughan of Little Stretton was not discovered until nearly two months after he was posted missing on the first day of the Third Battle of Ypres, or Paschendaele as it is better known. One of his officers wrote to his parents as soon as he heard to break the news:

I deeply regret to say that your son has been killed in action on 31ˢᵗ July. He was counted as missing and I delayed writing in the hope that we should discover his whereabouts and that he may have been wounded and passed down, unknown to us. It was only yesterday we heard that he had been buried in a cemetery nearby.[94]

Yet other families learned of the fate of their missing menfolk after working parties, clearing the battlefields in the days and weeks following, found their loved ones' bodies. The man who discovered and buried the body of Thomas Dean of Ludford wrote to Thomas's wife to let her know that her husband had died at Polygon Wood during the Battle of Paschendaele and was thoughtful enough to enclose her last letter to him, which he had found in one of his pockets.[95] Similarly, it was a member of the Rifle Brigade who wrote in late August 1915 to the siblings of Herbert James in Eardington after finding his body. In it he tried to console them as to the way their brother died:

You will not hear officially from the War Office perhaps for some weeks, so I thought you had rather a fellow soldier (although of another regiment) dropped you a line as soon as possible. He fell at the last battle, at the beginning of the month. My regiment were clearing the ground afterwards for the killed and wounded and judging from the expression on his face and his surroundings he had evidently died bravely and without a second's pain ... We buried the poor fellow with every reverence one comrade can show another and I have put up a cross with his name and particulars over his last resting place, amongst so many of his regiment. The enclosed photo and letter were on his person and I am forwarding them to you for your disposal.[96]

A number of families, not knowing what had happened to their husband or son, refused to await the apparently slow official channels of communication and chose to make their own enquiries. A few turned to the local vicar for help and asked him to try to find out more from regimental sources. For the parents of Harold Wellings of Clun, who went missing in March 1918, this brought not only further news on what had happened to him but also some hope. One officer wrote back to the clergyman that:

On March 22nd last, he, with a lot more of his company, were surrounded by the Germans and cut off and in consequence they are all presumed to have been taken prisoner ... Please convey to his parents my deepest sympathy during their trial, but I hope that their feelings will soon be relieved by the receipt of good tidings from Germany.[97]

This turned out to be the case and Harold returned safely home after the war.

Enquiries by the vicar of Chetton on behalf of the family of Walter Thomas also brought fresh news, but of a more sombre nature. Walter's Company Sergeant Major, recovering from wounds in an Eastbourne hospital, wrote to the vicar of a conversation that he had had about the events four months before at the Battle of Bellewaerde Ridge 1915:

> I have just found out from a fellow who was with Cpl Thomas in the engagement on the 25th May that there were three of the KSLI and one of the East Surrey's lying in a shell hole close to the German lines and Cpl Thomas and another, as they were afraid of being captured, said they were going to try and get back, but in the attempt they were both killed. Previous to Cpl Thomas being killed he had killed a German officer with his bayonet. What became of the East Surrey man I cannot say but the other man of the KSLI I saw the other day and in talking about things I find that he was wounded at the same time and is probably the only one who can certify that Cpl Thomas was killed. Trusting this information will settle all doubts.[98]

Other families contacted a missing man's comrades to ask if they had any news. The parents of Thomas James of Bridgnorth, who was posted missing in October 1917, wrote to friends in his unit with the result that in the following April a letter arrived from a man who was with Thomas when he died:

> Your son and I went up to our gun position together and were with each other all the way back, but halfway from our camp I had to stop to put my pack on firmer. As I stopped I saw a shell burst in the midst of our boys in front of me. When I got up to them the first man I saw was your son. He seemed rather dazed or in a semi-conscious condition, so I called for the Corporal to assist me. I managed to put him on a horse and rode him to the dressing station. I could see it was only a matter of minutes, and when I got him there the officer in charge told me he was dead ... the only words I heard him say were 'Tell them I am alright; God help me'.[99]

Some families, knowing that many at the front had the local newspaper sent to them, placed advertisements asking for information about missing relatives. The mother of Edward Harry Cook placed a notice in the *Bridgnorth Journal* giving details of when he was posted missing and asking that 'she would gladly receive any news of him', whilst the family of Arthur Hayward of Onibury placed a similar request for help, together with a photograph, in the *Wellington Journal*.[100] That newspaper also carried pleas for news from a Mrs Cross of Much Wenlock asking about the whereabouts of her brother Fred Anslow, and from the mother of Henry Wilcox who waited in hope for news at her home in Bridgnorth and Cardington.[101] The mother of Bob Halford, who had also been listed as missing, placed a similar plea in the *Ludlow Advertiser*.[102] Though most apparently failed to elicit a reply, an advertisement placed by the wife of James Morse of Ludlow, who had been posted as missing during the Battle of Polygon Wood in September 1917, did bring a response though not the one she wanted. In the following January she was informed that a Sergeant Palmer had seen 'her husband lying dead in front of the farm at 9 am'.[103]

The news that all families never wanted to hear of course was that their husband or son had been killed. Such tragic tidings, addressed to the next of kin, usually came in a telegram sent via the main regimental depot. This meant that a girlfriend or fiancée would often have to rely on receiving such news from her young man's family. For a Miss Gladys Preece of Bishop's Castle the first that she knew of the death of her fiancée, Francis Hancocks of Dorrington, was reading his name in the casualty column of her local newspaper.[104] For some families letters of condolence were also received from a man's commanding officer or from one of his comrades and these, at times, arrived before the official telegram.

When men from the same village or town served together, often in the same platoon, they could well witness a best friend's death and have to break the news to his parents or wife. Harry Langford of Much Wenlock found himself in the position of having to write to Annie Owen, the wife of his pal Charles, about how he had died:

> He was on sentry duty in my trench and was shot through the head. I helped take him to the hospital but he passed away before we could get him there. I can tell you I am broken-hearted, for he was my oldest chum and I can guess what your grief will be. He called your name and mine up to the time he died. He was shot at 2.30 on Thursday morning and died at 3 o'clock.[105]

Many men made pacts with each other that if anything should happen to one of them, the other would write back home to break the news. Ernest Kershaw of East Hamlet, Ludlow explained such a promise in a letter to his parents written in a dugout on the coast of Turkey during the Dardanelles campaign. He shared his hole in the ground with a friend from Lancashire:

> In case anything should happen to either of us we have arranged mutually to write to one another's parents. Of course, we all hope that nothing untoward will happen to either of us but you never know out here, as their high explosives come screaming through the air bringing their messages of death, and if they drop amongst troops they are sure to account for a lot of them.[106]

The company quartermaster of the 7th Battalion KSLI found himself having to honour such a pledge when his friend Ernest Tuckley was killed. He wrote to Ernest's sister in Bridgnorth as promised:

It appears he was at a Dressing Station having his wounds bandaged up when a shell struck the station and nothing more was seen of him ... Before Ern went up into action ... he told me to write and let you know if anything should happen ... Would you please convey the same to his father and all his relations.[107]

Alice Fewtrell, the wife of Walter William Fewtrell of Wentnor, at home with her six children, the youngest having just been born, first received news of her husband's death from 'one of his chums', whilst Geoffrey Roden wrote to his mother at the Post Office, Claverley with a heart-rending story of another such letter home from a close friend to break the news to a freshly widowed wife:

They were two chums (with both of whom I was very familiar); one got killed on the Thursday so the other wrote to his own wife and asked her to break the news to the dead one's wife, thinking it would be better than getting the news from the War Office. Then the one who wrote got killed on Friday – blown several yards by a shell – and we found the letter, ready to post, in his pocket. We wrote a letter breaking the news of her husband's death as gently as possible and we enclosed the letter her husband had written the night before asking her to break the news to his chum's wife. Fancy the sorrow that poor woman is suffering.[108]

A close friend of Charles Gwilliam kept his word and wrote to Charles' parents in Bishop's Castle to inform them of the death of their son, suffered as he was taking part in a charge against the German lines at Bazentin Ridge, whilst at the same time attempting to minimise the pain they must have felt:

I was not far from poor Charles when he got killed. He was killed at 3.00 o'clock in the morning of July 14th, an enemy bullet striking him in the body. It may be of some comfort to know that he could not have suffered much pain, as death was instantaneous. Through his death I have lost a good chum, for we have stuck loyally together since we joined up at Shrewsbury and I can assure you a better and nicer chap never lived. He was a true pal.'[109]

The parents of Harry France of Alveley first heard of his death when a letter arrived from their eldest son who had been serving with his brother.[110] News of the death of Horace (Frank) Bill of Eardington on the first day of the battle of the Somme, was broken to his family via the local stationmaster whose son had written to him to say:

I am sorry to tell you that poor Frank Bill has gone under as he was going over the top in our attack on July 1st. He and his Captain were killed ... Will you please let his people know, as they may not hear officially for some time ... I may add that we spent three nice evenings together prior to his regiment going into action.[111]

Often it was a man's officer who wrote to break the news. At the time such letters, with their apparent personal touch, must have been comforting to the bereaved. However, when looked at together and in hindsight, many appear to be written to formulae by officers who sometimes found themselves writing many similar letters, sometimes about soldiers they barely knew. A major in the Scots Guards wrote to Mrs Mary Ann Davies of Ludlow regarding the death of her son John:

> I expect by now you will have heard of the death of your son L.Cpl. J. Davies, killed in action on September 15th near Givenchy, while attacking a German trench. The captain of the company, Captain Norman, was killed at the same time, but as I formally commanded the company I should like to write you a word of deep sympathy from us all, for your son was much respected and left us a fine example of courage and self sacrifice. He was an excellent corporal, a gallant soldier, and will be greatly missed here, and I feel much for you in losing such a fine son.[112]

Many officers appear to be at pains not to cause further suffering by giving the true details of how that person died. Letters often stress the fact that the soldier in question never suffered and that death was immediate and virtually painless. Such was conveyed to John Blakeway's mother who also lived in Ludlow:

> It is with the profoundest regret that I have to inform you that your son Pte. J E Blakeway was killed last night June 4, by an enemy shell ... Your son was on duty at the time of his death and his two horses, to which he was very devoted and looked after splendidly, were killed at the same time ... It may be a little comfort to you to know that he was killed instantly and suffered no pain.[113]

A similar letter was penned and sent to the parents of James Keenan in Little Stretton. His commanding officer wrote that 'your brave son, I know you will be glad to hear, died without pain at all. Indeed he was killed instantaneously by a shell.'[114] Robert (Bob) Tong's parents in Clun were also informed by his captain that 'at the time he was gallantly advancing against the enemy under heavy rifle and machine gun fire. He was hit in the head by a bullet and killed instantly.'[115] One platoon commander wrote to the widowed mother of William Evans, also of Clun, in a very imaginative way in order to try to alleviate the pain she must be feeling. Not only did he tell her that her son's death by shellfire was 'instantaneous' but that 'afterwards he wore a smile and expression of happiness'.[116]

Some officers admitted that their knowledge was secondhand but still insisted that death was painless. The parents of Sydney Milman at the Cock Inn, Stottesdon were told by their son's commanding officer that 'I was not present when he was hit but I believe his death was instantaneous and that he did not suffer any pain'. Similarly the commanding officer of Sidney Fellows of Bridgnorth wrote to his family to say:

> I was not with the company and did not see him but I have been making enquiries from his friends and I find that it was quite instantaneous and he did not suffer. He was hit between the shoulders with a piece of shell but was not knocked about much.[117]

Only occasionally did such letters give a true hint of the pain that many casualties suffered before dying. The commanding officer of George Brocklehurst of Ludlow was quite honest about what happened to him in his letter:

> With deepest sympathy I have to inform you that your gallant son died in hospital on September 1st of wounds received in action on the 29th August. It was about midnight and a German shell struck three bombs [presumably primed grenades] which fell and exploded in a crowded trench wounding eight men. Your son was wounded by small splinters all over his body and I expect the doctors found it impossible to keep the wounds in a healthy condition.[118]

The chaplain attached to a hospital at the front wrote to the wife of Thomas Jones at her home in Bishop's Castle where she lived with her four children:

> I am very sorry to have to tell you that your dear husband died here from severe gas poisoning ... He did not suffer very much and received every care and attention from the medical officer and men.[119]

To what extent the phrase 'very much' preyed on her mind in the future is uncertain, but at least she had a glimmer of the reality of his passing.

Some of the news that came from chaplains in hospitals must have soothed the heartache felt by a wife or parent. One poignant letter to the mother of Mark Jones of Bridgnorth must have eased the pain that she felt:

> He was brought to the hospital three days ago with penetrating chest wounds ... I am sorry to say that he gradually lost ground and died yesterday evening. I never saw anyone pass away more peacefully and just like a child going to sleep – no sign of a struggle or distress – in fact it was hard to believe that the boy was really dead. I was with him at the time and as he was passing away I gave him a kiss on the forehead 'from his mother' ... I cut a lock of your dear boy's hair directly after he passed away as I thought you would value it.[120]

Perhaps because of their medical training, nurses also tended to be more open when writing to inform families of a death. When George Henry Humphries died in a casualty clearing station in France, the sister in charge wrote to his parents near Middleton in quite graphic detail of the wounds that he had finally succumbed to:

> Your son was admitted here on the 4th September and, I regret to say, died the same day at 2.00pm. He was severely wounded in the chest and both forearms and also had a penetrating wound of the abdomen.[121]

Whether such knowledge helped or hindered the grieving process is not known.

The amount of detail passed on to relatives as to how a man died appears to be different if the casualty was an officer. This can perhaps be partly explained by the fact that the person writing the letter would have been far closer to the deceased and partly because he may have believed that the parents of a fellow officer would expect to be informed as to the exact circumstances of how their son met his end.

When Lt Derwent Christopher Turnbull was killed, his parents in Church Stretton were told about their son's last hours in full. As a doctor he volunteered to leave his post in a dressing station 200 yards behind the front line to go to the forward trenches to help bring back a fellow wounded officer. After treating him he found himself exposed to fire whenever he attempted to stand to carry the stretcher back:

> He spent the rest of the day lying in the mud and water at the bottom of the trench, pressing the artery of the wounded officer to prevent loss of blood. When towards dusk they tried again to get to the dressing station, the handles of the stretcher were smashed by rifle fire and Lt. Turnbull received a shot through the right lung and fell back into the trench.

He died of his wound four days later.[122]

Mrs Garnett-Botfield of Bishop's Castle was given a full account of how her youngest son Alfred, also an officer, met his death:

> On the 9th an assault in the early morning had been attempted on the enemy trenches. This was unsuccessful so another was made in the afternoon when our Battalion was detailed to carry it out on one part of the line. Your son's platoon, during the artillery bombardment, had to crawl along an old trench in front of the breastwork in order to get nearer the enemy line. This they had to do under heavy fire but they succeeded so far. When the time came for the assault your son jumped up to lead his men and was shot at once before he

had got any distance. Several attempts were made at night to recover his body but owing to the enemy fire it was found impossible to do so before we were relieved at midnight, but it is still hoped to do so.

A letter from her son's batman indicates that he was killed by a shell burst rather than a bullet, but included what he claimed were his last words:

> The trenches were only ninety yards apart. There was a heavy bombardment going on and the enemy was thick as could be in their trenches and putting a terrible fire on us both from rifles and machine guns. To advance meant wholesale slaughter. But the order came for us to advance. Your son said to his platoon, or at least to what was left, 'Well boys I am going, who is going to follow?' and the reply was 'If you are going we will all follow' and on that instant we made a rush but we had not got over the ridge of the trench when a shell came and killed your son and a few more men and also wounded a lot more.

This rather heroic exchange of words between the lieutenant and his men was slightly contradicted by Edward Lowe from Clun who was present during the action. In a letter to his parents he claimed that what the lieutenant actually said was 'Don't blame me. Go on lads, it's not my fault', probably realising the futility of the attack.[123] Whatever the truth of his last words, at least his mother knew the circumstances surrounding his death.

On occasions families of enlisted men were given some details of the circumstances surrounding a loved one's death. The story of the last minutes of Nairn Jones's life can be pieced together from the letters received by his parents in Clun from his lieutenant and the chaplain attached to his unit. His officer explained that:

> He was dispensing in the dressing station just behind the lines in a fairly safe place when a wire came down to say that the RAMC teams up the line were too tired to go on and we're done up. Nairn was one of the first to go on the relief.

The chaplain then took up the story.

> He had gone up with another NCO and eight men to bring out wounded from one of the Regimental Aid Posts. The particular one he went to was an old German aid post which, now it is in our hands, the enemy shell very heavily. When within twenty yards of the entrance, the shell fell which killed your son, wounded the other NCO and knocked all the bearers down. Your boy was badly hit in the head and died at once. He was carried into the Aid Post where he now lies.[124]

The parents of other soldiers were sometimes informed of the circumstances of their son's death in a letter from one of his officers. Other families, starved of such knowledge, tried various ways to find out the circumstances of their relative's death, no doubt in an attempt to bring closure as near as possible. Daisy Hailstone, the wife of the Bishop's Castle scoutmaster, desired to know more about how her brother Cecil Brown had met his end. She therefore wrote to his battalion asking for further information and received a reply from a senior officer:

> I am sorry no one has written to you to give details of your brother's death. At the time he was killed the casualties were very severe. He and two others died like heroes. I saw them buried on Xmas Day where they fell, just outside the wood in front of the trenches which we still hold.[125]

Though her request only generated very generalised information, one fact did emerge which must have been upsetting. Since Cecil was killed on 7 November 1914 and he was only buried on Christmas Day, his decomposing body must have lain in no-mans-land for over six weeks.

In Bridgnorth, the parents of Leslie Smith were informed of the bare details of their son's death but desired to know more since they had not seen him since he emigrated to Canada after leaving school. His uncle, therefore, wrote to his unit requesting more information. The circumstances of Leslie's death were finally received from one of his comrades who wrote from his hospital bed. It appears that their battalion was sent to plug a gap in the line after a German gas attack:

> We advanced under heavy shell and rifle fire across open country (the fire came from three sides) and it fell to the lot of our platoon to occupy one of these gaps. Leslie was about 50ft away on my left when we reached our

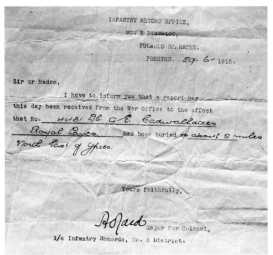

When a loved one was killed the grieving process was not helped by the fact that the body was buried abroad, that the funeral could not be attended and that a visit to the grave was not allowed until the war was over. For most, of course, a visit to the graveside would never be possible due to the prohibitive cost. Matters were not helped when the official notification of a burial was so short and terse due to the sheer number of them being sent out. (Courtesy of Shropshire Museum Services)

Many families not only could not attend the funeral of their son, brother, husband or lover but also had little idea of where he was even buried. A few army chaplains managed to photograph either the cemetery or even the grave itself and send a copy home to the serviceman's family. After the war a family could request a photograph of a grave by writing to the Director General of Graves Registration at the War Office. Above is the grave marker of Sidney George Garbett of Netchwood near Ditton Priors, who died of wounds in France, aged 22, in April 1917 at the 8th Casualty Clearing Station at Pas de Calais. The photograph appears to have been sent to his sister Nellie.
(Courtesy of Hugh and Di Bryan)

position. We had got separated in the rush but during a lull in the attack he waved his hand to me. A short while after this the German artillery opened up and got our range, point blank ... and here word was passed along to me that Leslie was killed by shrapnel. A few moments afterwards I was 'blown' up.[126]

Nelly Cadwallader of Bishop's Castle, in her search for further news about how her brother Alfred died, tracked down one of his wounded comrades in an Edinburgh hospital and travelled there to speak to him. She discovered that after spending eleven consecutive days in the trenches that included a gas attack, he volunteered, during yet another German offensive, to fetch reinforcements and ammunition for his comrades. Shortly after his successful return he was shot.[127]

One other desire of all of the bereaved relatives was to know if their loved one had received a proper and decent burial. Some army chaplains and officers made a special point of informing families of where and how their relatives had been interred. The parents of Samuel Price of Ludlow received one such letter from the Chaplain who had buried their son:

He has been buried by me in a well-kept soldiers cemetery behind the line.
The Church burial service was said and his officer and many of his comrades

were present. On his grave there will be placed a wooden cross with his name and regiment so that when the war is over there should be no difficulty in finding the place.[128]

In a letter to the widow of Charles Tristram of Ludlow his commanding officer, realising how important it was for her to know where her husband lay, stressed that he 'had been buried in a beautiful garden of a Latin Monastery in the hills near Jerusalem. I have had a cross, made by his comrades, erected over the grave.'[129]

Yet another chaplain took the trouble to photograph the cemetery in which he conducted burial services. This was 'in a mulberry grove just outside the village and down by the bank of a river'. After developing the picture when back in England on leave, he sent a copy to each of the bereaved families of the men interred there. The wife of William Nicholas of Bishop's Castle received such a snapshot and with it the chaplain enclosed her husband's watch.[130] Local vicars back in south Shropshire also obtained photographs of graves, presumably through church connections. The vicar of Lydbury North obtained such a snapshot of the grave in France of Alexander Lyndon for his parents.[131]

One officer went far out of his way to grant the wishes of one of his men's parents and ease their grief. After hearing of the death of their son Samuel Edwards, his parents arranged for a laurel wreath to be sent from Cleobury Mortimer to his platoon commander at the front and asked him if he would place it on their son's grave. A few days later they received a second letter from the lieutenant:

> As I had a few hours to spare, I cycled down to the place where Edwards is buried and put it on his grave. Some men of the Medical Corps had already put some flowers there and it looked very nice.[132]

Such acts of thoughtfulness must have been of great help at a time of deep grief.

With so many casualties occurring, some errors were bound to be made and these led to a further cruel twist of events for a number of families. News of the death of William Marston of Bishop's Castle came in a letter from his unit and was confirmed in a further letter sent home by another local soldier. After the flags were flown at half-mast and a remembrance service held, came an official notification that their son 'had been wounded on November 20th, place not known'. The sudden raising of hope that this news brought can only be imagined as can the despair when a week later any dreams of seeing their son again were dashed when one of his friends who had returned home to Colebatch on leave told them that he had seen him die.[133]

This was not just an isolated case. Charles Taggart of Bridgnorth had emigrated to Australia but returned to serve with their forces on the Western Front. In late July

1916 his name appeared on the casualty lists and then on 25 August his mother, who still lived in Bridgnorth, received the official notification that he had died of a compound fracture of his skull and leg on 3 July at a casualty clearing station. Imagine her shock and joy when in early September two letters arrived from him dated 22 and 24 July posted in Melbourne, Australia. He explained that he had been invalided home after suffering a bayonet wound. It appears that the cause of the error was that his name was Charles Bertram Taggart whilst in the same unit there was also a Charles Baird Taggart. It was he who had died and the wrong family informed.[134]

The parents of John Allen of Oldbury Wells must have ridden the same roller coaster of emotions. Within a space of two months they were at first told that their son was wounded and missing, then officially told that he had been killed, only then to be further notified that he was, in fact, a POW. At home in Ludlow, the parents of Charles Harold Badlan must have experienced a similar emotional heaven and hell. They were at first told that their eldest son had been seriously wounded at Ypres and had lost his right arm. Some days after came an official communication informing them that their son was dead. On the same day a letter of sympathy was received from their son's platoon commander breaking the news that a shell had killed Charles. Then, in the following day's post, the family received a letter from their 'dead' son saying that he was back in England and in hospital in Newcastle.[135]

The family of Donald Easthope of Hayton's Bent underwent a similar experience, though without the happy ending. After their son landed at Suvla Bay during the Gallipoli campaign they were told that he had been killed. Then came the news that he was in fact lying wounded in a hospital in Alexandria, Egypt after being evacuated there. The relief that this news brought was then dashed when they were told in November 1915 that he had died of his wounds back in August.[136]

The experience of the family of George Millichamp of Bitterley perhaps best shows the frequency of such errors. In the autumn of 1917 they were told in a letter from his regiment that their son had almost certainly been mortally wounded. The letter left 'but small room for hope'. But, as fellow villagers pointed out, 'on two previous occasions reports of his death proved to be without foundation'. This time, however, it was true since he had died at a casualty clearing station.[137]

Two other south Shropshire families also received letters from 'dead' sons. Arthur Benbow's mother, who lived at Nordley, Astley Abbots, was told that her son had been killed on 28 June 1916. The circumstances in which his death occurred were also relayed to her: he had been killed by machine gun fire whilst returning from a bombing raid on a German trench. Imagine her shock and joy when, two months later, a letter arrived from him saying that he had been wounded and taken prisoner and was now safe in a German hospital.[138] Similar news from beyond the grave landed on the doormat in Bridgnorth at the parental home of Lt Douglas Cunnington. He had been officially reported killed in action and letters of sympathy had been received from both his colonel and the battalion's chaplain. However, it appears that he had been left for dead after being shot in the lung and when he recovered consciousness he found himself in German hands. He was then sent to a hospital in Dusseldorf where he underwent a successful operation and made a good recovery. The tears of joy shed in that household must have been many.[139]

For families in south Shropshire the constant waiting for either good or bad news must have been stressful in the extreme, and each sight of a postman or telegram boy must have brought about feelings of apprehension. For those who received partial, misleading or even incorrect information the worry and pain caused is difficult to imagine. The serving men may have suffered untold privations or seen sights that would haunt them for years, but it should also never be forgotten that those who waited back home also suffered mental torments. For many these would continue after the war ended. There were those who would constantly grieve for the men who would never return, whilst others would have to care for loved ones who had been broken in mind or body. Suffering occurred not only at the front but also among the 'blue remembered hills' of south Shropshire.

6   PEACE AND THE AFTERMATH OF WAR

The first reaction to the news of the armistice of those at home was one of celebration. In Ludlow, word was received at the Post Office at 11am. It was a Monday morning.

> Within a very short time the centre of the town was be-flagged and the joy bells were raging. It being auction day the town was crowded. There was, throughout the day, plenty of flag waving and boisterousness among the younger generation – and no-one could blame or censure them.

But the celebrations took place against a backdrop of a new threat: a worldwide influenza epidemic. The elementary schools within the borough were already closed because of the epidemic, but as news reached the secondary schools the scholars were given a holiday. At the Grammar School, before being dismissed, the boys assembled around the flagstaff and saluted as the Union Jack was hoisted. The headmaster then gave a short address before the national anthem was sung. To allow the celebrations to continue, the town council rushed to declare the next day a holiday.[1]

At Bridgnorth peace was heralded by the sounding of the hooter at Park Meadows Mills, soon to be followed by the ringing of the church bells. People began putting out bunting and all businesses closed for the day at lunchtime. 'As the day wore on the holiday spirit increased.' By the time evening descended many of the townsfolk were dancing in the High Street as local musicians played.[2]

Joy was also unconfined in the smaller towns and villages. The bells pealed out in Church Stretton and within moments the 'whole place [was] adorned with flags'. Crowds gathered around the memorial fountain and sang the national anthem. The fountain itself was decorated, and a portrait of the king was hung there, as was the town's Roll of Honour alongside a laurel wreath. In the evening a dance was held at the Silvester Horne Institute, whilst others cavorted around a bonfire that was lit on Burway Hill. The ringing of school and church bells brought the news of the armistice to Newcastle. The following evening the church organised a procession

The workhouse in Knighton was taken over by the Red Cross in 1914 to be used as a hospital for wounded military personnel. Just after the armistice was declared in November 1918 a Victory Tea was organised for the patients and staff. (Courtesy of A.T.D. Evans)

After victory had been secured, some towns lobbied for war trophies that could be placed on permanent display. In January 1919, with the help of the Earl of Powis, Ludlow secured a German field gun. At first it was placed in Castle Square outside the Girls' High School before being moved a short distance to Dinham. It was donated for scrap as part of the war effort in the Second World War. (Courtesy of Shropshire Museum Service)

from the school to the square led by the pupils carrying banners and lights and singing patriotic songs. Once in the square speeches were made and hymns sung. When news of the end of fighting arrived in Bishop's Castle the town was soon 'a blaze of colour'. Church bells were rung, rockets fired into the air and the Boy Scout Bugle Band paraded round the streets. Clun too was soon festooned with flags and people walked the streets wrapped in the Union Jack whilst the Clun Valley official car, decorated with bunting, gave free rides to all. Children carried an effigy of the Kaiser round the streets accompanied by the beating of tins and the playing of mouth organs until it was finally burnt on the old castle grounds.[3]

A second round of celebrations occurred after the signing of the Peace Treaty at Versailles on 28 June 1919. At Much Wenlock the town was 'bedecked with flags, the church bells rang out with merry peals and there was dancing in the Square and the Corn Exchange, the town band supplying the music'. On the following Monday night an effigy of the Kaiser was carried in procession through the streets, again headed by the town band, and burnt in the Square. The large crowd that watched then took part in an impromptu dance.[4]

As regards organised celebrations, Saturday 19 July was designated as a national 'Joy Day' and events were planned throughout the area, although torrential rain on the day caused a number to be postponed to the following week. In Ludlow, despite the weather, the timetable was carried on mainly as planned. At 6.15am maroon rockets were launched from Castle Green followed by the pealing of the church bells. Detonators were then set off by the railway company to wake up any inhabitant still asleep in bed. A planned full day's sports programme for the youth of the town began at

This unknown local demobbed soldier poses with his wife and a presentation watch. Throughout 1919 such gifts were widely given by a grateful community as a way of showing their appreciation to those men who had served in the armed forces. They were often handed out at welcome home dinners held in parish and village halls, schools or local public houses. (Courtesy of Shropshire Museum Services)

9am. Then, following a church service at 10am, a large crowd gathered to see a Victory Oak planted on the Castle Walk. A civic reception followed for the servicemen who had returned from the war and Castle Square was 'packed with a dense a crowd as had assembled in Ludlow for many a long day'. Afterwards 570 discharged soldiers sat down to a cold luncheon washed down with beer in the town and market halls, which had been decorated with bunting and laurel wreaths. The children's sports then continued in the afternoon, though those for men were postponed to the following Thursday evening. The rain also caused the planned carnival procession to be abandoned and instead the floats were placed on view in the town hall and improvised entertainment put on. The lighting of a bonfire on Whitcliffe and a firework display completed the day.[5]

In Bridgnorth the celebrations were held over three separate days. On the Saturday, as in Ludlow, there was a civic reception followed by men's sports competitions. The rain eased off enough to allow the carnival procession to proceed,

All towns and villages welcomed back their returning soldiers in different ways. In Ludlow, on Saturday 19 July 1919, the town's returnees were given a civic reception in Castle Square. All 570 of them were then invited to a sit-down cold luncheon, washed down with beer, in the town and market halls, which had been decorated for the occasion. (Courtesy of Shropshire Museum Services)

though the dancing in the evening, which was planned for the High Street, had to move into the Drill Hall. The day ended with flares and signal rockets being sent up into the sky. The following Thursday was designated Children's Day and after their sports competitions 1,200 children aged between 3 and 15 sat down to tea. The next day it was the turn of the ex-servicemen. They sat down to dinner in a marquee erected behind the Falcon Hotel that had been decorated with flags and a Welcome Home banner. This meal was then followed by more rockets along with fireworks sent skywards attached to balloons.[6]

Similar events took place all over south Shropshire. At Cleobury Mortimer, the ex-servicemen were entertained to dinner in the Oddfellows Hall on Friday evening, and a pageant procession was staged on the Saturday headed by the town band and followed by sports and tea for all. In the evening the Oddfellows Hall was used as the venue for a dance. Much Wenlock saw a procession followed by sports. Here, schoolchildren, the over sixties and the wives and mothers of ex-servicemen were given tea whilst the ex-servicemen themselves were given lunch at the Corn Exchange. Due to rain the lighting of a bonfire on Windmill Hill was postponed until Monday.

In this photograph taken at Much Wenlock on 'Joy Day', recently demobilised men paraded in their uniforms that they were allowed to keep, though they had to hand back their equipment including belts. On the right are those who had probably been discharged earlier and no doubt included those discharged due to wounds or ill health. Sitting in front is the local boys' band which led the procession.
(Courtesy of Ina Taylor)

The town of Clun went to some effort to celebrate national 'Joy Day' in 1919. A few ladies chose to dress in costumes meant to represent the allies who fought with Britain against Germany. In the centre in the top photograph is Britannia complete with trident. On the extreme left is Japan whilst to the left of Britannia is the USA. The other three costumes probably represent Belgium, France and Serbia. The entourage then mounted a decorated wagon, ready to take its part in the planned procession through the streets. (Courtesy of Ray Farlow [top] and A.T.D. Evans [bottom])

The 'Joy Day' parade makes its way through the main street in Clun headed by Minnie Gittins on horseback, dressed as 'Peace', flanked to the left by Susie Roberts representing the Royal Navy, and to the right by Norah Morris representing the Army. (Courtesy of A.T.D. Evans)

Following the parade there was open air dancing to the strains of 'Bonnie' Hudson on the piano. (Courtesy of A.T.D. Evans)

In the top photograph returned local soldiers and one airman are given pride of place in the Bishop's Castle parade on a cart decorated with the laurel leaves of victory. Sitting amongst them is a nurse, many of whom volunteered to serve just behind the front lines in casualty stations. In the lower photograph young women are dressed up to represent the various occupations that women had taken over whilst the men were serving in the armed forces. Among the occupations represented here are chimney sweeping, postal delivery, and agricultural and munitions work. (Courtesy of Janet Preshous)

At Bishop's Castle a similar procession was held and a reminder was seen of the cost of victory when two of the town's wounded war veterans were given pride of place. These were Timothy Tipton, who had lost a leg, and Vincent Lennox, who had spent two years in and out of various hospitals undergoing at least eight operations. Later James Wilson joined them 'in his spinal carriage'.[7] 1,050 guests then sat down to tea in two marquees erected at the Pound Ground. The main procession, however, of decorated cars, cycles and people in fancy dress had to be postponed until the Monday evening due to a heavy downpour of rain. Also postponed was the dance. However, despite the deluge a huge bonfire was lit on the Saturday night on Colebatch Hill and it is said that from there 15 other bonfires could be seen. One was possibly that organised by the villages around the Stiperstone Hills that joined together to build a large bonfire on the Devil's Chair. At Knowbury too it was noted that at the end of the day the 'surrounding countryside, stretching for miles, was illuminated with bonfires and flares' as villages all over the county held their own smaller, but no less boisterous, celebrations.[8]

A few places, due to the weather, postponed all celebrations until the following week. Church Stretton held theirs on the Wednesday. Here, after a service was held on the Longhills, an oak tree was planted on the Recreation Ground that had just been given to the town. Over 200 ex-servicemen then sat down to lunch. Then, in the early afternoon, a fancy dress parade wended its way through the streets headed by a jazz band. A programme of sports attended by over 2,000 people then preceded 700 wives, widows and children of the area's servicemen sitting down to tea in the Parish Hall. Finally, a dance was held in the Barn theatre that lasted until 3am. Celebrations at Clun were also held over to the Wednesday when a procession through the streets was followed by sports on the Old Castle grounds and tea in a marquee for 1,100 guests.[9]

As servicemen were demobilised and returned home many villages and parishes organised welcome home dinners and celebrations.
At More Village such a meal, held in September 1919, was accompanied by sports and a dance.
(Courtesy of Janet Preshous)

However, between the armistice celebrations of November 1918 and those of the following July, some inhabitants of south Shropshire had faced further heartbreak. News of fatalities in the final days of the war were only received after the armistice had been announced. Two families in All Stretton received such devastating news. The wife of John George, at home with her child, opened a telegram informing her that her husband had died of wounds in a casualty clearing station at the end of October, whilst the parents of Edward (Ted) Lewis read in a letter that their son, in the last days of the war, had been 'hit by splinters from an H E shell and died painlessly within half an hour'.[10] Clement Price's mother at Mainstone only received a letter in the first week of December informing her of how her son met his death whilst going to the aid of a comrade three weeks before the armistice:

> Your son went on patrol on the afternoon of the 18th October 1918 and was wounded in the leg; another of the patrol was seriously wounded and your son went to his aid and bandaged him up. During the time a shell burst near and a piece of stone hit your son in the stomach and injured him internally. When they brought him in he was quite cheerful and had some soup but, poor lad, he was bleeding internally and it could not be stopped and he died the same day.[11]

The parents, brothers and sisters of Pte Ernest George Corfield, aged 23, of Ditton Priors must have been overjoyed when news of the armistice arrived on 11 November 1918 in the belief that they would see him come home again. One can only imagine their shock when news later arrived that he had in fact died of wounds just seven days before the war ended. The distress caused by the arrival of such shattering news following the celebrations of peace was one that happened to a number of South Shropshire families.
(Courtesy Hugh and Di Bryan)

The parents of Albert Egan of Highley, in the heady first days of peace, also received the sad news that their son had died of wounds on 23 October after just seven weeks in France. Ernest Corfield's father was another who heard that his son would never return to the family farm at Ditton Priors as he had succumbed to wounds received in action just one week before fighting halted. The wife of Frank Edwards of Bridgnorth received news that she would never see her husband again as he too had died of wounds suffered just over a week before the armistice.[12]

The profound, long-term consequences of the war for families is epitomised in what happened to the Edwards family of Inwood near All Stretton. Thomas Edwards, a farmer, had five sons, four of who joined the army. Of the three proudly pictured with him, Percy, on the far right, was killed whilst Will and Stanley returned home. A fourth son, Rio, came back with only one arm. (Courtesy of All Stretton History Group)

News of missing men also began to filter back after German hospital records and cemeteries fell into British hands. Sitting at home with her two young sons, the wife of Harry Darby of Bitterley, whose husband had been listed as missing and possibly a POW back in April 1918, finally heard in early 1919 'after months of anxiety' that he had died six days after his capture in a German hospital at Tournai as a result of being shot through the lungs. The death of Edwin Mason of Culmington whilst being cared for in German hands was also confirmed. He had died of a head wound nearly two weeks after going missing in late March 1918.[13]

Also, tragically, a few families who had been notified that their relatives were safe in captivity now discovered that they had died whilst incarcerated. Of the 29 prisoners from the Ludlow area, four had died whilst prisoners. George Simkiss of Craven Arms fell victim to dysentery a week after the war ended, and Alfred Roberts's sister, who lived in Bridgnorth, learned as late as February 1919 that her brother had died in a prison hospital of pneumonia back in June 1918. Meanwhile, the villagers of Lydbury North who had been sending parcels to the three men from their parish who had been in German hands since March 1918, discovered that one of them, Charles Wilcox, had died of disease just three weeks before the armistice.[14] Returning prisoners also brought back news as to how some of their comrades had died. Rumours had abounded that Edward (Ned) Davies of Ludlow had died of ill treatment at the hands of the Germans, but his family's minds could now be put at rest as a fellow prisoner informed the mayor that Ned had in fact 'died of dysentery and he had all the assistance it was possible to give him'.[15]

The prisoners that did return were often malnourished, largely because of the economic blockade of Germany that the allies had carried out, as explained in a leaflet handed to one Bridgnorth prisoner on his release by the German authorities:

> Our country blockaded, our civil population and army suffering for want of sufficient food and materials, the enormous demands made upon our harassed land from all sides – these and many other afflictions made it impossible to do all that we would have liked to do. Under the circumstances we did our best to lessen the hardships of your lot.[16]

Due to the poor physical shape of some POWs it was decided in Ludlow that, on medical advice, each returning prisoner would receive two free pints of milk daily, paid for by the local POW committee. In addition, each man was given £2 (as were the families of the four deceased POWs) and the residue of the fund was distributed on the basis of need. The local branches of the Queen Mary's Needlework Guild also gave each ex-prisoner three shirts, three pairs of socks and a muffler.[17]

It was the release of POWs that brought about another flurry of requests for information from families that had menfolk listed as missing, as hope soared that these men might miraculously be traced or at least what had happened to them might be discovered. One POW was able to confirm the death of John Morgan of Ludlow since he had seen his body on the field of battle.[18] The clamour for information resulted in entire columns of the *Wellington Journal* being filled with pleas for news. The mother of Tom and George Law of Dinchope, near Craven Arms, asked for any sightings of her sons. Sadly both were later listed as killed, though Tom's body was located having been found and buried by the German Army. Others hoping for news included the father of William Griffiths of Ludlow, missing since 30 December 1917; the Bridgnorth parents of Edgar Ball, whose only son had last been seen on 26 April 1918; and the mother and father of Thomas Lewis of Stanton Lacy who had been missing since March. All were later confirmed dead, though at least the grave of Thomas Lewis was found since the Germans had buried him after he had died in their care the day after his capture.[19]

As regards a welcome home, at first each community tended to greet the returning POWs individually. George Edwards of Bishop's Castle was met by his brother at Craven Arms railway station and brought home to his wife by motorcar. His neighbours hung out flags from their windows to greet his return.[20] Then in both Ludlow and Bridgnorth the ex-POWs, both from the boroughs and the surrounding rural districts, were all entertained and welcomed home as a group. The 25 surviving prisoners from Ludlow and district attended a dinner at the Studio on Broad Street, whilst in Bridgnorth they were given a civic welcome at the Town Hall before marching, led by a bugle band, to the Crown Hotel, where they sat down to dinner. Each man who had not already received a gift was now presented with one.[21]

Meanwhile the influenza epidemic, or the 'Spanish Flu' as it was known in Britain, was wreaking its own havoc on the surviving servicemen. This worldwide pandemic broke out in 1918 and lasted until 1920, causing an estimated 30 to 70 million deaths worldwide. Edward Bate, whose parents lived in Ludlow, died in France from influenza just five days before the war ended. Norman Gilkes of Church Stretton actually died on Armistice Day whilst George Dunn, who had been a groom at Lydham Manor, was yet another local serviceman to die of influenza whilst still in France, in his case three weeks into the peace. A week later Thomas Lewis of Bitterley died in Belgium.[22] Robert Morris of Colebatch fell a victim to the pandemic whilst serving in Greece where he had been for three years with no home leave, whilst Harry Humphreys of Ledwyche succumbed in Serbia just two days after the armistice. It was the same on the other side of the world, where William Wilding of Bridgnorth met his death from influenza in the Punjab.[23] Fate was being cruel to many families who had assumed that once peace came they would be reunited.

Other local servicemen died from the outbreak whilst in the United Kingdom. George Richards of Alveley, recuperating from wounds suffered at Cambrai in October 1918, died of influenza in hospital at Sheffield. Wallace Delo of Bridgnorth succumbed to the disease at the Prees Heath Camp in north Shropshire, and Frederick Davies of Bitterley died after contracting it on Armistice Day at Pembroke Dock.[24]

As regards the bulk of the servicemen who had survived the war years, they slowly trickled home throughout 1919, and each community honoured them in its own way. In June, the landlord of the Cape Inn treated all those from Billingsley to dinner. July saw all returned ex-servicemen from the parishes of Stokesay, Halford and Sibdon invited to a supper dance at the Town Hall in Craven Arms along with the next of kin of those who had died. During August, all the ex-servicemen from Claverley marched through the village, cheered by the local populace, to be given dinner in the schoolroom, which had been decorated with garlands and banners for the occasion. In the same month the village of Bromfield honoured 41 of their ex-servicemen with a meal at the Race Course Buildings, and each man was presented with a 'handsome cigarette case or silver match box as a gift from the people of the parish'.[25]

In the remaining months of the year Bucknell honoured its ex-servicemen with a dinner in the village school, whilst at Ashford Carbonel their counterparts sat down to a dinner in the Parish Room. Meanwhile, Sir Henry Ripley hosted a dinner at Bedstone House for the 30 men from his two estates at Bedstone and

L. Cpl George Husbands, a gamekeeper living in Clungunford, pictured here with his wife Elizabeth Ellen and their only son Frederick Christopher, volunteered and joined the KSLI in February 1915. In 1918, whilst serving as a stretcher-bearer, he fell victim to mustard gas and spent until May 1919 in hospital. It appears that he was then discharged so that he could die at home with his family around him. Like many other widows, Elizabeth Husbands now had to become the breadwinner. At first she took on two or three jobs including milking and cleaning, often walking ten miles a day and taking her young son with her. Later Elizabeth success-fully set up her own coal delivery firm. (Courtesy of Philip Husbands)

Hopton Castle who had joined the forces. At Highley the ex-servicemen were given dinner at the local Picture Palace, whilst on New Year's Day all returning soldiers at Ditton Priors sat down to a supper in the Howard Arms and were each presented with a cigarette box. Similarly the returning soldiers of Church Stretton each received a silver mounted walking stick and a cigarette case. Victory dinners carried on into the first two months of 1920 as the last few local men were demobbed. Eighty men sat down to dine in the schoolroom at Stanton Lacy where 'after dinner they were regaled with cigars, cigarettes and tobacco', and just under 30 men from the parish of Ludford sat down to a 'sumptuous dinner' at the Charlton Arms Hotel as the parishioners honoured the men who had fought for them. Here each man was presented with a silver mounted briar pipe and an ounce of tobacco.[26]

Sadly, not all returning men sat down to such meals. Many men, crippled in either mind or body, died after coming home or were still in hospital. Arthur Hayward, suffering from the effects of mustard gas poisoning, was released from Berrington Hospital, Shrewsbury so that he could spend Christmas with his wife in Bridgnorth but he died two days before. William Jones, an only son aged 20, who had been gassed at the Battle of Lens in August 1917, 'after much suffering passed away at his home at Titterstone' in January 1919.[27] George Husbands of Clungunford had also been admitted to hospital suffering from the effects of mustard gas but was sent home to his wife and son in May 1919, presumably to allow him to die surrounded by his family. This duly occurred just six weeks later. Another discharged soldier, George Bywater of Chelmarsh, died at home, his body weakened by malaria, gassing and seven separate woundings. As his local vicar explained:

> I visited him regularly for some three months before his death and in all that time, though he was in constant pain and suffering, he never murmured.

George Brunt of Kempton died in the autumn of 1919 whilst still a patient in a military hospital and was given a full military funeral in Clunbury village church-yard. This followed the death from wounds in a Birmingham hospital of Alfred Rutter of Bridgnorth. Such deaths occurred quite frequently throughout 1919 as the war continued to exert its toll.[28]

A number of men, weakened by their war service, succumbed to diseases such as tuberculosis (TB) after returning home. The Medical Officer of Health for Ludlow, in his report for 1918, highlighted the fact that the death rate from TB within the borough totalled thirteen, the highest for many years. As he explained:

> Discharged soldiers figure frequently in the death returns for TB and the increase in the death rate from this cause may be accepted as one of the results of the war.[29]

A weakened Edward Sheldon, the eldest son of the mayor of Ludlow, who had been discharged from the army on medical grounds, succumbed to TB in February 1919.[30]

As for mental trauma, many men would suffer from it for the rest of their lives and it often had physical side effects. One local resident, during his childhood after the Second World War, recalls a number of men who suffered from uncontrolled twitching or trembling. His father warned him never to laugh at such people on pain 'of a good hiding' since they had fought and suffered for their country and deserved every respect.[31]

As the death toll continued to mount, it was also time for communities as a whole to take stock of the slaughter of their young men. In Bridgnorth and Ludlow, where just over 1,000 men from each town served in the forces, 144 and 138 respectively lost their lives. But the cost of war was probably more fully felt in the small rural parishes. Of the 101 men who served from Stanton Lacy, 20 did not return. The small hamlet of Quatt lost 10 men, Alveley 14, Ditton Priors 20, Diddlebury 14, Little Wenlock 8 and Culmington 14. To such deaths must be added the even greater number of men who returned home either physically or mentally maimed in some way and whose future life would be far different from that envisaged before the war. In the parish of Lydbury North, a community of just 800, 150 men left their homes to join the forces of whom 26 never returned and a further 42 received wounds – a total of 45% of all those who had left this small, rural enclave.[32]

The tragedy was not just in the sheer number of men these communities lost or who returned maimed in some way, but that they were almost all of the same age. Of those in Lydbury North who rushed to enlist in the New Army between August and November 1914, 12 were killed. Seven of them were teenagers whilst a further two were aged 21 and 22. In the parish of All Stretton, with its 670 inhabitants, 20 of its men died. Of these six were teenagers when the war began and a further nine were in their early 20s. In the even smaller parish of Ditton Priors (pop. approx. 620), of the 20 men who were killed, seven were teenagers in 1914 and eight in their early 20s.[33] In the parish of Clun, 18 of the 27 men listed as having given their lives on the roll of honour inside the church were aged 22 or under in 1914. A swathe had been cut through a generation.

The effect on individual families could be tragic, as the experience of a Mrs Emily Minton of Ludlow highlights. This woman lost a son, two son-in-laws and two nephews, all of whom lived in nearby streets. It is not known how many other family members returned home having suffered wounds.[34] Such a scale of loss was common to many extended families.

To add further tragedy, a few returning soldiers came home to find that death had visited their homes in their absence. In September 1918 the influenza epidemic had reached south Shropshire and by October it was reported that the 'scourge has found its way to Ludlow'. Schools were closed as a preventative measure, including Sunday schools, children were excluded from the cinema and posters were displayed around the town setting out measures to prevent infection and what to do if a person contracted the disease. The town, it appears, got off comparatively lightly compared to other areas. Even so, ten people within the borough died from it during those three months.[35] Bridgnorth, the only other major centre of population in the south of the county, also escaped lightly.'[36] It was in the rural districts that influenza claimed most of its victims. The Medical Officer of Health for Ludlow RDC wrote in his 1918 report:

> A widespread and fatal epidemic of the disease overcame the district during the closing three months of the year. It commenced on Clee Hill and the first school closed was Bitterley in the middle of October followed by Clee Hill, Knowbury and Munslow in the next fortnight. In November virtually every school was closed.

He reported that 24 deaths had been recorded by the end of the year and that the epidemic was still far from over.[37] The situation was the same in the area of the Bridgnorth RDC where 21 deaths caused by influenza were recorded by the end of

December.[38] Here too the epidemic was still in full flow. In the west of the county, in the first week of November, the inhabitants of Bishop's Castle were beginning to feel the full force of the outbreak as all schools were closed until further notice:

> The influenza epidemic has claimed many additional victims this week. In several homes the whole family are suffering and business houses and office staff are seriously affected. The borough postal delivery and despatch of telegrams in the district have been undertaken by outside helpers.[39]

It was the same situation in Clun, where 'the epidemic is attacking both old and young and has spread very rapidly during the last week or two, in some households nearly every member being down with it at the same time'.[40]

In the surrounding villages the situation was no different and in the village of Brockton one of the first two fatalities was the mother of five young children.[41] Much Wenlock suffered too. In early November a husband and wife died within two days of each other, leaving three young orphans. Within days the youngest son of Alderman John Davies fell victim to influenza and, to make matters worse, on the morning of his funeral, his parents received the news that another of their sons, Norman, had died of wounds in France. By the first week in December six deaths from the outbreak had been reported.[42]

Nothing changed during the first months of 1919. In Bucknell 'the influenza epidemic [was] very bad ... and not many houses have escaped without one or more succumbing to it'.[43] Further east in Bitterley and Middleton it was stated that 'few houses in the parish have escaped the prevailing attack of influenza during the past three months and the mortality rate has been unusually high. A fresh grave has been opened nearly every week.' It was the same in nearby Culmington where a Mr Jones of Parting Hollow, who had lost two sons in the war, now lost two daughters and finally his wife. Further east at Astley Abbotts the epidemic 'had been very severely felt in our midst and has been no respecter of persons. Old and young have suffered from it', whilst at Tuck Hill 'hardly a household' had escaped.[44]

Whilst the Angel of Death still flapped her wings over south Shropshire, everyday life struggled to return to normality. Blackout regulations covering private property ended immediately on the war's end and streetlights were once again lit, but only at half power because of the fuel shortages. Prohibitions on lights in shop windows and advertising hoardings were only lifted two days before Christmas.[45]

The regulations pertaining to food rationing lasted longer. That on lard ended in December as did that on pork, game, horse, pressed, canned and potted meats and sausages. All other rationing remained in force, though the amounts that could be purchased weekly were raised on remaining meats and sugar. During 1919 rationing on a number of items was gradually removed, starting with margarine in February, jam in April, butter in May and all remaining meat in December, over a year after the fighting ended.

Fuel rationing also remained for many months. Petrol rationing ended in June 1919, but that of coal and gas supplies lasted much longer. By the end of the winter of 1918/19 the shortage of coal was particularly severe. It was claimed that in Ludlow a number of families had no coal at all, and this at a time when coal was often not only the sole method of heating for most households but was also needed for all cooking. In addition, due to the coal shortage, gas supplies were liable to be cut off without warning, leaving many households in darkness. As a result the theft of coal increased. Hannah Harrington of Clee Hill was convicted of taking 28lbs of coal from a rail truck in her apron, whilst the vicar of Knowbury caught his verger putting 13lb of coal in his pockets.[46] When the matter of shortages was raised at a Fuel Committee meeting, it was reported that a member quipped, to much laughter, that they were suffering from a shortage of paper. This incensed one person so much that they penned an angry letter to the local newspaper:

> Last week a poor woman, who has had two sons fighting for our country, had to cut up her furniture to make a fire to get a meal through being unable to get any coal and there are many instances of this. I ask, Sir, if this is a state of affairs for members of our committee to sit and do nothing except laugh … I wondered at the time how many of them got up in the morning and there was no fire for them to cook a meal.[47]

Rumours were meanwhile sweeping Ludlow that one of the town's elite had more coal delivered than was allowed. To make matters worse it was claimed that the committee had only issued a warning and not prosecuted, on the grounds that it would be unfair to the coal merchant to be held responsible for his workers being prepared to accept the price of a few beers to leave extra coal. To add insult to injury, no criticism was apparently made of the gentleman who had successfully offered the bribe.[48]

Coal restrictions were still in place during the winter of 1919/20, when it was decided that no individual customer could receive more than 2cwt of coal at a time, and they could not have any at all if they already held a stock of 10cwt. These measures, designed to ensure that everyone had some coal whilst allowing sufficient to produce the gas for lighting, were nullified when a rail strike disrupted the transport of what little coal there was. The result was that at the beginning of October the Ludlow area was to have its gas supply cut off at 7pm every Saturday evening until the following morning until further notice. Since the reservoir that fed the local water supply relied on a gas turbine to pump it, this service was now restricted to just two hours per day.[49]

Whilst all this was happening, local profiteering committees were set up throughout the country in the latter part of 1919 to try to stop wholesalers and retailers from making excessive profits from the various shortages. This responsibility was given to the Food Control Committees. Complaints were invited from the public but these were apparently few and decisions to prosecute were also quite rare. This was possibly due to two main reasons: fear of victimization by a shopkeeper if a customer reported them, and the low 10/- maximum fine for each offence, often less than the cost of prosecution. Different committees reacted to the few reports they did receive in different ways. The one covering the village of Bucknell successfully prosecuted a local butcher for a number of offences, whilst the Ludlow borough committee took a more relaxed and lenient view of events. The first trader to have complaints levied against him was William Brown, a local chemist who just happened to be a sitting councillor. The committee, made up mainly of his colleagues, upheld the complaint that he had overcharged by 33% for saccharine tablets but decided that as long as he refunded the difference to the aggrieved customers then, 'as this was the first case which had been before them, and as it was a small case, the committee did not direct any prosecution'. Such apparently biased decisions appear to have dissuaded further complaints.[50]

The returning servicemen, meanwhile, came home hoping to take up their previous employment, but many were bitterly disappointed. Unlike the Second World War, employers did not have to offer returning servicemen their old jobs back. To their credit, in this area local councils did do so, whilst some major organisations such as the post office took on those who had been severely wounded. Charles Badlan left his Ludlow home at the age of 19, to lose an arm and suffer a shrapnel wound in his hip area so large that 'you could put your fist in it'. On his discharge from hospital in 1921 he was

After discharge from the army, Charles Cornes, after losing his right arm, could no longer carry on his previous occupation as a wagoner. He found a job with the post office as the postman for Worfield and kept it until retirement, managing to ride a bike whilst carrying a heavy postbag. (Courtesy of his grandson Ron Cornes)

taken on by the post office as a postman delivering letters by bicycle throughout the Hope Bagehot area, and so joined two other one-armed ex-servicemen employed to deliver the post: one at Stoke St Milborough and ex-gunner Charles Cornes at Worfield.[51] But many other employers would not employ such men, as one local ex-soldier pointed out:

> A discharged soldier with one arm has applied for his previous employment and although quite capable of doing a light job, he has been refused employment and myself think it a great scandal after serving the colours as he has done.[52]

But employers ignore the pleas not just of disabled ex-employees, but also of the able-bodied. Councillor Randles, who had sat on the Ludlow and District Recruiting Committee, reminded his fellow members that in the early months of the war they had passed a resolution that when the war was over they would do all they could to persuade employers to reinstate their ex-workers when they returned from fighting. Both Richard Marsden, who had been the chief recruiting officer, and the other members of the committee now hid behind the excuse that the original minutes had been lost and there was no official record of such a resolution. As a result:

> What did men find now when they did come back? That their places had been filled by female labour and female labour being cheaper the employers stuck to it and the discharged men were left to find other jobs.[53]

It was the same in Church Stretton, where one inhabitant wrote to his local newspaper to give vent to his feelings on this subject:

> I think it very unfair that after our boys have risked their lives (while their late employers have been safe at home) and are discharged or thinking of coming home, they find they are not wanted at their previous employment. They did not want to leave their homes and their work to face untold dangers and hardships, any more than their master did, but they went to do their duty, expecting, on their return, to have their old employment again, as they ought, instead of being refused as some have been done. Do the employers call this patriotic?[54]

In Ludlow this attitude meant that of the 192 men who were unemployed in July 1919, 151 of them were ex-servicemen. The borough's General Purposes Committee therefore resorted to 19th-century solutions and investigated whether these men could be given temporary employment breaking stone for roads.[55]

Unsurprisingly, the numbers of families both in Ludlow and the surrounding rural area given out relief by the Poor Law Guardians to help them survive increased dramatically. Such expenditure had risen by 10% during the war years as wives and children left at home found it difficult to survive on meagre army allowances, but once peace came it rose a further 60% as allowances stopped and all income ceased until the man could find work.[56] For many this proved difficult and caused a number of ex-servicemen to leave their families yet again in order to search out work in other towns and cities. If successful, they would then send for their families to join them. Others went 'on the tramp' in search of a job. Until one was found they were often forced to bed down at night in the casual ward of a workhouse, where a large increase in the demand for accommodation was seen compared to the pre war years. The 'land fit for heroes to live in' promised by David Lloyd George at the general election that followed the armistice was not one that was inhabited by many ex-soldiers in south Shropshire.

This situation also brought to the surface the bitterness still felt by many who had served, or had sent sons to serve, against those who, in their eyes, had chosen to stay safely at home. This can be seen when it was decided that the Ludlow premises of the Comrades of the Great War should have central heating installed. The choice of the man asked to undertake the task was soon questioned, it being argued that *he* was not 'a comrade of the war, ... having stayed at home to gather in the harvest whilst others were risking their lives daily and even hourly under severe hardships'. This complainant to the local newspaper went on to argue that the work should be given to a tradesman whose sons had 'paid the supreme sacrifice. Now, I ask, is it fair to these and our returned heroes to find themselves ignored and a stay-at-home placed on a pedestal?'[57]

Against this backdrop, discussions were being held in towns and villages everywhere to decide how to remember those who had answered their country's call to arms and especially those who had given their lives. The collective need for local memorials began whilst the war was still going on. The compiling and display of rolls of honour in churches and even schools was widespread from the first few months of war, but this was given added impetus when the news of the massive casualties suffered at the opening of the Battle of the Somme in July 1916 filtered back to Britain. The result was the construction of war shrines fixed to a wall in a street. This was apparently done first in south Hackney, London and the custom rapidly spread throughout the country. The core of these shrines was a list of men who had died and those who were still serving whose homes were in the street or adjoining streets where the shrine was placed. Such shrines were decorated with fresh flowers, flags and various patriotic symbols. The practice was not universally welcomed, for to some it smacked of 'Popish Catholicism'. However, it certainly caught on in Ludlow with the full blessing of the local parish church.

The first two were erected on Mill Street and Raven Lane in September 1916. The cost was covered by donated funds given to the church, and a service was held to bless them. Then, as a churchman explained, 'the shrines are handed over to the people living in the street where they are placed, to be protected from damage, and to be decorated with flowers'. Within a month twelve more appeared around the town, ten paid for by the church, and two, on New Road and New Street, by local people. All were blessed by the church, which asked everyone who passed by them to halt a while and offer up a short prayer, not only for those who had died, but for the safe return of those still fighting.[58] Sadly, after a year the shrines were beginning to show signs of wear:

> The flags have faded and bleached and in many cases the rain has beaten in and made the ink run; and the sun, where the shrines have been exposed to it, has almost taken all the colour out of the names, so that they have become very difficult to read.[59]

Consequently, many such memorials had disappeared by the end of 1918, but there was now a growing feeling, shared by all communities, that more permanent memorials were needed. The form the memorials would take differed from place to place and, of course, depended to a great extent on the amount of finance that could be raised locally. In most small villages it was usually a tablet with the names of the fallen inscribed upon it and placed within the parish church. At Lydham it was one of beaten copper and brass, at Acton Scott and Tuck Hill it was of oak, and at Middleton Scriven it was a brass tablet encased in oak. In addition to a tablet, at Ditton Priors a new memorial clock was installed in the church tower, whilst at

When a man was buried at the Front his grave was at first marked by a wooden cross made by local carpenters and his name and unit stamped out on a piece of metal and affixed to it. The names were also stencilled on. After the fighting ended the stone headstones that can now be seen replaced the crosses. It was possible for relatives to arrange for those crosses to be sent home. Three of them, which once marked the resting places of three local men who died in 1918, can be seen in Lydham Church. (Author's collection)

TO PERPETUATE THE GLORIOUS MEMORY OF
THE MEN OF THE PARISH OF STOKESAY
WHO FELL IN THE GREAT WAR 1914-1918
AND WHOSE NAMES ARE INSCRIBED BELOW

W. H. BEAMAN	C. LUCAS
W. C. BIGGS	P. H. MAWSON
C. BLAKEWAY	J. A. MORRIS
E. C. DAVIES	C. A. PREECE
W. C. DAVIES	S. SALMON
J. EVANS	C. SIMKISS
J. FARR	H. SLAYMAKER
W. HIGGINS	W. THOMAS
H. HOTCHKISS	A. WILLIAMS
S. JACKS	H. WRIGHT
E. LOCKLEY	

The war memorial at Craven Arms, originally situated on the corner of the A49 and the Corvedale Road, was unveiled in 1920. As well as listing the 24 men of the parish who gave their lives, the remainder of the plinth lists all 98 men who served and returned home. The memorial now stands in Stokesay churchyard.
(Courtesy of Ray Farlow)

Oldbury church it was a plaque and a memorial window and at Caynham it was a memorial lychgate.[60] At a few places, to satisfy the needs of those of all religious denominations and none, memorials were erected in a public place, as was done at Claverley where one was erected at the entrance to Chykell Park. At Clun, again to keep all persuasions happy, the memorial was placed in the parish churchyard wall, on consecrated ground but accessible from the road.

In the larger communities, a more substantial memorial could be considered. At Bishop's Castle the first step was to ask the relatives of the fallen what they would like. A small majority favoured a stone memorial in the churchyard, which is what was erected. At Much Wenlock the construction of a memorial hall was decided upon, whilst at Bridgnorth, at a public meeting, the three main suggestions were a memorial swimming baths, a memorial hall and a stone memorial. The final suggestion was chosen, though the material chosen was bronze, and the memorial was erected in Castle Park.[61] According to the memorial committee set up in Church Stretton 'every householder has been consulted as to its form. The majority voted for a "visible memorial" on the Longhills.' A Celtic Cross was chosen and the cost of £550 raised through a house-to-house collection.[62]

It was only in Ludlow where real difficulties emerged, as it proved impossible for religious differences to be amicably settled. At a public meeting it was decided to set up a memorial committee and that to take a vote at a second meeting as to the erection of a stone memorial cross just outside

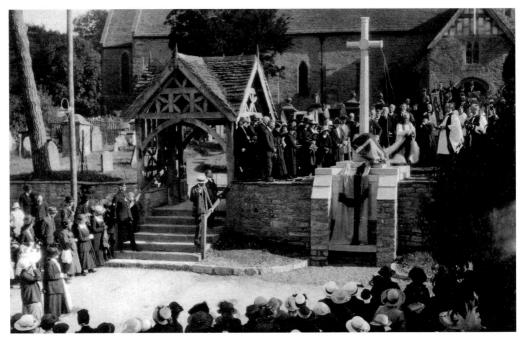

In a few places there was dissension about where to place a war memorial, especially from nonconformists if the grounds of the parish church was mooted. In Clun, any such opposition was forestalled by placing it in the churchyard wall with access from the road. (Courtesy of A.T.D. Evans)

the entrance to the parish church. The non-conformists in the town then began to mobilise, thinking that the cross should be erected elsewhere in the town.[63] Others felt that the relatives of the fallen should be consulted as to what they wanted. The result was that at the next meeting the motion was defeated and the committee immediately resigned.[64] Following this, the rector called a meeting of the church-wardens and sidesmen, and a decision was taken for the church to go ahead on its own. They decided to hang memorial boards to be hung in the porch of the church and, if enough money was left over, to erect a marble cross in the churchyard. As for consulting the relatives, the Rector was adamant in his refusal:

> It ... seemed to him that the last people to consult would be the soldiers or their relatives. It is we who have been saved from suffering and sorrow and it is we who are erecting a memorial to commemorate the sacrifices made for us and it would be altogether beside the mark to ask them what we should do to show our gratitude to them.[65]

Meanwhile a new war memorial committee was formed in the town and the decision was made to have honours boards hung in the town hall: one set listing the dead and a second set listing all those Ludlovians who had served in the forces. This

188

latter set was to be divided according to the year in which the men had enlisted, helping to perpetuate the difference between those who had volunteered to fight and those who had to be conscripted.[66] Further evidence of the bitterness still felt by some of those who fought towards those who had not was shown when the local populace was asked to contribute towards the cost:

> Re the subscription list to the War Memorial and Celebration Fund, I am willing to give my mite in proportion to the so-called 'indispensable' business men of military age who stayed at home and made large profits out of soldier's wives and others, while we and our sons have done our bit ... I suggest that the committee call upon those individuals first and publish the sums they give which ought in themselves be sufficient to pay for the greater portion, if not the whole. It would then be a guide to us men 'who sacrificed in loss of business and in other ways' to contribute to the above fund.[67]

One way or another the money was raised and the boards erected, whilst the collection of funds by the church for its separate memorial ran out of steam. Instead of the bronze panels originally envisaged, the

From Armistice Day 1919 it became the tradition that a two minute silence would be held at 11am. It also became the norm for a religious service to be held in each town and village at the local war memorial once it was erected. Here at Bridgnorth such a remembrance service is being held, attended by many of the local community. The internationally renowned Ludlow sculptor Adrian Jones, whose most famous work can be found on top of the Wellington Arch at Hyde Park Corner, London, was responsible for the design of the memorial.
(Author's Collection)

church erected panels of oak, whilst the cross never came to pass.[68] As a consequence, Ludlow ended up with two sets of memorial boards and no stone memorial.

લ

The 'war to end all wars' lasted just over four years. Pre-war planning had been based on the premise that any future war would be of relatively short duration. However, after the war became static due to the advent of trench warfare, such planning was shown to have been inadequate. The number of men now required to fight meant that a volunteer army could never provide the ever-growing numbers required, with the result that conscription had to be introduced. In addition, the advent of trench warfare and the conditions that the soldiers had to endure meant that their equipment and supplies were also inadequate. As a consequence there grew a need for the civilian population to provide everything from warm clothing to shaving equipment and cigarettes for the troops. The volume of men being sworn into the armed forces also depleted the nation's workforce at a time when the demand for war production dramatically increased. In rural Shropshire this mainly affected farming and meant that women and even children came to work on the land. At the same time the need to feed the army, allied to a reduction in food imports due to submarine warfare, together brought about shortages and finally rationing.

The overall result was that, for the first time, the population of rural Shropshire found that a war was fought not only in far-off battlefields but at home. It was being fought in the fields growing food, in parish rooms making and packing 'comforts' for the troops, and on the streets collecting money for countless causes including providing for the wounded and those local men in far-away prison camps. Most living in the towns and villages of south Shropshire eventually found themselves playing a role in the war effort, whilst waiting in worried anticipation for news of loved ones at the front. And when that war was over they found that the dislocation of their lives had still not ended. For many, life would never be the same again.

Ways of celebrating peace differed from place to place. Following a thanksgiving church service on 'Joy Day' in Ludlow, the mayor, Edward Sheldon, planted a 'Victory Oak' on Castle Walk for both present and future generations. (Courtesy of Paul Sheldon)

Local servicemen mentioned in the book

Allen, S. John   Pte.24985 KSLI whose parents lived at Oldbury Wells, nr Bridgnorth.

Amphlett, Charles E.   Air Mechanic 408592 RAF of 13 Fishmore, Ludlow.

Anslow, Frederick C.   Pte.26951 7th Battalion KSLI whose sister lived at Smithfield Road, Much Wenlock. Killed in action, aged 20, on 26 September 1917.

Armstrong, A.W.   Cpl. 4th Battalion KSLI.

Armstrong, Harold T.   Sniper KSLI whose father lived at Deuxhill, nr Bridgnorth.

Ashwood, William   Sgt. 1st Battalion KSLI of Hop Pole Yard, Bridgnorth.

Badlan, Charles H   Pte.2457 Queens Royal West Surrey Regiment (Transferred from 4th Battalion KSLI) of 6 Warrington Gardens, Ludlow.

Ball, Edgar A.   Pte.53042 3rd Battalion Worcestershire Regiment of 7 Mill Street, Bridgnorth. Killed in action, aged 24, 26 April 1918.

Baron, John Henry   Pte.10346 1st Battalion KSLI of 27 St. John's Road, Ludlow.

Bate, Edward B.   Pte.29749 6th Battalion South Wales Borderers whose parents lived at 45 Upper Galdeford, Ludlow. Died, aged 38, of influenza on 2 November 1918.

Benbow, Arthur J.   Pte.3485 Buffs (East Kent) Regiment whose mother lived at Nordley, Astley Abbotts.

Bennett, Llewellyn   Pte. of Kerry Lane, Bishop's Castle.

Bill, Horace (Frank)   CSM12083 9th Battalion, Devonshire Regiment whose parents lived at Eardington. His wife lived at 4 Pound Street, Bridgnorth. Killed in action 1 July 1916.

Bishop, George B.H.   Chaplain attached to 6th Battalion Northumberland Fusiliers. He was killed on 27 May 1918.

Bishop, James Elisha   Pte.1531 3rd Battalion Monmouthshire Regiment whose parents lived at Diamond Cottage, Clee St Margaret.

Bishop, Thomas H.   Pte.1526 3rd Battalion Monmouthshire Regiment whose parents lived at Diamond Cottage, Clee St Margaret.

Bishop, William   Pte.1631 3rd Battalion Monmouthshire Regiment whose parents lived at Diamond Cottage, Clee St Margaret.

Bissell, Thomas   Pte.1967 23rd Battalion Middlesex Regiment, aged 39, of 100 Lower Galdeford, Ludlow.

Blakeway, J. Edward   Pte.9622 1st Battalion KSLI Transport Section whose mother lived at 24 St John's Road and prior to that at Taylor's Court, Lower Broad Street, Ludlow. Killed in action, aged 28, on 4 June 1918.

Boucher, Cyril B.   Pte. 5th Battalion KSLI of 5, Rudge Heath, nr Claverley.

Bowen, Edward A.   Pte.131151 6th Battalion KSLI whose mother lived at 45 Bernard's Hill, Bridgnorth. He was killed, aged 29, on 22 March 1918.

Bowen, Stanley   Pte.13155 6th Battalion KSLI whose mother lived at 45 Bernard's Hill, Bridgnorth.

Bowen, T. Alfred   Pte.7975 5th Battalion KSLI killed in action 25 September 1915.

Brereton, Frederick C.   Pte.27779 2nd Battalion Royal Warwickshire Regiment of The Cottage, Lydbury North. Killed in action 9 October 1917.

Bright, Albert   Pte.17269 2nd Battalion KSLI of 62 Church Street, Bishop's Castle.

Bright, Frederick   Pte. 5th Battalion KSLI of Griffiths Green, Claverley.

Bright, Thomas W.   Pte.11290 2nd Battalion King's Own Scottish Borderers whose parents lived at Griffiths Green, Claverley.

Brocklehurst, George   Sgt.8093 6th Battalion KSLI whose parents lived at East Hamlet Nurseries, Ludlow. Died of wounds on 1 September 1916.

Brookes, Frederick C.   Pte.2019 4th Battalion KSLI of 23 St John's Road, Ludlow.

Brookes, George   Pte.4459 2nd Battalion KSLI whose parents lived at Rose Cottage, Slaney Street, Oakengates. Died at home, aged 43, from effects of gassing on 28 August 1915.

Brown, Archie   Stretcher Bearer 6th Battalion Cheshire Regiment of Highley.

Brown, Cecil F.   Pte. Hampshire Regiment whose sister, Daisy Hailstone, lived at 37 High Street, Bishop's Castle. Killed in action, aged 34, on 7 November 1914.

Brown, George	Sgt.5906 Royal Veterinary Corps of Castle Mill Cottage, Ludlow.
Brunt, George Henry	Pte. South Wales Borderers of Kempton, nr Clunbury. Died, aged 21, in St John's military hospital, Shrewsbury, Autumn 1919.
Burton, Eric F.	Pte.1553 Princess Patricia's Canadian Light Infantry whose parents lived at 33 High Street, Bridgnorth. Died of wounds, aged 23, on 9 May 1915.
Bywater, George	Of Dean Farm, Chelmarsh. Died of wounds 3 December 1919.
Cadwallader, Alfred E.	L.Cpl.4431 1st Battalion King's Own (Royal Lancaster) Regiment of 39 Welsh Street, Bishop's Castle. Killed in action, aged 41, on 6 May 1915.
Chapman, George A.	Pte.46887 163rd Labour Battalion of 21 Bell Lane, Ludlow.
Charlton, Gustave	Pte.7380 3rd Battalion KSLI of 54 Lower Broad Street, Ludlow.
Cook, Edward H.	Pte. 36918 6th Battalion Gloucestershire Regiment (Formerly 4th Battalion KSLI) of Railway Street, Bridgnorth. Killed in action, aged 22, on 2 December 1917.
Cooper, Edward	Sgt.12837 4th Battalion Worcestershire Regiment of 62 Cartway, Bridgnorth. Died of wounds, aged 24, on 11 January 1918.
Corbishley, F. Harry	32nd Field Ambulance RAMC and later 2nd Lt. Machine Gun Corps. His father lived at 152 Corve Street, Ludlow.
Corbishley, Thomas K.	RAMC whose father lived at 152 Corve Street, Ludlow.
Corfield, Ernest G.	Pte.24080 4th Battalion KSLI of Ruthall, Ditton Priors. Died of wounds, aged 23, on 4 November 1918.
Cornes, Charles R.	Gunner 1349 122nd Howitzer Brigade RFA of 9 Hollybush Road, Bridgnorth.
Cunnington, Douglas	Lt. 50th Battalion Canadian Expeditionary Force whose parents lived at 3 Church Street, Bridgnorth.
Darby, Harry	Pte.266723 2nd Battalion Monmouthshire Regiment of the Old School House, Bitterley. Died of wounds in German hands, aged 38, on 18 April 1918.
Davies, Arthur	Sgt. ASC of 70 New Street, Ludlow.
Davies, Edward R.	Pte.16823 4th Battalion KSLI of 15 Raven Lane, Ludlow. Died in captivity 22 July 1918.
Davies, Frederick	Pte.401439 10th Battalion Essex Regiment of 1, Colemore Green, Astley Abbotts. Died of wounds 27 April 1918.
Davies, Frederick N.	Pte.45169 4th (Reserve) Battalion KSLI of Springfield House, Bitterley. Died, aged 29, of influenza on 11 November 1918.
Davies, George	Pte.6064 2nd Battalion KSLI whose parents lived at 28 Union Street, Bishop's Castle.
Davies, John	L.Cpl.6900 1st Battalion Scots Guards whose mother lived at 47 Mill Street, Bridgnorth. Killed in action, aged 27, on 15 September 1916.
Davies, Joseph E.	Sgt. (later Company Quartermaster) 4th Battalion KSLI of 19 Mill Street, Ludlow. He died in France on 30 November 1918.
Davies, Norman	Pte.111065 21st Squadron Machine Gun Corps (Cavalry) whose parents lived at The Bungalow, Much Wenlock. Died of wounds, aged 27, on 27 September 1918.
Davies, T. Bernard	Trooper 1560 Shropshire Yeomanry of Wistantstow.
Davis, Charles J. (MM)	Pte.19596 7th Battalion KSLI of 112, Corve Street, Ludlow. Died, aged 22, of lockjaw on 7 November 1918.
Dean, Thomas	Sgt.9940 2nd and later 7th Battalion KSLI of Railway Crossing, Ludford, Ludlow. Killed in action 26 September 1917.
Deighton, Clement G.	Trooper 106190 1st Battalion Canadian Mounted Rifles. Parents lived in St Mary's Street, Bridgnorth.
Delo, Wallace L.	Pte.1109 5th Battalion KSLI of 69 St Bernard's Hill, Bridgnorth. His parents lived at no.32. Died of influenza, aged 28, on 8 February 1919.
Didlick, John Albert	Pte.8271 1st Battalion KSLI of 1 Brickyard, East Hamlet, Ludlow.
Downes, William	Sgt. KSLI of 95 Old Street, Ludlow.
Drew, Ernest A.	Pte. 5th Battalion KSLI of Broughton, Claverley.
Duck, R.G.	Bombardier who was a former employee of Mr C. Meredith, draper, of Clun.
Dunn, George William	Pte.203032 4th Battalion Royal Welch Fusiliers. He had previously been a groom at Lydham Manor. Died, aged 31, of influenza on 2 December 1918.

Dyke, Albert H.   Pte.14510 10th Battalion Sherwood Foresters (Notts and Derby Regiment) of Upper Galdeford, Ludlow. Killed in action July 1916.

Easthope, Donald E.   Pte.1329 1st Battalion Herefordshire Regiment of The Willows, Hayton, Stanton Lacy. Died of wounds, aged 21, on 17 August 1915.

Edwards, Albert   Cpl. KSLI of The Priory, Church Stretton.

Edwards, Alfred J.   Pte.18065 5th Battalion KSLI, aged 35, of 8 Sheinton Street, Much Wenlock.

Edwards, Francis L.   Staff Sgt.4991 Army Service Corps of 31 Severn Street, Bridgnorth. Died of wounds, aged 29, on 29 October 1918.

Edwards, George   Pte.2064 2nd Battalion KSLI of 3 Union Street, Bishop's Castle.

Edwards, Percy G.   Pte 19304 7th Battalion KSLI of Castle Villa, All Stretton. Killed, aged 22, on 14 July 1916.

Edwards, Samuel   L.Cpl.10823 5th Battalion KSLI whose parents lived at Clematis Cottage, Hopton Bank, Cleobury Mortimer. Killed in action, aged 28, on 3 June 1915.

Egan, Albert Leonard   Pte.35179 7th Battalion KSLI of 26 Clee View, Highley. Died of wounds, aged 19, on 23 October 1918.

Evans, Henry (Harry)   Cpl.9785 1st Battalion KSLI of 11, Severn Street, Bridgnorth.

Evans, William   L.Cpl.30239 10th Battalion Welsh Regiment. Mother lived at 5 Cluns Green, Clun. Killed in action, aged 29, on 5 September 1917.

Fellows, Sydney   Pte.14498 6th Battalion KSLI of 68 St Bernard's Hill, Bridgnorth. Killed in action, aged 21, on 17 September 1916.

Foxall, Frank J.   Colour Sgt 1st Battalion KSLI whose parents were stationers at Postern Gate, Bridgnorth.

France, Edward   Pte. 5th Battalion KSLI of 95 Cook's Cross, Alverley.

France, Harry   Pte.1649 5th Battalion KSLI of 95 Cook's Cross, Alveley. Killed 15 July 1915.

Francis, Charles A.   Sgt.8880 1st Battalion KSLI of 41 Upper Galdeford, Ludlow.

Francis, Thomas   Pte.18035 7th Battalion KSLI, aged 23, whose parents lived at Patch House, Lawton, Diddlebury.

Francis, William O.   Pte.18036 7th Battalion KSLI, aged 25, whose parents lived at Patch House, Lawton, Diddlebury.

Garbett, Sydney G.   Pte 22350 7th Battalion KSLI of Netchwood, nr Ditton Priors.

Garmston, Harry   Signalman attached to KSLI of Woodlands farm, Stanton Lacy.

Garnett-Botfield A.C.F.   Lt. 1st Battalion South Wales Borderers. Mother lived at The Hut, Bishop's Castle. Killed in action, aged 22, on 9 May 1915.

Gatacre, George E.   Capt. 2nd Battalion Duke of Wellington's (West Riding) Regiment of Gatacre Hall, Claverley.

George, John Francis   Driver 901694 78th Brigade RFA of Laurel Cottage, All Stretton. Died of wounds, aged 32, on 25 October 1918.

Gilkes, Norman S.   Gunner 160580 5th Siege Battery RGA. Prior to enlistment he worked at Lloyds Bank, Church Stretton and his parents lived at 23 Broad Street, Ludlow. Died from influenza on 11 November 1918.

Gittens, William   Gunner 150885 RGA. His wife lived at the Victoria Hotel, Clee Hill.

Gough, F.W.   Pte.11514 5th Battalion KSLI.

Greatwich, Frederick J.   Cpl.13192 6th Battalion KSLI, aged 23, whose parents lived at 11 St Bernard's Hill, Bridgnorth.

Greatwich, Sidney   CQMS 6th Battalion KSLI whose parents lived at 11 St Bernard's Hill, Bridgnorth.

Green, Frederick   Pte.76767 Tank Corps whose parents lived at Violet Cottage, Lydham. Killed in action on 23 August 1918.

Griffiths, Frank   Pte.1953/200448 4th Battalion KSLI of Ivy Cottage, Ashford Bowdler.

Griffiths, J. Gilbert   Pte.9984 2nd Battalion KSLI of 10 Raven Lane, Ludlow.

Griffiths, Percy J.   Sgt.1381 6th Battalion Gordon Highlanders whose mother lived at 6 North Gate, Bridgnorth. Killed in action, aged 24, on 6 July 1918.

Griffiths, William   Pte.2020/200498 4th Battalion KSLI whose father lived at 1 Lower Mill Street, Ludlow. Killed in action on 30 December 1917.

Gwilliam, Charles	Pte.22377 7th Battalion KSLI. Parents lived at 8 Mount View, Bishop's Castle. Killed in action, aged 31, on 14 July 1916.
Halford, John Robert	Pte. 13602 7th Battalion KSLI of 9 Raven Lane, Ludlow. Killed in action, aged 25, on 14 July 1916.
Hamer, George	Pte.200748 4th Battalion KSLI of The Cabin, Bishop's Castle.
Hancocks, Francis	Pte.8854 5th Battalion KSLI of 4 Main Road, Dorrington. Killed in action, aged 23, on 25 September 1915.
Handley, Herbert	Pte.6913 2nd Battalion Duke of Wellington's Regiment of 13 Railway Terrace, Craven Arms.
Harley, C. Maurice	Pte.46212 14th Battalion Worcestershire Regiment of 51 Ivy Place, Alveley. Killed in action, aged 19, on 25 March 1918.
Harries, Harry	Pte. 9th Battalion Royal Welch Fusiliers of Magpie Cottage, Church Stoke.
Harrington, John (Jack)	Pte.241381 5th Battalion Royal Welch Fusiliers. Parents lived at 95 Green Lane, Onibury. Died, aged 21, whilst in Turkish hands on 2 April 1917.
Hatfield, Harry Alfred	L.Cpl. Liverpool Regiment. Discharged on medical grounds. Lived at 21 Dinham, Ludlow.
Hayward, Arthur	Driver 52nd Div. Ammunition Column RFA of 13 Severn Street, Bridgnorth. Died of effects of gas poisoning on 23 December 1918.
Hayward, Arthur E.	Pte.11796 1st Battalion Welsh Guards of Wooton, Onibury. Parents lived at 3 Woodhouses, Bromfield. Killed in action, aged 29, on 2 October 1915.
Henson, George	Pte.8065 1st Battalion KSLI of 2 Lower Mill Street, Ludlow.
Higgins, Alfred H.	Pte.20499 of 44 St Mary's Street, Bridgnorth.
Holder, Thomas	Pte 394834 M T Army Service Corps of Kerry Lane, Bishop's Castle.
Holland, Charles G.	Pte KSLI of Temeside, Ludlow.
Hoskins, Lewis	Pte.270 2nd Battalion Lancashire Fusiliers whose wife lived in New Street, Bishop's Castle.
Hughes, Leslie O.	Pte.2873 Shropshire Yeomanry (Attached to 1st Battalion Cheshire Regiment) of 50 Mill Street, Bridgnorth.
Humphreys, Harry T.	Pte.170275 ASC of Ledwyche whose parents lived in St Mary's Lane, Ludlow. Died, aged 33, of influenza on 13 November 1918.
Humphries, E.	Pte.35114 Essex Regiment.
Humphries, George H.	Pte.230342 10th Shropshire and Cheshire Yeomanry Battalion KSLI of 3 Roundthorn, Middleton. Died of wounds on 4 September 1918.
Husband, John	Pte.200809 4th Battalion KSLI whose parents lived at 17 Bull Lane, Bishop's Castle. Died in German hands on 15 April 1918 after being reported missing on 30 December 1917.
Husbands, George R.	L.Cpl. Military Foot Police (formerly KSLI) of Saddle Hill Cottage, Clungunford. Died aged, 34, of effects of gas poisoning on 26 June 1919.
Jacks, Thomas	Pte. KSLI of 5 Old Field, Bromfield.
James, Herbert	Pte.10107 1st Battalion KSLI of 29 Eardington. Killed in action on 9 August 1915.
James, Thomas W.	Driver 73728 83rd Brigade RFA. His parents lived at 30 Severn Street, Bridgnorth. Killed in action, aged 22, on 15 October 1917.
Jenkins, A.	Church Stretton.
John, David	Trooper 1541 Shropshire Yeomanry of Stanton Lacy.
Johnson, Albert John	Pte.50716 11th Battalion Cheshire Regiment whose parents lived at 19 Glen Place, High Churchyard, Bridgnorth. Died of wounds, aged 23, on 26 March 1918.
Johnson, Harry	Sgt.16910 5th Battalion KSLI of 3 St Mary's Street, Bridgnorth and later 38 Mill Street, Bridgnorth.
Jones, Alfred	Pte.12524 6th Battalion KSLI, aged 22, whose parents lived at Duxmore, Onibury.
Jones, Alfred W.	Pte.7122 1st Battalion Royal Welch Fusiliers whose parents lived at 74 Lower Broad Street, Ludlow.
Jones, Edward A.	Pte 523797 423rd Agricultural Company, Labour Corps of 10 Kerry Lane, Bishop's Castle.

Jones, Eli	Pte.11014 Coldstream Guards of 25 St Mary's Street, Bridgnorth.
Jones, George W.	Pte. Naval Division whose parents lived at the Shakespeare Hotel, Castle Street, Bridgnorth.
Jones, Horace	Pte.18579 5th Battalion KSLI of 13 Riverside, Bridgnorth. Killed in action on 16 September 1916.
Jones, Mark	Pte.201929 10th Battalion Worcestershire Regiment of 84 High Street, Bridgnorth. Died of wounds on 5 May 1918.
Jones, Nairn	Sgt.37581 RAMC 58th Field Ambulance Unit whose parents lived at 23 High Street, Clun. Killed in action, aged 20, on 26 July 1916.
Jones, Phillip Henry	Pte.7300 2nd Battalion KSLI of Hayton's Bent. He died at home as a result of gassing in April 1917.
Jones, R.A.	Sgt. RAMC.
Jones, Richard	Pte.12525 6th Battalion KSLI, aged 19, whose parents lived at Duxmore, Onibury.
Jones, Thomas	Gunner 220421 RFA D Battery 256th Brigade of 10 Welsh Street, Bishop's Castle. Died, aged 31, as a result of gas poisoning on 9 September 1918.
Jones, William E.	Sgt.17179 Army Service Corps of 9 Bell Lane, Ludlow.
Jones, William G.	Pte.93829 51st Battalion King's Liverpool Regiment of Titterstone. Died, aged 19, from effects of gas poisoning on 31 January 1919.
Keenan, James A.	L.Cpl.14783 7th Battalion KSLI. Formerly assistant teacher at Bishop's Castle boys school and whose parents lived at Little Stretton. Killed in action on 27 March 1916.
Kellock, David	Sgt.13757 Royal Welsh Fusiliers (later 292066 of the Welsh regiment) who lived at 48 Broad Street, Ludlow.
Kershaw, Ernest G.	Signaller 39628 32nd Field Ambulance 10th Division and later Pte.31914 10th Battalion KSLI whose parents lived at Rosedene, East Hamlet, Ludlow.
Kershaw, Harold V.	Signaller 5403/25968 RAMC (Attached to KSLI) whose parents lived at Rosedene, East Hamlet, Ludlow.
Kimber, George	Cpl. 4th Battalion KSLI of Knowbury. He was the adopted son of William and Sarah Waterfield of Angel Lane, Bitterley.
Langford, Harry (DCM)	Pte. 1st Battalion KSLI of Bourton Road, Much Wenlock.
Lavender, Franklin	Hon. Artillery Company. Prior to enlisting he had been articled to Mr E. Griffiths, solicitor, Bishop's Castle.
Law, George	Pte.33240 10th Battalion KSLI of Dinchope, nr Craven Arms. Killed in action on 22 August 1918.
Law, Thomas	Pte.16692 1st Battalion KSLI of Dinchope, nr Craven Arms. Killed in action on 21 March 1918.
Lawley, Frederick A.	Pte.24285 1st Battalion KSLI of 5 Whitburn Place, Bridgnorth.
Lennox, Vincent E.	L.Cpl.22103 7th Battalion KSLI of 12 Castle Green, Bishop's Castle.
Lewis, Edward	Gunner 80570 79th Brigade RFA of Plush Hill, All Stretton. Died of wounds, aged 24, on 8 October 1918.
Lewis, Ernest Arthur	Pte.11357 5th Battalion KSLI of Brook Cottage, 5 Fishmore, Ludlow.
Lewis, John	Pte. of Bedlam, Bitterley.
Lewis, Thomas	Sgt.200363 4th Battalion KSLI whose parents lived at The Hope, Stanton Lacy. Killed in action on 26 March 1918.
Lewis, Thomas	Gunner 153842 RHA whose parents lived at 4 Titterstone Cottages, Bitterley. Died, aged 28, of influenza on 7 December 1918.
Lloyd, George Thomas	Cpl.200599 Signal Section 4th Battalion KSLI of 3 Severn Street, Bridgnorth. Killed in action, aged 22, on 26 March 1918.
Lowe, Edward	Cpl. 1st Battalion South Wales Borderers whose parents lived at Castle Street, Clun.
Lucas, George	Pte.7290 2nd Battalion KSLI of 3 Cunnery Terrace, Church Stretton.
Lucas, John	Pte. 79th Field Ambulance RAMC of Wigley Cottage, Fishmore, Ludlow.
Lyndon, W. Alexander	Rifleman 1351 3rd Battalion Rifle Brigade of Brockton Lydbury North. Killed in action, aged 19, on 20 July 1915.

Lythall, Leonard	Pte.8175 1st Battalion South Wales Borderers.
Maddocks, Frank	Pte. RAMC of 5 Castle Street, Bishop's Castle.
Marston, William D.	Pte.33626 6th Battalion KSLI of Station Road, Bishop's Castle. Killed in action on 20 November 1917.
Mason, Arthur	Gunner 106537 RGA of Quatford, nr Bridgnorth.
Mason, Edwin	Pte. 57963 51st Battalion Machine Gun Corps. Died of wounds in German hands, aged 33, on 10 April 1918.
Massey, John	Pte.6084 1st Battalion KSLI of 34 Lower Broad Street, Ludlow. Killed in action on 22 March 1918.
McMichael, Colin John W.	Pte.514977 London Scottish Regiment whose parents lived on the High Street, Bridgnorth. He died, aged 19, on 6 September 1918.
Meadmore, Edward W.	Pte.266668 2nd Battalion Monmouthshire Regiment of Stanley Cottage, Lydbury North.
Mellings, Harold T.	DSC and Bar, DFC Capt. 210th Squadron RAF of Bromfield. Killed in action on 22 July 1918.
Meyrick, Thomas	Pte. KSLI of 7 Walmet Terrace, Lower Down, Lydbury North.
Millichamp, George	Pte.37288 9th Battalion Lancashire Fusiliers whose parents lived at Nine Springs, Bitterley. Died of wounds on 4 September 1917.
Milman, Sydney	Pte.13144 6th Battalion KSLI whose parents lived at The Cock Inn, Stottesden. Killed in action, aged 20, on 24 February 1916.
Minton, William	L.Cpl.5189 1st Battalion KSLI of 34, Lower Broad Street, Ludlow. He died from wounds on 3 June 1917.
Mitchell, Ewan	Trooper whose parents lived at Home farm, Cleobury Mortimer.
Morgan, John Ernest	L.Cpl.200635 4th Battalion KSLI whose parents lived at 58 Corve Street, Ludlow. Killed in action, aged 30, on 26 March 1918.
Morris, Robert	Pte.16680 2nd Battalion KSLI of 17 Colebatch. Died of influenza on 5 October 1918.
Morse, James	Cpl.23715 7th Battalion KSLI of 77 Lower Galdeford, Ludlow. Killed in action, aged 27, on 26 September 1917.
Munns, William J.	Pte.27478 1st Battalion KSLI of 18, Mill Street, Ludlow.
Nash, William	Pte.13597 7th Battalion KSLI and then L.Cpl.260759/206109 Royal Engineers of Ludlow.
Nicholas, Benjamin	Sgt.889/12038 4th Battalion KSLI of 5 Waterside, Ludlow. Died from wounds on 30 December 1917.
Nicholas, William	Pte.12038 2nd South Wales Borderers of Quality Square, Ludlow.
Nicholas, William	Sgt.34996 99th Brigade RFA of 22 Castle Green, Bishop's Castle. Killed in action, aged 35, on 19 February 1917.
Oliver, Charles	Pte 5th Battalion KSLI. His father lived at 37 Severn Street, Bridgnorth.
Oliver, George	Pte 5th Battalion KSLI. His father lived at 37 Severn Street, Bridgnorth.
Oliver, John	Pte.11200 5th Battalion KSLI. His father lived at 37 Severn Street, Bridgnorth.
Ovens, Ernest	Pte.16825 5th Battalion KSLI of 28 Lower Broad Street, Ludlow.
Owen, Charles	Pte.7630 1st Battalion KSLI of Smithfield Road, Much Wenlock. Killed in action, aged 26, on 25 August 1915.
Owen, W. Owen	Pte. (Probably of 2nd Battalion King's Own Scottish Borderers) whose parents lived at Upper Farmcote, Claverley.
Packer, Francis W.	Pte.83910 66th Battalion Machine Gun Corps of The Hollies, Gravel Hill, Ludlow. He was killed in action, aged 20, on 29 March 1918.
Painter, W.	Pte. 1st Battalion KSLI whose stepbrother George Owen lived at 24 Church Street, Bishop's Castle.
Parr, Thomas	Discharged on medical grounds. Lived at 2 Gravel Hill, Ludlow.
Peachey, Joseph E.	Lance Sgt.135690 2nd Battalion KSLI of 144 Corve Street, Ludlow.
Penny, John	Pte.6769 3rd Dragoon Guards of 1, Old Bell Cottages, Ludford, Ludlow.
Phillips, Arthur	Pte. 6th Battalion Gloucester Regiment (later Leicestershire Regiment) of Lydbury North.

Pinches, Thomas W.   Pte. 1st Battalion KSLI of 27 Gravel Hill, Ludlow.
Piper, W. Edgell   Pte.963 1st Birmingham City Battalion of 9 Victoria Road, Bridgnorth.
Pounds, Francis   Cpl.8880 1st Battalion KSLI of 88 Upper Galdeford, Ludlow.
Powell, John   Pte.10360 1st Battalion KSLI of 11, Bell Lane, Ludlow.
Preece, Edward   Pte.10114 1st Battalion KSLI whose mother lived at 55 Upper Galdeford, Ludlow.
Preece, John   Pte.6807 2nd Battalion KSLI of 3 Holdgate Fee, Ludlow.
Price, Benjamin   Pte.6129 1st Battalion KSLI of 92 Lower Galdeford, Ludlow. He died of wounds on
                          22 May 1916.
Price, Clement M.   Pte.355866 25th Battalion Royal Welsh Fusiliers (Mont. and Welsh Horse Yeomanry)
                          of The Ashes, Mainstone, Bishop's Castle. Died of wounds, aged 21, on
                          18 October 1918.
Price, Samuel   Pte.20039 4th Battalion KSLI attached to 190th Coy Machine Gun Corps of
                          43 Oldgate Fee, Ludlow. Killed in action on 30 December 1917.
Pugh, John   2nd Lt. 48 Squadron RAF whose mother lived at 7 Castle View, Ludlow.
Reynolds, Alfred T.   Pte.13610 KSLI of 43 Old Street, Ludlow.
Richards, George H.   Cpl.58493 15th Battalion Welsh Regiment whose parents lived at 68 Rose Villa,
                          Alveley. Died, aged 25, of influenza on 29 October 1918.
Roberts, Alfred   Pte.202775 4th battalion KSLI of 14 Colemore Green, Astley Abbotts. Died, aged 41,
                          of pneumonia in German POW camp on 23 June 1918.
Roberts, Clement J.   Trooper 1437 Shropshire Yeomanry who boarded at 63 Old Street, Ludlow.
Robinson, Albert   Pte. 2nd Indian Cavalry Supply Column, Motor Transport Section, Army Service corps
                          whose parents lived at Church Street, Bishop's Castle. Later transferred to the
                          Rifle Brigade and was killed in action 30 October 1917.
Roden, Geoffrey E.   L.Cpl.1086 1st West Yorks Regiment whose mother lived at the Post Office, Claverley.
Rogers, George   Sgt.9805 1st Battalion KSLI of 132 Corve Street, Ludlow.
Rogers, John (Jack)   Pte.61387 1st Battalion KSLI of 132 Corve Street, Ludlow and later 11 St Mary's
                          Lane, Ludlow.
Rutter, Alfred Henry   Pte.58002 13th Battalion Royal Welch Fusiliers (formerly South Wales Borderers) of
                          59, Cartway, Bridgnorth. Died, aged 19, of wounds on 4 June 1919.
Sanders, Walter C.   Acting Sgt.130068 16th (Manitoba) Canadian Regiment.
Sheldon, Edward   Sgt.20011 RGA whose father was landlord of the Horse and Jockey public house, Old
                          Street, Ludlow. Died of TB after weakening by wounds on 24 February 1919.
Sherry, Walter   Pioneer 10170 1st Battalion KSLI of 84 Cartway, Bridgnorth. He died of wounds on
                          3 July 1915.
Shingler, Francis John   L.Cpl.15353 6th Battalion KSLI of Drawell farm, Ditton Priors. He died of wounds
                          on 11 November 1915.
Shuker, Thomas   Pte. of Greenfields, All Stretton.
Shutt, Edwin T.   Discharged on medical grounds. Lived at 1 Taylor's Court, Lower Broad Street,
                          Ludlow.
Simkiss, George   Pte.63500 8th Battalion Machine Gun Corps. Parents at Nortons Camp nr Craven
                          Arms. Died of dysentery in German POW Camp on 18 November 1918.
Smith, Archie   Pte.123591 RAMC of 69, Broad Street, Ludlow.
Smith, Leslie Charles   Pte.23442 7th Battalion Canadian Infantry. Killed in action on 24 April 1915.
                          Previously lived in Bridgnorth.
Smith, Thomas   Pte.5932 2nd Battalion KSLI of 38 Union Street, Bishop's Castle. Officially listed as
                          killed in action on 25 May 1915.
Southerton, William J.   Pte.24318 5th Battalion KSLI formerly of the King's Head, Bishop's Castle. Died of
                          wounds on 23 September 1916.
Southwell, Arthur H.S.   Served in ranks of 6th Battalion KSLI but when promoted to 2nd Lt. he was transferred
                          to the 7th Battalion. Killed on 13 November 1916. His father lived at Fairfield,
                          Oldbury, nr Bridgnorth.
Spink, Henry M.   Lt. Northumberland Fusiliers whose father lived at 19 Castle Street, Bishop's Castle.
Stead, Ernest Stanley   L.Cpl.9100 York and Lancaster Regiment of 12 Tower Street, Ludlow.

Steenton, Henry	Pte.2425 4th Battalion KSLI of 45 Lower Broad Street, Ludlow.
Stokes, Alfred W.	Pte.1689 14th Battalion Royal Warwickshire Regiment of Hopstone House, Claverley. Killed in action, aged 22, on 3 September 1916.
Sutton, R. Harold	Pte. 2nd Battalion Lancs and Yorks Regiment whose father lived at 16 Union Street, Bishop's Castle.
Swain, Walter John	Pte. 2nd Battalion KSLI of Brockton nr Lydbury North.
Taggart, Charles B.	Pte. 51st Battalion Australian Imperial Force whose mother lived at 12 St Bernard's Hill, Bridgnorth.
Taggart, Thomas H.	Pte.6926 1st Border Regiment of 12 St Bernard's Hill, Bridgnorth.
Taylor, George Henry	Pte.39391 5th Battalion South Wales Borderers of 6 Pound Street, Bridgnorth.
Taylor, Thomas	Worcestershire Regiment of Highley.
Tennant, John	Pte.27776 1st Battalion Royal Warwickshire Regiment whose parents lived at 2 Cornbank Bridge, Clee Hill. Died of wounds, aged 36, on 11 January 1917.
Thomas, Walter J.	Cpl.9796 2nd Battalion KSLI of 10 St Bernard's Hill, Bridgnorth. Killed in action, aged 21, on 25 May 1915.
Thornley, Thomas	Pte. Cheshire Regiment whose parents lived at 3 Church Lane, Woodbine Terrace, Bishop's Castle.
Tipton, Herbert P.	Rifleman 1707 King's Royal Rifles of Roveries Lodge, Churchstoke.
Tipton, Timothy R.	Pte.55520 17th Battalion Royal Welsh Fusiliers of Roveries Lodge, Churchstoke.
Tong, Edwin Robert	Pte.201110 6th Battalion KSLI of The Crown Inn, Clun. Killed in action, aged 25, on 16 August 1917.
Tristram, Charles	L.Cpl.38719 Royal Engineers 5th Siege Field Company whose wife lived at 18 Spring Gardens and later 28 St John's Road, Ludlow. Killed in action on 10 December 1917.
Tuckley, A.Ernest	CSM14414 7th Battalion KSLI whose father lived at 12 The Waterworks, Mill Street, Bridgnorth. Killed in action, aged 41, on 26 September 1917.
Turnbull, Derwent C.	Lt. 84th Field Ambulance RAMC attached to 1st Battalion Cheshire Regiment. Parents lived at Burway House, Church Stretton. Died of wounds on 14 March 1915.
Turner, Bernard W.	Sgt. 4th Battalion KSLI of 7 West Castle Street, Bridgnorth.
Vale, A. Harold	Pte. KSLI and later Cpl.187231 134th Labour Company of 22 Bell Lane, Ludlow.
Vaughan, Arthur	Pte.2207 South Wales Borderers. His parents lived at Bridge Cottage, Little Stretton. Killed in action, aged 29, on 31 July 1917.
Vaughan George H.	Pte.41263 777 Area Employment Company of 13 Bridge Cottage, Colebatch.
Wait, Arthur	Pte.6880 3rd Battalion KSLI of 111 Lower Galdeford, Ludlow.
Ward, Robert	Pte. 3rd Battalion KSLI of 69 Lower Galdeford, Ludlow.
Wellings, Harold	Pte. KSLI of Pitts farm, Clun.
Whittall, Joseph	Sgt.20258 10th Battalion South Wales Borderers of 20 Station Road, Bishop's Castle.
Wilcox, Charles	Pte. 26582 6th Battalion KSLI formerly a cowman at Choulton, Lydbury North. Died of Disease in German POW camp on 18 October 1918.
Wilcox, Harry	Pte.23572 1st Battalion KSLI of Little Villa, Cardington. Killed in action, aged 22, on 21 March 1918.
Wilding, William A.	L.Cpl.22365 1st Garrison Battalion Yorkshire Regiment whose parents lived at 19 Salop Street, Bridgnorth. Died, aged 31, of influenza on 28 November 1918.
Williams, Arthur	Discharged on medical grounds and lived with his mother at 13 Bell Lane, Ludlow.
Wilson, James	Pte.97576 8th Battalion machine Gun Corps of 22 Church Street, Bishop's Castle.
Woodhouse, Charles	Pte.53737 7th Battalion Cheshire Regiment of 4 Taylors Court, Lower Broad Street, Ludlow. His parents lived at New Inn, Hopton Bank. Killed in action, aged 31, on 1 June 1918.
Woodhouse, Thomas J.	L.Cpl.6118 1st Battalion KSLI of 127 Corve Street, Ludlow.
Woosnam, William E.	Rifleman King's Royal Rifles of Acton Bank Farm, Brockton, nr Lydbury North.
Wright, Albert	Pte 2nd Battalion KSLI of Bishop's Castle.

References

Chapter 1

1. *Church Stretton Advertiser* 8 August 1914.
2. *Ludlow Advertiser* 8 August 1914.
3. *ibid.*
4. Major W. de B. Wood (ed.), *The History of the KSLI in the Great War 1914-1918,* (London, 1925) pp.95-97.
5. *Ludlow Advertiser* 8 August 1914; *Bridgnorth Journal* 8 August 1914.
6. *Ludlow Advertiser* 15 August 1914.
7. *Wellington Journal* 6 August 1914.
8. *Bridgnorth Journal* 8 August 1914; *Ludlow Advertiser* 15 August 1914; *Church Stretton Advertiser* 15 August 1914.
9. *Ludlow Advertiser* 15 August 1914.
10. *Bridgnorth Journal* 13 March 1915, *Ludlow Advertiser* 13 March 1915 and 3 & 10 April 1915; *Church Stretton Advertiser* 20 August & 10 September 1914.
11. *Ludlow Advertiser* 29 August & 14 November 1914; *Church Stretton Advertiser* 20 August 1914 & 9 September 1915.
12. *Ludlow Advertiser* 29 August and 7 & 14 November 1914; *Bridgnorth Journal* 5 May 1917.
13. *Ludlow Advertiser* 15 May 1915.
14. Arthur Marwick, *The Deluge: British Society and the First World War* (London, 1965) pp.35-37.
15. *Bridgnorth Journal* 29 August 1914; *Ludlow Advertiser* 26 September 1914.
16. *Bridgnorth Journal* 12 June 1915.
17. Evidence of Clifford Smout of Rock Cottage, Haytons Bent whose father Andrew Smout was a under gardener at Downton Hall in 1914 and was one who enlisted.
18. *Bridgnorth Journal* 21 November & 12 December 1914; *Parish of Lydbury North War Record 1914-1918,* privately published (Bishop's Castle Local History Collection); *Church Stretton Advertiser* 24 September 1914; *Ludlow Advertiser* 31 October & 28 November 1914; *Bitterley and Ludlow Parish Magazine* Oct. and Dec. 1914 in Shropshire Archives.
19. *Ludlow Advertiser* 29 September 1914; *Bridgnorth Journal* 29 August & 12 September 1914.
20. *Ludlow Advertiser* 5 September, 10 October & 19 December 1914; *Church Stretton Advertiser* 15 October 1914.
21. *Church Stretton Advertiser* 10 June 1915.
22. *Rural Deanery of Bridgnorth Parish Magazine* Jan. 1915, Shropshire Archives P40/H/1/5 1911-1916; *Bridgnorth Journal* 12 & 19 September & 26 December 1914.
23. *Church Stretton Advertiser* 3 June 1915; *Bridgnorth Journal* 12 September 1914; *Wellington Journal* 5 September 1914.

24. *Ludlow Advertiser* 26 September & 19 December 1914; *Bridgnorth Journal* 28 November 1914; *Church Stretton Advertiser* 21 January 1915.
25. *Clun Valley Parochial Magazine* Oct. 1914, Shropshire Archives ref. P137/H/1.
26. *Bitterley and Ludlow Parish Magazine* Sept. 1914, Shropshire Archives. For a discussion of invasion fears and those of possible sabotage prior to invasion see Christopher Andrew *The Defence of the Realm: The Authorized History of MI5* (London, 2009) pp.3-28.
27. *Ludlow Advertiser* 8 August 1914; *Bridgnorth Journal* 15 August 1914.
28. *Church Stretton Advertiser* 13 & 20 August 1914; *Bridgnorth Journal* 29 August 1914; *Ludlow Advertiser* 5 June 1915.
29. *Bitterley and Ludlow Parish Magazine op.cit.* Jan. 1915.
30. *Ludlow Advertiser* 21 November 1914 & 23 January 1915; *Church Stretton Advertiser* 13 August 1914 & 1 December 1915; *Bridgnorth Journal* 21 November 1914, 26 June & 6 November 1915, and 1 July 1916; *Wellington Journal* 5 December 1914, 21 August & 25 September 1915; *Rural Deanery of Bridgnorth Parish Magazine op.cit.* June 1915.
31. *Ludlow Journal* 15 August 1914; *Church Stretton Advertiser* 13 August & 3 September 1914.
32. *Church Stretton Advertiser* 13 August 1914; *Ludlow Advertiser* 15 August 1914.
33. *Ludlow Advertiser* 14 November & 19 September 1914.
34. *Bridgnorth Journal* 20 March & 8 May 1915.
35. *Ludlow Advertiser* 15 May & 5 June 1915.
36. *Ludlow Advertiser* 8 August 1914.
37. *Church Stretton Advertiser* 8 August 1914; *Bridgnorth Journal* 8 August 1914.
38. *Ludlow Advertiser* 8 August 1914.

Chapter 2

1. *Ludlow Advertiser* 8 May 1915.
2. *Church Stretton Advertiser* 29 April 1915; *Ludlow Advertiser* 8 May & 16 October 1915; *Bridgnorth Journal* 8 May 1915.
3. *Bridgnorth Journal* 25 December 1915; *Ludlow Advertiser* 4 September 1915.
4. *Ludlow Advertiser* 29 May, 3 July & 4 September 1915.
5. *Ludlow Advertiser* 17 & 24 October 1914 and 8 January 1916; *Church Stretton Advertiser* 1 February 1917.
6. *Church Stretton Advertiser* 21 January 1915.
7. *Bridgnorth Journal* 19 April 1914, 5 June & 9 October 1915; *Ludlow Advertiser* 26 June 1915; *Church Stretton Advertiser* 31 May 1917.

8. *Ludlow Advertiser* 17 July 1915.

9. *Ludlow Advertiser* 11 September 1915.

10. *Bridgnorth Journal* 9 October 1915 and *Church Stretton Advertiser* 7 October 1915

11. *Bridgnorth Advertiser* 9 October 1915.

12. *Bridgnorth Journal* 10 June 1916; *Ludlow Advertiser* 24 June & 1 July 1916 and 8 December 1917.

13. Letter, dated 4 November 1914, from Edward Preece in *Ludlow Advertiser* 21 November 1914.

14. Letter, dated 2 January 1915, from Frank J. Foxall to his family in *Bridgnorth Journal* 23 January 1915.

15. Letter from A. Jenkins in *Bridgnorth Journal* 16 January 1915.

16. Letter from Franklin Lavender to his mother in London in *Ludlow Advertiser* 9 January 1915.

17. Letter, dated 29 January 1915, from J. Gilbert (Gill) Griffiths to Mr John Diggle, headmaster of the National School, in *Ludlow Advertiser* 6 February 1915; *Ludlow Advertiser* 6 March 1915; letter from Lewis Hoskins to his wife in *Ludlow Advertiser* 16 January 1915.

18. Letter from Albert (Bert) Bright in *Ludlow Advertiser* 15 January 1916.

19. Interview with F.W. Gough in *Ludlow Advertiser* 18 September 1915.

20. Letter from George Davies to his mother in *Ludlow Advertiser* 29 May 1915.

21. Letter from R.G. Duck to his former employer Mr C. Meredith, draper of Clun, in *Ludlow Advertiser* 10 April 1915.

22. Letter from Albert H. Dyke to John Diggle, headmaster of the National School, in *Ludlow Advertiser* 25 September 1915.

23. Letters from Ernest G. Kershaw to his parents in *Ludlow Advertiser* 11 September & 9 October 1915.

24. Letter from Charles Francis to John Diggle, headmaster of the National School, in *Ludlow Advertiser* 28 November 1914.

25. Letter from George Davies in *Ludlow Advertiser* 12 June 1915.

26. Letter from Albert (Bert) Robinson to his parents in *Ludlow Advertiser* 5 June 1915.

27. Letter from Charles A. Francis to his former headmaster John Diggle at the National School, Ludlow in *Ludlow Advertiser* 26 June 1915.

28. Letter, dated 1 October 1915, from Arthur Horace Steadman Southwell to his father in *Bridgnorth Journal* 9 October 1915.

29. Letter from Franklin Lavender to his aunt Mrs M.S. Green who formerly lived at Prospect Place, Bishop's Castle in *Ludlow Advertiser* 9 January 1915; and letter from Eric F. Burton to his parents in *Bridgnorth Journal* 20 March 1915.

30. Letter, dated 20 August 1915, from Thomas John Woodhouse to John Diggle, headmaster of the National School in *Ludlow Advertiser* 28 August 1915.

31. Letter from John Preece writing from Wharncliffe War Hospital, Sheffield to John Diggle, headmaster of National School in *Ludlow Advertiser* 19 June 1915.

32. Letter, dated 1 August 1915, from Geoffrey E. Roden to his mother in *Bridgnorth Journal* 14 August 1915.

33. Letter from Thomas Jacks quoted in *Bitterley and Ludlow Parish Magazine* Jan. 1916, Shropshire Archives *op.cit.*

34. Letter from Herbert Tipton in the *Ludlow Advertiser* 30 October 1915.

35. *Ludlow Advertiser* 21 August 1915.

36. *Wellington Journal* 9 October 1915.

37. *Ludlow Advertiser* 8 January 1916.

38. *Ludlow Advertiser* 12 February 1916.

39. *Ludlow Advertiser* 29 January 1916.

40. *Bridgnorth Journal* 19 June 1915; *Rural Deanery of Bridgnorth Parish Magazine* May 1918, Shropshire Archives P40/H/1/6 1917-1921; and Revd George Bernard Hamilton Bishop Chaplain in *Church Stretton Advertiser* 22 August 1918.

41. *Church Stretton Advertiser* 2 March 1916; *Ludlow Advertiser* 4 March 1916; *Bridgnorth Journal* 10 June 1916; *Wellington Journal* 24 June 1916.

42. *Ibid.*

43. *Church Stretton Advertiser* 30 March 1916; *Ludlow Advertiser* 27 May 1916.

44. *Ludlow Advertiser* 13 July, 2 September, 21 October & 11 November 1916.

45. J.W. Graham, *Conscience and Conscription 1916-1919* (London, 1922) pp.139-140; E.C. Gould 'The Home Office Scheme' in *For His Names Sake 1914-1918* (Heanor, 1921). My thanks to Rona Cobb of Ditton Priors and Alfred Hinton, the son of one of the C.O.s, for bringing this to my attention.

46. *Ludlow Advertiser* 11 March & 16 December 1916 and 6 January 1917; *Church Stretton Advertiser* 20 April 1916; *Bridgnorth Journal* 3 June 1916.

47. *Ludlow Advertiser* 4 March 1916.

48. *Church Stretton Advertiser* 24 February 1916.

49. *Bridgnorth Journal* 27 May 1916; *Ludlow Advertiser* 13 July 1916.

50. *Bridgnorth Journal* 30 June 1917.

51. *Ludlow Advertiser* 23 September 1916.

52. *Ludlow Advertiser* 1 July & 28 October 1916.

53. *Ludlow Advertiser* 20 January 1917.

54. *Church Stretton Advertiser* 15 June 1916; *Ludlow Advertiser* 2 September & 21 October 1916; *Bridgnorth Journal* 12 August 1916.

55. *Ludlow Advertiser* 24 November 1917 and 26 January 1918

56. *Ludlow Advertiser* 23 September 1916 and 5 May 1917.

57. *Ludlow Advertiser* 4 & 10 March 1916.

58. *Bridgnorth Journal* 10 & 24 June 1916.

59. *Church Stretton Advertiser* 30 March 1916.

60. *Church Stretton Advertiser* 15 June & 21 October 1916.
61. *Ludlow Advertiser* 12 January 1918.
62. *Ludlow Advertiser* 23 December 1916.
63. *Ludlow Advertiser* 21 July 1917
64. *Ludlow Advertiser* 4 August 1917.
65. *Ludlow Advertiser* 17 July 1917.
66. *Church Stretton Advertiser* 24 February & 5 October 1916.
67. *Bridgnorth Journal* 28 October 1916; *Ludlow Advertiser* 12 & 22 January 1918.
68. *Ludlow Advertiser* 17 March 1917.
69. Letter from ex-Councillor William Joseph Perry of 14 Galdeford, Ludlow in *Ludlow Advertiser* 15 September 1917.
70. *Church Stretton Advertiser* 4 March 1916 and 1 August 1918.
71. *Ludlow Advertiser* 3 November 1917.
72. Letter from John Penny in *Ludlow Advertiser* 17 June 1916.
73. Letter dated 18 November 1916 from Revd Alex Hawken of Lydham to Frederick Green. (Permission of Gwynneth Evans)
74. *Ludlow Advertiser* 25 November 1916 and 27 October 1917; *Church Stretton Advertiser* 28 February 1918.
75. *Church Stretton Advertiser* 20 December 1917 and 16 May 1918.
76. *Ludlow Advertiser* 25 November 1916.
77. *Ludlow Advertiser* 26 August, 2 September & 29 December 1916; *Bridgnorth Journal* 6 October 1917 and 2 December 1916.

Chapter 3
1. *Bridgnorth Journal* 19 October1914; *Ludlow Advertiser* 31 October & 7 November 1914.
2. *Bridgnorth Journal* 17 October 1914; *Ludlow Advertiser* 7 November 1914.
3. *Church Stretton Advertiser* 29 October & 5 December 1914 and 14 & 28 January 1915; *Bridgnorth Journal* 13 February 1915; *Ludlow Advertiser* 31 October & 12 December 1914, and 20 & 30 January & 27 March 1915; *Bitterley and Ludlow Parish Magazine* Dec. 1914, Shropshire Archives; *Clun Valley Parochial Magazine* Sept. – Dec. 1914, Shropshire Archives Ref. P137/H/1.
4. *Bridgnorth Journal* 21 November 1914 and 23 January 1915; *Church Stretton Advertiser* 26 November 1914; *Ludlow Advertiser* 31 October, 21 & 28 November 1914 and 1 & 30 January 1915.
5. *Ludlow Advertiser* 30 January, 13 March, 9 October & 4 December 1915 and 19 February 1916; *Church Stretton Advertiser* 4 March 1915; *Bridgnorth Journal* 22 May 1915.
6. *Ludlow Advertiser* 14 October & 2 December 1916 and 31 March 1917; *Bridgnorth Journal* 27 January 1917; *Church Stretton Advertiser* 25 October 1917.

David Kellock Royal Welsh Fusiliers of 48, Broad Street, Ludlow.
7. *Bridgnorth Journal* 23 February & 16 March 1918; *Ludlow Advertiser* 9, 16 March & 22 June 1918.
8. *Church Stretton Advertiser* 17 September 1914; *Ludlow Advertiser* 7 November 1914 and 16 January 1919; *Bridgnorth Journal* 22 August 1914 and 17 April 1915; *Bitterley and Ludlow Parish Magazine op.cit.* Sept. and Oct. 1914; *Clun Valley Parochial Magazine* Sept., Oct. and Dec. 1914, Shropshire Archives Ref. P137/H/1; *Rural Deanery of Bridgnorth Parish Magazine*, Shropshire Archives Ref. P.40/H/1/5 1911-1916.
9. *Church Stretton Advertiser* 8 July 1915, 21 December 1916 and 14 February 1918; *Bridgnorth Journal* 5 January 1918; *Ludlow Advertiser* 22 March 1919.
10. Letter from George Rogers of 132 Corve Street in *Ludlow Advertiser* 30 October 1915.
11. Letter from Arthur Phillips in *Church Stretton Advertiser* 15 July 1915.
12. *Rural Deanery of Bridgnorth Parish Magazine op.cit.* April 1916 regarding George Edward Gatacre.
13. *Ludlow Advertiser* 29 August, 24 October & 14 November 1914.
14. *Ludlow Advertiser* 17 October 1914, 17 April & 24 July 1915 and 24 February 1917.
15. *Ludlow Advertiser* 24 April, 12 June, 10 July & 25 September 1915; *The Ludlovian* Feb. 1915.
16. *Ludlow Advertiser* 23 September 1916.
17. Letter from W. Painter to his stepbrother George Owen of Church Street, Bishop's Castle quoted in *Ludlow Advertiser* 5 December 1914.
18. Letter from Ernest Ovens to his sister from a hospital bed in France dated 30 August 1915 in *Ludlow Advertiser* 11 September 1915.
19. *Clun Valley Parochial Magazine op.cit.* Nov. 1915 to Jan. 1916; *The Ludlovian* Feb. 1916; letter dated 7 February 1916 from John Lucas in *Ludlow Advertiser* 4 March 1916.
20. *Ludlow Advertiser* 11 November & 2 December 1916; *Church Stretton Advertiser* 18 January 1917 and 2 December 1915.
21. *Ludlow Advertiser* 17 March 1917 and 2 December 1916.
22. *Ludlow Advertiser* 8 December 1917.
23. Letter from George Brown in *Ludlow Advertiser* 5 January 1918.
24. Letter from William John Munns in *Ludlow Advertiser* 5 January 1918.
25. Letter from George Ashton Chapman in *Ludlow Advertiser* 5 January 1918.
26. *Ludlow Advertiser* 25 November 1916, 30 November & 7 December 1918; *Church Stretton Advertiser* 6 December 1917.
27. Letter from Charles Edward Amphlett in *Church Stretton Advertiser* 23 January 1919.

28. Letter from Alfred William Jones and Herbert Handley in *Ludlow Advertiser* 15 May 1915.

29. *Ludlow Advertiser* 17 July 1915. The soldier was James Elisha Bishop.

30. Letter from Leonard Lythall in *Bridgnorth Journal* 12 June 1915.

31. Interview with Pte Herbert Handley in *Ludlow Advertiser* 29 September 1917.

32. Letters from James Bishop, Herbert Handley & Alfred Jones in *Ludlow Advertiser* 16 October & 25 September 1915.

33. Interview with Herbert Handley *Ludlow Advertiser op.cit.* and speech by William Ashwood in *Bridgnorth Journal* 18 January 1919.

34. For information on work of the KSLI POW Fund I am indebted to Major W. De B. Wood (ed.) *The History of the KSLI in the Great War 1914-1918* (London, 1925) pp.331-338 and speech by committee member made at Bridgnorth Town Hall in *Bridgnorth Journal* 22 June 1918.

35. *Ludlow Advertiser* 16 March 1918.

36. *Bridgnorth Journal* January 1919.

37. Arthur Phillips, Thomas Meyrick & Charles Wilcox in *Ludlow Advertiser* 18 May 1918; Harry Harries in *Ludlow Advertiser* 22 June 1918; *Bridgnorth Journal* 15 June 1918.

38. *Bridgnorth Journal* 1 June 1918.

39. Letter from John Powell in *Ludlow Advertiser* 5 October 1918.

40. Arthur Phillips in *Parish of Lydbury North War Record 1914-1918* p.15 held in Bishop's Castle History Record Centre, ref. 0289.

41. George Hamer in *Ludlow Advertiser* 26 January 1918.

42. *Ludlow Advertiser* 12 January 1918.

43. *Ludlow Advertiser* 26 January & 9 February 1918.

44. *Ludlow Advertiser* 16 February 1918.

45. *Church Stretton Advertiser* 7 October 1915; *Ludlow Advertiser* 5 January & 16 March 1918.

46. *Bridgnorth Journal* 2 June 1917; *Ludlow Advertiser* 4 August 1917, 22, 29 September & 6 October 1917.

47. William John Munns in *Ludlow Advertiser* 27 October 1917.

48. *Ludlow Advertiser* 20 April, 28 September 1918 and 18 September 1915.

49. *Bridgnorth Journal* 9 June 1917 and 9 March 1918; *Rural Deanery of Bridgnorth Parish Magazine op.cit.* Dec. 1917 and Dec. 1918; *Ludlow Advertiser* 2 February 1918.

50. *Ludlow Advertiser* 17 June & 9 September 1916; *Church Stretton Advertiser* 7 September 1916; *Bridgnorth Journal* 9 September 1916.

51. *Bridgnorth Journal* 21 October 1916; *Church Stretton Advertiser* 1 November 1916; *Ludlow Advertiser* 27 October 1917.

52. *Ludlow Advertiser* 9 September & 4 October 1916, 24 November 1917, 25 May & 8 June 1918; *Church Stretton Advertiser* 17 May & 21 June 1917.

53. *Church Stretton Advertiser* 25 October 1917; *Ludlow Advertiser* 20 July 1918; Pamela Horn 'The employment of elementary schoolchildren in agriculture 1914-1918' in *History of Education* (Journal of the History of Education Society) (1983), 12:3, pp.203-215; *Ludlow Rural Deanery Magazine* Oct. 1916, Shropshire Archives.

54. Wood, *History of the KSLI op.cit.* pp.325-331; *Bridgnorth Journal* 22 August 1914 and 22 March & 26 April 1919; Valerie Roberts *The Story of Much Wenlock Hospital* (priv. pub. 2003) pp.13-16. See also *The Red Cross in Shropshire 1915-1917* (Shrewsbury, 1918).

55. *Church Stretton Advertiser* 15 June 1915, 14 September 1916 and 22 May 1919; *Wellington Journal* 12 December 1914 and 28 December 1918.

56. Churchstoke Recorders, *Memories are made of this* (priv. pub.); *Church Stretton Advertiser* 18 February 1915 and 30 March 1916.

57. *Leintwardine History Group Journal* Issue 15, March 2006; *Bitterley and Ludlow Parish Magazine op.cit* Feb. 1915; *Clun Valley Parochial Magazine* April 1919, Shropshire Archives ref. P137/H/1; *Wellington Journal* 28 December 1918; *Bridgnorth Journal* 13 February 1915.

58. Information supplied by the archivist of The Red Cross; *Ludlow Advertiser* 17 August 1918; *Church Stretton Advertiser* 20 February 1920; *Wellington Journal* 28 December 1918.

59. *Ludlow Advertiser* 13 April 1918; *Lydbury North War Record op.cit.* p.24; *Wellington Journal* 28 December 1918.

60. *Church Stretton Advertiser* 7 January 1915.

61. *Bridgnorth Journal* 2 & 9 January & 20 March 1915.

62. *Ludlow Advertiser* 15 May 1915; *Bridgnorth Journal* 15 May & 9 October 1915, 16 & 23 September & 21 October 1915.

63. Roberts *Much Wenlock Hospital op.cit.; Ludlow Advertiser* 5 July 1915, 15 & 22 June 1918; *Wellington Journal* 12 June 1915; *Church Stretton Advertiser* 23 September 1915.

64. *Ludlow Advertiser* 30 September & 7 October 1916, 5 January & 15 June 1918.

65. *Ludlow Advertiser* 12 October 1918; *Bridgnorth Journal* 29 December 1917 and 12 & 19 January 1918.

66. *Bridgnorth Journal* 11 November 1916; *Ludlow Advertiser* 12 May 1917. The soldier was Walter Chisholm Sanders.

67. *Ludlow Advertiser* 15 & 22 September 1917.

68. E. Humphries quoted in *Church Stretton Advertiser* 18 July 1918.

69. Letter from 412352 Cpl Thomas K. Court 21st Canadian Regiment dated 24 November 1916. www.canadianletters.ca.

70. *Bridgnorth Journal* 9 February 1918; *Ludlow Advertiser* 30 March 1918.

71. *Leintwardine Historical Group Journal* Issue 15 March 2006; *Church Stretton Advertiser* 16 November 1916.

72. Churchstoke Recorders *Memories op.cit.; Ludlow Advertiser* 24 August 1918, 1 September 1917 and 10 August 1918; *Church Stretton Advertiser* 23 & 30 September 1915.

73. *Bridgnorth Journal* 3 June 1916; *Church Stretton Advertiser* 18 October 1917; *Ludlow Advertiser* 8 May 1915 and 9 December 1916.

74. *Ludlow Advertiser* 6 May 1916; *Church Stretton Advertiser* 14 September & 1 November 1916; *Bitterley and Ludlow Parish Magazine op.cit.* June 1915; *Rural Deanery of Bridgnorth Parish Magazine op.cit.* June 1915.

75. *Ludlow Advertiser* 8 July 1916; *Church Stretton Advertiser* 14 February 1918.

Chapter 4

1. *Ludlow Advertiser* 19 September 1914.

2. *Ludlow Advertiser* 2 January 1915.

3. *Ludlow Advertiser* 15 May 1915.

4. *Ludlow Advertiser* 17 October 1914.

5. *Bridgnorth Journal* 13 March & 17 April 1915.

6. *Ludlow Advertiser* 4 March 1916; *Bridgnorth Journal* 12 February 1916.

7. *Bridgnorth Journal* 21 October 1916.

8. *Ludlow Advertiser* 9 December 1916, 13 January & 6 October 1917.

9. *Ludlow Advertiser* 15 April, 7 October, 14 October & 4 November 1916; *Bridgnorth Journal* 21 October 1916.

10. Letter in *Ludlow Advertiser* 22 September 1917.

11. *Church Stretton Advertiser* 15 November 1917 and 19 January 1918; *Ludlow Advertiser* 6 & 20 October 1917, 9 February & 7 September 1918.

12. *Ludlow Advertiser* 20 October 1917, 23 February & 18 May 1918; *Bridgnorth Journal* 24 August 1918.

13. *Ludlow Advertiser* 17 August & 5 October 1918.

14. *Church Stretton Advertiser* 19 & 26 September 1918; *Ludlow Advertiser* 26 October 1918.

15. *Ludlow Advertiser* 29 January 1916 and 20 October 1917.

16. *Ludlow Advertiser* 3 April 1915.

17. *Ludlow Advertiser* 15 January 1916.

18. *Ludlow Advertiser* 29 January & 15 February 1916.

19. *Ludlow Advertiser* 3 April 1915; *Wellington Journal* 4 March & 24 June 1916; Heather Williams *The Lure of the Land: A Century of Education at Harper Adams* (priv. pub. 2000) Chapter 5.

20. *Bridgnorth Journal* 17 April & 11 December 1915, 22 January & 26 February 1916; *Church Stretton Advertiser* 22 August 1918; *Wellington Journal* 15 April 1916.

21. *Rural Deanery of Bridgnorth Parish Magazine* July 1916, Shropshire Archives Ref. P40/H/1/5 1911-1916; *Church Stretton Advertiser* 17 January 1918; *The Lure of the Land op.cit.* Chapter 5.

22. *Bridgnorth Journal* 11 December 1915 and 22 January 1916; *Ludlow Advertiser* 6 November 1915.

23. *Church Stretton Advertiser* 30 August 1917 and 1 August 1918; *Bridgnorth Journal* 1 June 1918.

24. *Ludlow Advertiser* 19 June 1915; *Church Stretton Advertiser* 17 May 1917; *Bridgnorth Journal* 26 June 1915.

25. Frank Large and Mike Stammers *Finnish Sailors in British Forests'* (priv. pub.). My thanks to Rona Cobb of Ditton Priors and Dermot Edwards of Lismore, Co. Waterford for drawing my attention to this.

26. *Church Stretton Advertiser* 30 November 1916; *Ludlow Advertiser* 8 December 1919; *Wellington Journal* 3 March 1917 and 3 August 1918.

27. *Bridgnorth Journal* 9 March & 31 August 1918; *Ludlow Advertiser* 16 & 30 March 1918; *Church Stretton Advertiser* 22 August 1918; *Clun Valley Parochial Magazine* Oct. 1918, Shropshire Archives ref. P137/H/1.

28. *Ludlow Advertiser* 24 August 1918.

29. *Ludlow Advertiser* 6 July 1918 and 12 July 1919.

30. *Ludlow Advertiser* 19 & 26 July 1919.

31. *Ludlow Advertiser* 5 May 1917; *Bridgnorth Journal* 20 October 1917; *Church Stretton Advertiser* 14 March 1918.

32. *Bridgnorth Journal* 20 October 1917; *Ludlow Advertiser* 17 November 1917; *Church Stretton Advertiser* 10 May 1917.

33. *Church Stretton Advertiser* 24 May 1917; *Ludlow Advertiser* 13 January 1917.

34. *Ludlow Advertiser* 10, 17 March & 5 May 1917; *Bridgnorth Journal* 20 October 1917; *Church Stretton Advertiser* 24 May 1917.

35. *Church Stretton Advertiser* 3 & 24 May 1917; *Ludlow Advertiser* 1 November 1917.

36. *Ludlow Advertiser* 27 December 1916.

37. *Ludlow Advertiser* 29 January & 28 April 1917.

38. *Ludlow Advertiser* 14 & 21 October 1916 and 12 May 1917.

39. *Ludlow Advertiser* 25 August 1917.

40. *Bridgnorth Journal* 20 October 1917.

41. *Ludlow Advertiser* 6 October & 27 October 1917.

42. *Ludlow Advertiser* 15 December 1917.

43. *Ludlow Advertiser* 2, 16 & 30 March 1918.

44. *Bridgnorth Journal* 3 August 1918.

45. *Bridgnorth Journal* 10 November 1917.

46. *Church Stretton Advertiser* 29 November 1917; *Ludlow Advertiser* 16 March, 15 June & 19 October 1918.

47. *Ludlow Advertiser* 19 February 1918; *Church Stretton Advertiser* 28 February 1918.
48. *Ludlow Advertiser* 12 & 19 January 1918; *Bridgnorth Journal* 2 February 1918.
49. *Ludlow Advertiser* 7 June & 5 July 1917; *Church Stretton Advertiser* 18 April 1918.
50. *Ludlow Advertiser* 14 & 21 July 1917 and 6 April 1918.
51. *Church Stretton Advertiser* 4 October 1917; *Ludlow Advertiser* 23 March 1918; *Ludlow Rural Deanery Magazine op.cit.* Sept. and Nov. 1917; Rural Deanery of Bridgnorth *op.cit.* July 1917n.
52. *Ludlow Advertiser* 23 February 1918.
53. *Ludlow Advertiser* 26 January 1918.
54. *Ludlow Advertiser* 2 & 9 March 1918.
55. *Ludlow Advertiser* 16 March & 13 April 1918.
56. *Ludlow Advertiser* 11 September 1915.
57. *Church Stretton Advertiser* 19 April & 1 November 1917.
58. *Ludlow Advertiser* 22 September & 10 November 1917, 6 April & 27 July 1918.
59. *Ludlow Advertiser* 14 September 1918.
60. *Church Stretton Advertiser* 19 September 1918.
61. *Ludlow Advertiser* 14 September 1918.
62. Most details regarding allowances and pensions are taken from E. Sylvia Pankhurst *The Home Front* (London, 1932).
63. Her husband was Alfred Joseph Edwards. See *Wellington Journal* 8 January 1916.
64. *Ludlow Advertiser* 10 March & 27 October 1917 and 7 September 1918.
65. *Ludlow Advertiser* 16 March 1918.
66. *Church Stretton Advertiser* 15 February 1917.
67. *Church Stretton Advertiser* 10 May & 26 April 1917.
68. *Church Stretton Advertiser* 4 November 1915; *Ludlow Advertiser* 18 September 1915.
69. *Church Stretton Advertiser* 14 June & 12 July 1917 regarding George Henry Vaughan.
70. *Church Stretton Advertiser* 19 July 1917; *Ludlow Advertiser* 17 August 1918.
71. *Ludlow Advertiser* 15 September 1917 regarding Arthur Williams.
72. *Church Stretton Advertiser* 15 March 1917 regarding Thomas Bissell; *Church Stretton Advertiser* 3 May 1917.
73. Minute Book of the Ludlow Poor Law Guardians 28 October 1918, Shropshire Archives PL9/2/1/26.
74. Arthur Davies in *Ludlow Advertiser* 5 May 1917; Gustave Charlton in *Church Stretton Advertiser* 30 August 1917; *Ludlow Advertiser* 16 February 1918.
75. Harry Hatfield in *Ludlow Advertiser* 21 July 1917; Edwin Thomas Shutt in *Church Stretton Advertiser* 19 July 1917; William Downes in *Church Stretton Advertiser* 7 June 1917.
76. Thomas Parr in *Church Stretton Advertiser* 3 July 1917; *Ludlow Advertiser* 5 January 1918.
77. *Church Stretton Advertiser* 15 February & 15 March 1917.
78. *Ludlow Advertiser* 12 January & 22 January 1918.

Chapter 5
1. *Clun Valley Parochial Magazine* June 1918, Shropshire Archives ref. P137/H/1 regarding Edward William Meadmore.
2. George Lucas in *Wellington Journal* 12 June 1915.
3. Neville Stones 'Eastward Voyage' in *The Cocaonut Tree and After: Memoirs of the 4th KSLI* (KSLI Regimental Museum, 2004 reprint) pp.5-8.
4. Letter from Henry Steenton to Mr J. Keyte of Old Street dated 29 December 1914 quoted in *Ludlow Advertiser* 20 February 1915.
5. Letter from Benjamin Nicholas to John Diggle, Headmaster of the National School dated 26 April 1915 quoted in *Ludlow Advertiser* 5 June 1915.
6. Letter from William Griffiths 4th to his father dated 4 April 1915 from Singapore quoted in *Ludlow Advertiser* 22 May 1915.
7. Letter from George Kimber quoted in *Church Stretton Advertiser* 3 June 1915.
8. Letter from Bernard William Turner quoted in *Bridgnorth Journal* 26 June 1915.
9. Letter from Frederick Charles Brookes to John Diggle dated 12 February 1915 quoted in *Ludlow Advertiser* 20 March 1915.
10. Stones 'Eastward Voyage' *Cocaonut Tree op.cit.* p.8.
11. Letter from Frederick Charles Brooke dated 12 February 1915 quoted in *Ludlow Advertiser* 20 March 1915.
12. Letter from Joseph Ernest Davies to John Diggle dated 18 March 1915 quoted in *Ludlow Advertiser* 24 April 1915.
13. Letter from A.W. Armstrong quoted in *Bridgnorth Journal* 29 April 1916; *The Cocaonut Tree op.cit* pp.19-22.
14. Letter from Frank Maddocks RAMC to Mr W. Hailstone quoted in *Ludlow Advertiser* 3 July 1915.
15. Letter from Thomas Kyffin Corbishley to his father dated 9 February 1917 quoted in *Ludlow Advertiser* 17 March 1917.
16. Letter from William Ernest Jones dated 28 July 1916 quoted in *Church Stretton Advertiser* dated 30 March 1916.
17. Anon Letter from a 'Ludlovian' quoted in *Ludlow Advertiser* 30 March 1918.
18. Letter from Edward Preece to his mother dated 4 November 1914 quoted in *Ludlow Advertiser* 21 November 1914. The other men he mentions are Francis Pounds, John Albert Didlick and John Henry Baron.
19. Interview with Owen Owen about Thomas William Bright in *Wellington Journal* 14 November 1914.

20. William Bishop, Thomas Henry Bishop and James Elisha Bishop in *Bitterley and Ludlow Parish Magazine* July 1915, Shropshire Archives.

21. Harry France, aged 19, and Edward France in *Rural Deanery of Bridgnorth Parish Magazine* Aug. 1915, Shropshire Archives ref. P40/H/1/5 1911-1916.

22. Sidney Greatwich and Frederick James Greatwich, aged 23, in *Bridgnorth Journal* 22 July 1916.

23. William Orlando Francis and Thomas Francis in *Ludlow Rural Deanery Magazine* May 1916, Shropshire Archives.

24. Alfred Jones, aged 22, and Richard Jones in *Ludlow Rural Deanery Magazine op.cit.* Sept. 1916.

25. Stanley Bowen and Edward Arthur Bowen in *Bridgnorth Journal* 2 September 1916.

26. Letter from John Lewis dated 30 Nov 1916 in *Ludlow Rural Deanery Magazine op.cit.* Feb. 1917.

27. Letter from John Oliver 5th Battalion KSLI to his father dated 27 September 1915 quoted in *Bridgnorth Journal* dated 2 October 1915. The two casualties mentioned are C. Harry Johnson and Thomas Alfred Bowen.

28. Postcard dated 28 September 1915 and reprinted in *Bridgnorth Journal* 16 October 1915.

29. Letter from Harold Victor Kershaw to his parents quoted in *Ludlow Advertiser* 29 June 1918. His brother was Ernest Granville Kershaw.

30. Letter from Thomas Kyffin Corbishley *op.cit.* quoted in *Ludlow Advertiser* dated 1 January 916. His brother was Frederick Henry (Harry) Corbishley.

31. Letter from George Davies to his parents quoted in *Ludlow Advertiser* dated 24 June 1915. His comrades mentioned were Robert Morris, Walter John Swain, and Albert Bright.

32. Letter from George Davies *op.cit.* to his father quoted in *Ludlow Advertiser* 9 Octber 1915. Thomas Smith was later officially listed as being killed in action.

33. Ernest A. Drew in *Bridgnorth Journal* 30 October 1915. The other men were Frederick Bright and Cyril Boucher.

34. *Ludlow Advertiser* 25 May 1918.

35. Letter from W. Scott to Albert Smallman, 5 St. Leonard's Steps, Bridgnorth quoted in *Bridgnorth Journal* 13 January 1917.

36. R.A. Jones in *The Ludlovian* Feb. 1916; letter from George Rogers to Mr J. Barker, headmaster of the British School, Old Street. Men mentioned were Ernest Stanley Stead, John (Jack) Rogers, Thomas William Pinches and George Benjamin (Ben) Price in *Ludlow Advertiser* 30 October 1915.

37. Letter from J. Gilbert Griffiths to John Diggle dated 24 October 1915 quoted in *Ludlow Advertiser* 6 November 1915. Men named were Harold Vale and Ernest Arthur Lewis.

38. Letter from Joseph Henry Peachey to John Diggle dated 28 November 1915 and quoted in *Ludlow Advertiser* January 1916. He refers to Joseph Ernest Davies.

39. Letter from Benjamin Nicholas quoted in *Ludlow Advertiser* 5 June 1915. The men mentioned were George Henson and William Minton.

40. Letter from Charles A. Francis to John Diggle quoted in *Ludlow Advertiser* 26 June 1915.

41. Edward Cooper. *Bridgnorth Journal* 19 January 1918.

42. Letter from Sister G.M. Allen to father of Walter Sherry dated 3 July 1915 and quoted in *Bridgnorth Journal* 10 July 1915.

43. *Ludlow Advertiser* 29 September 1917.

44. Colin John Wyld McMichael in *Bridgnorth Journal* 31 August & 14 September 1918.

45. *Ludlow Advertiser* 28 April 1917; *Church Stretton Advertiser* 28 June & 5 July 1917.

46. Letter from Robert Harold (Harry) Sutton to his father quoted in *Church Stretton Advertiser* 14 April 1917.

47. Letter from Harold T. Armstrong to his father quoted in *Bridgnorth Journal* 29 July 1916.

48. Thomas Thornley in *Ludlow Advertiser* 20 October 1917.

49. George Henry Taylor in *Bridgnorth Journal* 20 & 27 April 1918.

50. W.J. Southerton in *Church Stretton Advertiser* 28 September 1916.

51. Francis John Shingler in *Bridgnorth Journal* 27 November 1915.

52. Letter from a Cpl. Jennings 3rd Battalion KSLI. The soldiers were Robert Ward and Arthur Wait. *Ludlow Advertiser* 13 March 1915.

53. Eric F. Burton in *Bridgnorth Journal* 5 & 12 June 1915.

54. Arthur Mason, Charles R. Cornes and Alfred Herman Higgins in *Bridgnorth Journal* 24 November, 8 & 15 December 1917.

55. The brother who died was John Tennant. *Ludlow Advertiser* 17 February 1917.

56. Eli Jones in *Bridgnorth Journal* 8 April 1916.

57. Alfred Thomas Reynolds in *Ludlow Advertiser* 6 April 1918; Llewellyn Bennett in *Church Stretton Advertiser* 19 August 1915, and 28 June 1917 regarding George Wilkes.

58. Leslie O. Hughes in *Bridgnorth Journal* 23 September 1916.

59. William Gittens RGA and George Walter Jones Naval Division in *Bridgnorth Journal*.

60. Archie Brown in *Bridgnorth Journal* 8 December 1917.

61. Probably Archie Smith of 69 Broad Street, Ludlow in *Ludlow Advertiser* 30 March 1918.

62. Phillip Henry Jones in *Ludlow Advertiser* 21 April 1917.

63. George Brookes in *Church Stretton Advertiser* 9 September 1915.
64. W. Edgell Piper in *Bridgnorth Journal* 1 July 1916; H.M. Spink in *Ludlow Advertiser* 22 September 1917.
65. Thomas Henry Taggart in *Bridgnorth Journal* 28 August, 4 September & 18 December 1915.
66. Thomas Taylor in *Bridgnorth Journal* 2 October 1915.
67. William Edward Woosnam in *Ludlow Advertiser* 29 June 1918.
68. Timothy Tipton in *Ludlow Advertiser* 1 June 1918.
69. Thomas Thornley in *Ludlow Advertiser* 27 April 1918.
70. Joseph (Joe) Whittall in *Ludlow Advertiser* 27 May 1916.
71. Charles John Davis in *Ludlow Advertiser* 16 November 1918.
72. Frederick Davies in *Bridgnorth Journal* 6 July 1918.
73. Donald Edward Easthope in *Church Stretton Advertiser* 2 December 1915.
74. Alfred William Stokes in *Bridgnorth Journal* 16 December 1916.
75. Frederick (Fred) Charles Brereton in *Church Stretton Advertiser* 22 November 1917.
76. (Charles) Maurice Harley in *Rural Deanery of Bridgnorth Parish Magazine op.cit.* Oct. 1918.
77. Francis W. Packer in *Ludlow Advertiser* 22 June 1918.
78. Albert John Johnson in *Bridgnorth Journal* 20 July 1918.
79. Arthur Horace Steadman Southwell in *Bridgnorth Journal* 9 December 1916 and December 1917.
80. John Husband in *Church Stretton Advertiser* 12 September 1918.
81. Edward (Ned) Reginald Davies in *Ludlow Advertiser* 8 June 1918.
82. John (Jack) Harrington in *Ludlow Rural Deanery Magazine op.cit.* Sept 1917
83. Ewan Mitchell in *Bridgnorth Journal* 20 July 1918.
84. Clement G. Deighton in *Bridgnorth Journal* 8 July 1916.
85. Frank Griffiths in *Ludlow Advertiser* 8 June 1918.
86. Henry (Harry) Evans in *Bridgnorth Journal* 8 June 1918.
87. Frederick Arthur Lawley in *Bridgnorth Journal* 6 July 1918.
88. Albert Edwards KSLI of The Priory, Church Stretton and Thomas Shuker of Greenfields, All Stretton.
89. Harry Garmston in *Church Stretton Advertiser* 18 July 1918.
90. John Pugh in *Ludlow Advertiser* 30 November 1918.
91. Percy J. Griffiths in *Bridgnorth Journal* 27 July 1918.
92. Horace Jones in *Bridgnorth Journal* 2 December 1916.
93. Letter from Lt F. Kinchin-Smith about George Thomas Lloyd in *Bridgnorth Journal* September 1918.
94. Arthur Vaughan in *Ludlow Advertiser* 29 September 1917.
95. Thomas Dean in *Ludlow Advertiser* 15 December 1917.
96. Herbert James in *Bridgnorth Journal* 4 September 1915.
97. Harold Wellings in *Church Stretton Advertiser* 16 May 1918.
98. Letter from E. Crudge to Revd R.B. Southwell of Chetton regarding Walter James Thomas. *Bridgnorth Journal* 2 October 1915.
99. Letter from F. Hilton RFA to the parents of Thomas William James in *Bridgnorth Journal* 31 August 1918.
100. Edward Harry Cook in *Bridgnorth Journal* 23 February 1918; Arthur Edwin Hayward in *Wellington Journal* 18 December 1915.
101. Frederick Charles Anslow, Edward Harry Cook and Harry Wilcox.
102. John Robert (Bob) Halford in *Ludlow Advertiser* 9 September 1916.
103. James Morse in *Ludlow Advertiser* 19 January 1918.
104. Miss Gladys Maud Preece lived at Brook Villa, Kerry Road, Bishop's Castle and her fiancée was Francis Hancocks. *Church Stretton Advertiser* 21 October 1915.
105. Letter from Harry Langford to Annie Owen of Smithfield Road, Much Wenlock about her husband Charles Owen quoted in *Wellington Journal* 4 September 1915.
106. Letter from Ernest Granville Kershaw to his parents dated 12 September 1915 quoted in *Ludlow Advertiser* 9 October 1915.
107. Andrew Ernest Tuckley in *Bridgnorth Journal* 20 October 1917.
108. Letter from Geoffrey E. Roden to his mother quoted in *Bridgnorth Journal* 14 August 1915.
109. News of death of Walter William Fewtrell in *Ludlow Advertiser* 26 February 1916; letter from H. Bengry to the parents of Charles Gwilliam quoted in *Church Stretton Advertiser* 7 September 1916.
110. Harry France in *Bridgnorth Journal* July 1918.
111. Letter from Sapper E. Cooke to his parents regarding Horace (Frank) Bill quoted in *Bridgnorth Journal* 22 July 1916.
112. Letter from Major M Barnes 1st Battalion Scots Guards to Mrs Mary Ann Davies, mother of John Davies quoted in *Ludlow Advertiser* 7 October 1916.
113. Letter to Mrs Mary Blakeway from commanding officer of John Edward Blakeway quoted in *Ludlow Advertiser* 22 June 1918.
114. James A. Keenan in *Church Stretton Advertiser* 4 May 1916.

115. Letter to the parents of Edwin Robert (Bob) Tong quoted in *Ludlow Advertiser* 1 September 1917.

116. Letter to mother of William Evans quoted in *Ludlow Advertiser* 29 September 1917.

117. Sydney Milman in *Bridgnorth Journal* 8 April 1916 and Sydney Fellows in *Bridgnorth Journal* 7 October 1917.

118. Letter to parents of George Brocklehurst quoted in *Ludlow Advertiser* 30 September 1916.

119. Letter to the widow of Thomas Jones quoted in *Ludlow Advertiser* 21 September 1918.

120. Letter from the Chaplain of the 10th Casualty Clearing Station to the mother of Mark Jones quoted in *Bridgnorth Journal* 18 May 1918.

121. Letter from E.O. Schofield, Sister in charge of the 20th Casualty Clearing station at Hilly, near Amiens, to parents of George Henry Humphries quoted in *Ludlow Advertiser* 5 October 1918.

122. Derwent Christopher Turnbull in *Church Stretton Advertiser* 25 March 1915.

123. Letter from Major A.J. Reddie 1st Battalion South Wales Borderers to Mrs Garnett-Botfield of the Hut, Bishop's Castle dated 11 May 1915 regarding her son Alfred Clulow Fitzgerald Garnett-Botfield; letter from Pte Seabourne to Mrs Garnett-Botfield; letter from Edward Lowe to his parents quoted in *Ludlow Advertiser* 15 May 1915.

124. Letters to the parents of Nairn Jones quoted in *Ludlow Advertiser* 19 August 1916.

125. Letter from Major F.R. Hicks 1st Hampshire Regiment regarding Cecil Frederick Brown quoted in *Ludlow Advertiser* 10 April 1915.

126. Leslie Charles Smith in *Bridgnorth Grammar School Magazine* July 1915.

127. Alfred Edward Cadwallader in *Ludlow Advertiser* 12 June 1915.

128. Letter to William and Sarah Price regarding their son Samuel Price quoted in *Ludlow Advertiser* 2 February 1918.

129. Letter to the widow of Charles Tristram quoted in *Ludlow Advertiser* 26 September 1918.

130. Letter to widow of William Nicholas quoted in *Ludlow Advertiser* 14 April 1917.

131. William Alexander Lyndon in *Clun Valley Parochial Magazine op.cit.* March 1916.

132. Samuel Edwards in *Wellington Journal* 3 July 1915.

133. William Douglas Marston in *Church Stretton Advertiser* 6, 13 & 20 December 1917.

134. Charles Bertram Taggart in *Bridgnorth Journal* 9 September 1916.

135. S. John Allen in *Bridgnorth Journal* 9 February 1918; Charles Harold Badlan in *Ludlow Advertiser* 20 October 1917.

136. Donald Edward Easthope in *Bitterley and Ludlow Parish Magazine op.cit.* Dec. 1915.

137. George Millichamp in *Bitterley and Ludlow Rural Deanery Magazine op.cit.* Oct. and Dec. 1917.

138. Arthur James Benbow in *Bridgnorth Journal* 26 August 1916; *Rural Deanery of Bridgnorth Parish Magazine op.cit.* Sept. 1916.

139. Douglas G.L. Cunnington in *Bridgnorth Journal* 5 October 1918.

Chapter 6

1. *Ludlow Advertiser* 16 November 1918.

2. *Bridgnorth Journal* 16 November 1918.

3. *Church Stretton Advertiser* 14 November 1918; *Clun Valley Parochial Magazine* Jan. 1919, Shropshire Archives ref. P137/H/1.

4. *Wellington Journal* 5 July 1919.

5. *Ludlow Advertiser* 26 July 1919.

6. *Bridgnorth Journal* 2 August 1919.

7. Timothy Reginald Tipton, Vincent Eccles Lennox and James Wilson in *Bridgnorth Journal* 26 July 1919.

8. *Wellington Journal* 19 & 26 July 1919; *Bridgnorth Journal* 26 July 1919; *Church Stretton Advertiser* 24 July 1919; *Ludlow Advertiser* 26 July 1919.

9. *Church Stretton Advertiser* 31 July 1919; *Wellington Journal* 26 July 1919.

10. John Francis George and Edward Lewis in *Church Stretton Advertiser* 21 November 1918; *Ludlow Advertiser* 30 November 1918

11. Maurice Price (Permission of Miriam Ellison).

12. Albert Leonard Egan, Ernest George Corfield and Francis (Frank) Leonard Edwards in *Bridgnorth Journal* 16 & 30 November & 7 December 1918.

13. Harry Darby and Edwin Mason. *Ludlow Rural Deanery Magazine* Dec. 1918 – Feb. 1919 in Shropshire Archives.

14. George Simkiss, Alfred Roberts and Charles Wilcox in *Church Stretton Advertiser* 23 January 1919; *Bridgnorth Journal* 22 February 1919; Parish of Lydbury North War Record 1914-1918 in Bishop's Castle Local History Collection Ref. 0289 p.15.

15. Edward (Ned) Reginald Davies in *Church Stretton Advertiser* 23 January 1919.

16. *Bridgnorth Journal* 1 February 1919.

17. *Church Stretton Advertiser* 23 January 1919.

18. John Ernest Morgan in *Ludlow Advertiser* 6 September 1919.

19. Tom Law, George Law, William Griffiths, Edgar A. Ball and Thomas Lewis in *Wellington Journal* 30 November, 7 & 28 December 1918 and 18 January 1919.

20. George Edwards in *Church Stretton Advertiser* 23 January 1919.

21. *Church Stretton Advertiser* 30 January 1919; *Bridgnorth Journal* 18 January 1919; *Ludlow Rural Deanery Magazine* Oct. 1919, Shropshire Archives.

22. Edward Bradley Bate, Norman Stump Gilkes, George William Dunn and Thomas Lewis in *Church Stretton Advertiser* 9 January 1919; *Ludlow Advertiser* 14 December 1918; *Ludlow Rural Deanery Magazine op.cit.* March 1919.

23. Robert Morris, Harry Thomas Humphreys and William Henry Wilding in *Church Stretton Advertiser* 24 October 1918; *Ludlow Rural Deanery Magazine op.cit.* Feb. 1919; *Bridgnorth Journal* 28 December 1918.

24. George Henry Richards, Leonard Delo and Frederick N. Davies in *Bridgnorth Journal* February 1919; *Ludlow Rural Deanery Magazine op.cit.* Dec. 1918.

25. *Bridgnorth Journal* 14 June & 23 August 1919; *Ludlow Advertiser* 2 & 30 August 1919.

26. *Clun Valley Parochial Magazine op.cit.* Sept. and Oct. 1919; *Rural Deanery of Bridgnorth Parish Magazine* Aug. 1919, Shropshire Archives ref. P40/H/1/6 1917-1921; Ditton Priors Parochial Log Book Vol. 2 Feb 1920 (my thanks to Rona Cobb for bringing this to my attention); *Wellington Journal* 11 January 1919; *Ludlow Advertiser* 10 January & 7 February 1920.

27. Arthur Hayward and William George Jones in *Bridgnorth Journal* 28 December 1918; *Ludlow Rural Deanery Magazine op.cit.* March 1919.

28. George Richard Husbands, George Henry Brunt, Alfred Henry Rutter and George Bywater in *Bridgnorth Journal* 28 December 1918 and 14 June 1919; *Clun Valley Parochial Magazine op.cit; Rural Deanery of Bridgnorth Parish Magazine op.cit.* Jan. 1920.

29. MOH Report 1918 for Ludlow Borough reported in *Ludlow Advertiser* 13 September 1919.

30. Edward Sheldon.

31. Evidence of Bill Bradley of Ludlow.

32. Parish of Lydbury North War Record 1914-1918 held by Bishop's Castle Local History Centre, ref 0289.

33. *Ibid* and Hugh R. Bryan *The Fallen Heroes of Ditton Priors* (priv. pub., 2002).

34. Mrs E. Minton lived at 9 Taylors Court, Lower Broad Street, Ludlow and the soldiers were William Minton, John Massey, Charles Woodhouse, Benjamin Nicholas and William Nicholas. *Ludlow Advertiser* 24 May 1919.

35. MOH Report for Ludlow 1918 reported in *Ludlow Advertiser* 13 September 1919.

36. MOH report for Bridgnorth 1918 reported in *Bridgnorth Journal* 17 May 1919.

37. MOH Report for Ludlow RDC 1918 reported in *Ludlow Advertiser* 26 July 1919.

38. MOH Report for Bridgnorth RDC reported in *Bridgnorth Journal* 21 June 1919.

39. *Church Stretton Advertiser* 7 November 1918.

40. *Ludlow Advertiser* 2 November 1918.

41. *Ludlow Advertiser* 7 December 1918.

42. Norman Davies. *Wellington Journal* 9 & 14 November 1918.

43. *Clun Valley Parochial Magazine op.cit.* June 1919.

44. *Ludlow Rural Deanery Magazine op.cit.* April & May 1919; *Rural Deanery of Bridgnorth Parish Magazine op.cit.* April 1919.

45. *Ludlow Advertiser* 16 November & 28 December 1918.

46. *Ludlow Advertiser* 23 November 1918; *Church Stretton Advertiser* 1 March 1919.

47. *Ludlow Advertiser* 12 April 1919.

48. *Ludlow Advertiser* 29 March 1919.

49. *Ludlow Advertiser* 2 September & 4 October 1919.

50. *Ludlow Advertiser* 22 November 1919 and 28 February 1920.

51. Charles Harold Badlan. Evidence of his son, Alan 'Bill' Badlan. Charles Richard Cornes. Evidence of his grandson Ron Cornes.

52. *Church Stretton Advertiser* 13 February 1919.

53. *Ludlow Advertiser* 5 July 1919.

54. *Church Stretton Advertiser* 20 February 1919.

55. *Ludlow Advertiser* 9 August & 6 September 1919.

56. Minutes of Ludlow Union Poor Law Guardians 1913-1922, Shropshire Archives PL9/2/1/24-28.

57. *Ludlow Advertiser* 13 March 1920.

58. *Ludlow Rural Deanery Parish Magazine* Oct. & Nov. 1916, Shropshire Archives.

59. *Ludlow Rural Deanery Parish Magazine op.cit.* Sept. 1917, Shropshire Archives.

60. *Church Stretton Advertiser* 14 March 1919; *Ludlow Advertiser* 14 June 1919; *Bridgnorth Journal* 12 July 1919; *Rural Deanery of Bridgnorth Parish Magazine op.cit.* Dec. 1919 – June 1920.

61. *Church Stretton Advertiser* 19 June 1919; *Bridgnorth Journal* 15 July 1919.

62. Church Stretton War Memorial File, Shropshire Archives ref. DA/134/11/6.

63. *Ludlow Advertiser* 19 April 1919.

64. *Ludlow Advertiser* 26 April 1919.

65. *Ludlow Advertiser* 10 May 1919.

66. *Ludlow Advertiser* 19 July & 6 September 1919.

67. *Ludlow Advertiser* 14 June 1919.

68. *Ludlow Advertiser* 13 March 1920.

General Index

Index of Towns and Villages

213

Index of Names